STEWARDING THE earth

STEWARDING THE earth

RETHINKING PROPERTY AND THE EMERGENCE OF BIOCULTURAL RIGHTS

SANJAY KABIR BAVIKATTE

OXFORD
UNIVERSITY PRESS

OXFORD
UNIVERSITY PRESS

Oxford University Press is a department of the University of Oxford.
It furthers the University's objective of excellence in research, scholarship,
and education by publishing worldwide. Oxford is a registered trademark of
Oxford University Press in the UK and in certain other countries

Published in India by
Oxford University Press
YMCA Library Building, 1 Jai Singh Road, New Delhi 110 001, India

First Edition published in 2014

ISBN-13: 978-0-19-809866-9
ISBN-10: 0-19-809866-9

Typeset in Adobe Garamond Pro 11/13
by MAP Systems, Bengaluru 560 082, India
Printed in India by G.H. Prints Pvt. Ltd, New Delhi 110 020

To Tom Bennett for his unflagging support
To my family for their unconditional love
To the stewards of the earth for their quiet wisdom

Contents

Preface

We shall not cease from exploration
And the end of all our exploring
Will be to arrive where we started
And know the place for the first time.
Through the unknown, remembered gate
When the last of earth left to discover
Is that which was the beginning;

— T.S. Eliot, 'Little Gidding'

The story of this book is the culmination of my journey to arrive at the place I started from and to know it for the first time. I started my journey in jurisprudence as a law student many years ago and later worked my way as a lawyer assisting indigenous and local communities to secure their rights to their territories. The notions of property I set out with after law school were turned on their head when I began working with communities who had a radically different relationship with their lands. I felt as if I was remembering something primal and half forgotten and entered, to use Eliot's phrase, through an unknown, remembered gate. Peoples, whom the law had seen as the last, showed me the way to that which was the beginning and paradoxically the future.

This book is fundamentally about rethinking the jurisprudence around property and telling the story of stewardship as way of relating to the land. The book seeks to go back to the beginning and explore our cultural and spiritual relationships to land and the ways in which this informs our personhood and peoplehood. It relies on my own experience as a lawyer working with communities and governments and constructs its theoretical foundations on insights from economics, law, and anthropology.

Ultimately what you hold in your hands is an engaging narrative which blends personal experience, conversations with communities, and ideas of visionaries who had the courage to challenge dominant legal assumptions by asking the most important of questions: 'What is the good life and how can this inform our relationship with the land?'

The book in no way seeks to romanticize indigenous and local communities and their relationship to the land. On the contrary it acknowledges the contradictions therein. It nevertheless seeks to discover and learn from the hidden but strong pulse of stewardship that still beats amongst communities worldwide despite being ravaged by unchecked capitalism. In fact, all this book seeks to do is to provide a well-reasoned manifesto for the future of our relationship with the earth, based on the simple wisdom of those who tend it with love.

Not known, because not looked for
But heard, half-heard, in the stillness
Between two waves of the sea.
Quick now, here, now, always—
A condition of complete simplicity
(Costing not less than everything)

— T.S. Eliot, 'Little Gidding'

Acknowledgements

A moment's deliberation on the tangled web of great and small forces that resulted in this book leaves me despairing at the impossibility of listing everyone who deserves gratitude.

All I can do is thank those who played key parts in my fast failing memory of the events leading up to the book.

So to begin—I am indebted to Shabbir Banoobhai for his radical presence and for nudging me in the direction of this book. I am deeply grateful to Fatima Hassan for her infinite patience through the process of writing this book. Then comes my appreciation for the indomitable Natural Justice team for their inspiring commitment to the cause of the stewards of the earth.

Thank you Elisa Morgera for meticulously reviewing the manuscript and providing the most helpful suggestions.

Professor Thomas Bennett, words are a poor substitute to express the unabashed gratitude I feel. This book would not have been possible without your selfless support and painstaking editing that went far beyond any call of duty. Thank you, thank you, and thank you.

Finally a deep bow of appreciation in no direction in particular to thank all the seen and unseen people, forces, and events that have conspired to make this book possible.

Abbreviations

ABS	Access and Benefit Sharing
AU	African Union
CAMPFIRE	Communal Areas Management Programme for Indigenous Resources
CBD	Convention on Biological Diversity
CBNRM	Community Based Natural Resource Management
CBO	Community Based Organizations
CEMIRIDE	Centre for Minority Rights Development
CGRFA	Commission on Genetic Resources for Food and Agriculture
COMPAS-ED	Comparing and Supporting Endogenous Development
COP	Conference of Parties
CSIR	Council for Scientific and Industrial Research
EMRIP	Expert Mechanism on the Rights of Indigenous Peoples
FAO	Food and Agriculture Organization
FPP	Forest Peoples Programme
GRULAC	Group of Latin America and the Caribbean
GTLE	Group of Technical and Legal Experts
ICCA	Indigenous Peoples' and Community Conserved Areas
ICCPR	International Covenant on Civil and Political Rights
ICESCR	The International Covenant on Economic, Social and Cultural Rights
ICJ	International Court of Justice
IIED	International Institute for Environment and Development

IIFB	International Indigenous Forum on Biodiversity
ILC	Indigenous and Local Communities
ILO	International Labour Organization
ING	Inter-regional Negotiating Group
IPR	Intellectual Property Rights
ITPGRFA	International Treaty on Plant Genetic Resources for Food and Agriculture
KWS	Kenyan Wildlife Service
LMMC	Like-Minded Megadiverse Countries
MADENSA	Maderas y Derivados de Nicaragua, S.A.
MARENA	Ministry of Environmental and Natural Resources
MAT	Mutually Agreed Terms
OAU	Organization of African Unity
PC	Privy Council
PES	Payment for Ecosystem Services
PIC	Prior Informed Consent
PoWPA	Programme of Work on Protected Areas
PRATEC	Andean Project for Peasant Technologies
REDD	Reducing Emissions from Deforestation and Forest Degradation
SBSTTA	Subsidiary Body on Scientific, Technical and Technological Advice
SOLCARSA	Sol del Caribe, S.A.
TCE	Traditional Cultural Expressions
TEEB	The Economics of Ecosystems and Biodiversity
TK	Traditional Knowledge
TRIPS	Trade Related Aspects of Intellectual Property Rights
UDHR	Universal Declaration on Human Rights
UNCCD	United Nations Convention on Combating Desertification
UNFCCC	United Nations Framework Convention on Climate
UNDRIP	United Nations Declaration on the Rights of Indigenous Peoples
UNEP	United Nations Environment Programme
WGIP	Working Group on Indigenous Populations

WIPO	World Intellectual Property Organization
WIPO-IGC	World Intellectual Property Organization-Intergovernmental Committee on Intellectual Property and Genetic Resources, Traditional Knowledge and Folklore
WTO	World Trade Organization
WWF	World Wildlife Fund

Table of Cases

Alexkor Ltd. v. *The Richtersveld Community* 2003 (12) BLR 1301 (CC).
Amodu Tijani v. *The Secretary, Southern Nigeria* (1921) 2 A.C. 399.
Cal v. *Attorney General*, Claims Nos. 171 and 172 (2007).
Case of Moiwana Village v. *Suriname* Inter-Am. Ct. H.R. (ser. C) No. 124 (15 June 2005).
Central Control Board (Liquor Traffic) v. *Cannon Brewery Company Ltd.* (1919) AC 744
Cherokee Nation v. *Georgia* 5 Peters 1 (1831).
Clissold v. *Perry* (1904) 1 CLR 363.
Cooper v. *Stuart* (1889) 14 App Cas 286.
Delgamuukw v. *British Columbia* (1997) 3 S.C.R. 1010.
Endorois Welfare Council v. *Kenya*, Communication 276/2003, Decision of the African Commission on Human and Peoples Rights.
In Re Southern Rhodesia (1919) AC 211 (PC).
Johnson v. *M'Intosh* 21 US (8 Wheaton) 541 (1823).
Kaiser Aetna v. *US* 444 US 164 (1979).
Lyng v. *Northwest Indian Cemetery Protective Association* 485 US 439 (1988).
Mabo v. *Queensland (No.2)* (1992) HCA 23, (1992) 175 CLR 1.
Mayagna (Sumo) Awas Tingni Community v. *Nicaragua* Inter-Am. C.H.R., No. 79, Ser. C (2001).
Milirrpum v. *Nabalco Pty Ltd.* (1971) 17 FLR 141.
Moiwana Village v. *Suriname* Inter-Am. Ct. H.R. (ser. C) No. 124 (15 June 2005).
Mrs. Emily Hussey v. *P. Palmer* [1972] 3 All ER 744.
Navajo Nation v. *US Forest Service* 535 F.3d 1058 (9th Cir. 2008).
Navajo Tribe v. *US* 624 F2d 981 (1980).
Nkosi v. *Bührmann* (1/2000) [2001] ZASCA 98.

Introduction

Environmental law is at a political crossroads. It presents an optical illusion that on the face of it seems like a clear-eyed response by governments to stem the ecological crisis that confronts the planet. But beneath the surface a furious battle is being fought. The terrain of this battle is law itself and the battle is around the nature of solutions to solve environmental problems. The kind of solutions that could be implemented through law are either technocratic in nature or those that engender local self-determination. Herein lies the heart of the conflict that is also a fault-line within the environmental movement itself.

This book will examine the emergence of biocultural rights as an aspect of the third generation group rights—an aspect that seeks to resolve our current environmental predicament through affirming the stewardship role of indigenous peoples, tribal, and other traditional communities[1] over their lands and waters. In doing so the book will trace the origins of biocultural rights to the convergence of three of

[1] When the term 'community' is used in this work, it should be taken to include indigenous, tribal, and traditional communities whose ways of life are predominantly land-based and who have strong cultural and spiritual bonds with their lands and waters. While communities are fluid and are organized along various lines including ethnicity, shared resources, common interests, political bodies, etc., the term 'community' is used here to denote groups of people with a way of life that is intimately linked to the ecosystem. It is clear that even such communities don't have homogenous interests with many of them occupying the cusp between tradition and modernity. However, despite the diversity of views within such communities, at the level of law and policy there is a clearly recognizable advocacy for rights by these communities to govern and manage their resources based on historical stewardship. This book seeks to analyse and map this trend in

the most significant social movements of our times, all of which have a direct bearing on the fate of our planet—the post-development movement,[2] the commons movement,[3] and the movement for the rights of indigenous, tribal, and traditional communities.[4] The term 'biocultural' has a long pedigree and, as will be seen later, is used widely by communities, academics, civil society actors, and intergovernmental organizations to denote a way of life that emerges from a holistic dynamic between Nature and culture.

It is important to bear in mind that the aim of this book is to map the trajectory of biocultural rights as they emerge through multilateral environmental agreements, domestic legislation, case law, shifts in the development discourse, and the struggles of communities. Because biocultural rights are at an incipient stage, the examples that are provided here in support of these rights should not be viewed as unequivocal evidence that there are no cases to the contrary. Rather they should be seen as efforts to trace a preponderant tendency in environmental jurisprudence towards the affirmation of biocultural rights. It is only a matter of time before the long arc of this preponderant tendency bends undeniably towards biocultural rights. The rich and varied evidence presented in the following chapters bears testimony to this assertion.

The chapters that follow will make a clear case for biocultural rights by critically analysing the contemporary dominance of private property over common property discourses and the hegemony of market values over all other social values. The case for biocultural rights will be supported by theories of political economy from Karl Marx to Karl Polanyi, to theories of property from C.B. Macpherson

---

communities at the level of law and policy making, rather than focusing on local differences. Note: where the term 'peoples' has been used in the title of Chapter V, it should be understood as 'community' as explained here.

[2] *See generally*, Chapter One, note 9.

[3] *See generally*, John Tierny, 'The Non-Tragedy of the Commons', *The New York Times*, 15 October 2009, http://tierneylab.blogs.nytimes.com/2009/10/15/the-non-tragedy-of-the-commons/ (accessed 14 March 2012).

[4] *See generally*, Ronald Niezen, *The Origins of Indigenism: Human Rights and the Politics of Identity* (Berkeley: University of California Press, 2003).

to Margaret Jane Radin. Emerging biocultural rights jurisprudence in international and domestic law will also be mapped by:

a) Tracing the rights gains of communities in recent multilateral environmental agreements like the Nagoya Protocol on Access and Benefit Sharing (ABS)
b) Examining the decisions of regional tribunals such as the Inter-American Court of Human Rights and the African Commission for Human and Peoples Rights, and domestic courts like the High Court of Australia, Supreme Court of Canada, and the Constitutional Court of South Africa
c) Exploring the widespread development and use of biocultural community protocols by communities across the world to assert their biocultural rights

It is useful to note that the evidence presented here of a jurisprudential tendency in favour of biocultural rights is not restricted to one particular country but is of a widespread nature.

CHAPTER ONE

Self-determination as Political Ecology

The Roots of Biocultural Rights

Technocratic solutions are generally based on scientific reports about the ecosystem's carrying capacity and pollution thresholds. They are also supported by economic studies focused on ensuring that industrialization keeps step with the regenerative capacity of the ecosystem. They recognize the need to prevent the abuse of natural resources and seek to put forward expert solutions for the rational management of air, water, and land. They also propose policies for reducing waste and for recycling, along with the development of environment-friendly technologies.[1]

States implement technocratic solutions developed by experts through a variety of carrots-and-sticks such as taxes, subsidies, and penalties. The enforceability of these technocratic solutions ultimately depends on a class of experts and bureaucrats who are tasked with the role of rationally managing the environment in the interests of humanity.[2] The demarcation and management of protected areas to conserve forests is an example of the exercise of techno–bureaucratic power through environmental law. Often however, this power involves usurping of the decision-making authority of local communities by a professional class of experts. The case of the Raika pastoralists of Rajasthan and the denial of their historical monsoon grazing rights in

[1] *See generally,* Howard P. Segal, *Technological Utopianism in American Culture* (New York: Syracuse University Press, 2005).

[2] Andre Gorz, 'Political Ecology: Between Expertocracy and Self-Limitation', in *Ecologica* (Calcutta: Seagull Books, 2008), pp. 43–76.

the Kumbalgarh sanctuary by a 2003 decision of the Indian Central Empowered Committee is such an example.[3]

Indigenous peoples and community organizations fighting for the recognition of customary land rights, however, insist that communities who have historically conserved ecosystems (and are most affected by any adverse environmental impact) are best suited to make decisions about these ecosystems. These groups argue that the current ecological crisis is an outcome of an expertocracy imposing non-consultative top–down solutions resulting in the delegitimization of local knowledge and decision-making. Many of them rely on growing evidence of community conservation practices that have sustained ecosystems for generations. Much of this evidence as we shall see later has come to fore over the last two decades, and in some cases contradicts the established 'truths' of communities being in direct conflict with conservation objectives.[4]

The top–down solutions posed by experts for environmental conservation are what Andre Gorz terms 'locking technologies'. He distinguishes between 'locking' and 'open' technologies.[5] Open technologies facilitate communication, local autonomy, and sharing, and rely on the personal and creative energies of recipients thereby making them both users and creators. Locking technologies, on the other hand, are those that come pre-set and work on a principle of command and control. Their development and deployment is centralized, and provide recipients little or no freedom to adapt them to their local needs and context.

Community activism around environmental issues represents a break in the environmental movement from a techno–bureaucratic approach to ecology to a political ecology. The proponents of the latter trace the origins of the environmental movement to a time

[3] Ilse Kohler-Rollefson, 'Biocultural Community Protocols: A Tool for Pastoralists to Secure Customary Rights to the Commons', FES, *Common Voices*, Issue 2 (2010), pp. 16–18.

[4] *See generally* Grazia Borrini-Feyerabend 'Bio-cultural Diversity Conserved by Indigenous Peoples and Local Communities—Examples and Analysis', Companion document to the IUCN/CEESP Briefing Note No.10 (Tehran: CENESTA, 2010).

[5] Andre Gorz, *Ecologica* (2008) pp. 8–9.

before the current crisis when it manifested as a protest against the usurpation of the rights of communities to their lands and waters by the administrative and economic apparatus of colonial and settler states.[6]

The Nature that these communities sought to protect is not the Nature of the technocrats and bureaucrats, nor is it the 'unspoilt wilderness' of the naturalists. Rather it was a Nature that was so integrally intertwined with community life that it represented an entire way of being and knowing.[7] The defence of Nature for these communities represented a defence of a 'cosmovision'.[8] Nature for them was not something 'out there' that needed to be protected by scientists and administrators through 'command and cope' mechanisms but the very notions of self and community were constructed through an intimate and historical interaction with the ecosystem.

It is against this backdrop of political ecology that we shall highlight three social movements that have contributed to the emergence of biocultural rights: the post-development movement, the commons movement, and the movement for the rights of indigenous people.

Post-development: Developing a People-centred Ecology

The post-development[9] movement traces its origins to thinkers and activists ranging from E.F. Schumacher[10] and Ivan Illich[11] to Arturo Escobar and Gustavo Esteva.[12] In his seminal work

[6] Andre Gorz, *Ecologica* (2008), p. 50.

[7] 'Bio-cultural Diversity Conserved by Indigenous Peoples and Local Communities' (2010).

[8] '[T]he term cosmovision has to do with basic forms of seeing, feeling, and perceiving the world. It is made manifest by the forms in which a people acts and expresses itself. This means that a cosmovision does not necessarily correspond to an ordered and unique discourse (cosmology) through which it can be described/explained and understood. In some cases the only way to understand a cosmovision is through living it— by sharing experiences with people who sustain that mode of living and that life-world'. *See* Jorge Ishizawa, 'Affirmation of Cultural Diversity-Learning with Communities in the Central Andes', *Development Dialogue*, Vol. 2 (August 2009), p. 118.

[9] Post-development theories gained momentum in the 1990s as a critique of the ecological and social fallouts of dominant development

Encountering Development: The Making and the Unmaking of the Third World, Escobar best sums the post-development turn when he says:

> Development was— and continues to be for the most part — a top-down, ethnocentric and technocratic approach, which treated people and cultures as abstract concepts, statistical figures to be moved up and down in the charts of 'progress'. Development was conceived not as a cultural process (culture was a residual variable, to disappear with the advance of modernization) but instead as a system of more or less universally applicable technical interventions intended to deliver some 'badly needed' goods to a 'target' population. It comes as no surprise that development became a force so destructive to the Third World cultures, ironically in the name of people's interests.[13]

Post-development scholars presented a foundational critique of the large development projects of 1970s and 1980s as contributing to destabilizing communities, creating poverty, and destroying the environment.[14] In 1970s and 1980s, with the looming ecological crisis, post-development activists began to highlight local community conservation systems and the importance of affirming such systems.[15] The work of organizations such as the Andean Project for

---

paradigms that ranged from neo-liberalism to the Green Revolution. Post-development theorists critiqued these development paradigms as top–down, techno–bureaucratic solutions bound to fail due to their inability to genuinely engage with community needs and experiences.

[10] E.F. Schumacher, *Small is Beautiful: Economics as if People Mattered* (London: Blond and Briggs, 1973).

[11] Ivan Illich, *Tools of Conviviality* (London: Boyars, 1973); Illich argued that politics is no longer about choosing between Left and Right. The real choice is between 'vernacular values' and 'industrial values' or between 'conviviality' and 'technofascism'.

[12] Gustavo Esteva and Madhu Suri, *Grassroots Postmodernism: Remaking the Soil of Cultures* (London: Zed Books, 1998).

[13] Arturo Escobar, *Encountering Development: The Making and Unmaking of the Third World*, p. 44 (Princeton: Princeton University Press, 2012).

[14] *See generally*, Wolfgang Sachs (ed.), *The Development Dictionary* (New York: Zed Books, 2010) and Majid Rahenama and Victoria Bawtree (eds), *The Post-Development Reader* (New York: Zed Books, 1997).

[15] One of the most famous examples of this is the work of Vandana Shiva that critiqued the cultural and ecological devastation caused by the Green Revolution in India, stressing the importance of affirming traditional

Peasant Technologies (PRATEC)[16] and Comparing and Supporting Endogenous Development (COMPAS-ED)[17] epitomized the best of post-development thinking in practice.

PRATEC based in the central Andes (covering parts of Peru, Bolivia, and Ecuador), has worked extensively on cultural affirmation through the valorization of traditional agricultural practices. As Jorge Ishizawa from PRATEC points out:

---

agricultural practices, and recognizing their ability to adequately respond to increased demand for food. Vandana Shiva, *Monocultures of the Mind* (Penang: Third World Network, 1993).

[16] The 'Andean Project for Peasant Technologies' (Proyecto Andino de Tecnologías Campesinas, PRATEC) is a Peruvian NGO founded in 1988, devoted to the recovery and valorization of traditional agricultural practices and associated knowledge. PRATEC participates in the efforts of Andean-Amazonian peasant communities to counter the socially and ecologically destructive effects of industrial agriculture and governmental agrarian policies. By using local knowledge and the practice of traditional 'ritual agriculture' and through adopting a non-dualistic, eco-centric worldview, PRATEC supports the resurgence of local approaches to agriculture, which it sees as radically opposed to Western industrial agriculture. The Andean peasant practice of ritual agriculture embraces kinship-oriented visions of the land and encourages empathetic actions that illustrate respect for all living entities of the biosphere.

Agricultural activities include ritual actions, utterances, and offerings that express both a deep respect for Pachamama (Mother Earth) and communitarian aspects that characterize the worldview of the Andean people. *See* http://www.terralingua.org/bcdconservation/?p=244 (accessed 14 March 2012).

[17] The COMPAS network supports field programmes of Community Based Organizations (CBOs) and Non-Governmental Organizations (NGOs) to develop, test, and improve the endogenous development approach in dialogue with modern western-based science. COMPAS systematizes the experiences in such a way that other NGOs and government agencies can make use of the endogenous development approach. COMPAS facilitates intercultural dialogues amongst CBOs, NGOs, universities, and research centres across countries and continents to enable systematization beyond the national level. According to COMPAS-ED, endogenous development revitalizes ancestral and local knowledge and integrates external knowledge

> In our understanding, cultural affirmation is the process by which people who live in a place remember and regenerate their traditional practices, nurturing their *pacha* (local world) and letting themselves be nurtured by it. Since in the case of the central Andes, this local world is agrocentric, nurturance is the mode of being in the Andean *pacha*. Andean cultural affirmation is the continuous affirmation of this mode of being .... Cultural affirmation, then, is not an intellectual matter. For the people of the central Andes, it is the sustained regeneration of biocultural diversity through the activities of mutual nurturance undertaken by the *campesinos* [peasants] and the entities that make up their *pacha*.[18]

A statement by Julia Pacoricona Aliaga from Conima in Peru best exemplifies the kind of culture that PRATEC seeks to affirm:

> The potato is our mother because when it produces fruits it is feeding us, clothing us and giving us happiness, but we also nurture her. When the plants are small, we call them *wawas* (children) because we have to look after them, delouse (weed) them, clothe (hill) them, dance and feast them. This has always been done. My parents taught me to nurture them with affection and good will as we do with our children.[19]

Over the last sixteen years COMPAS-ED has worked on endogenous development in a sustained manner with partner organizations in Asia, Latin America, and Africa. Endogenous development encapsulates the essence of post-development thinking by basing itself on local peoples' own criteria of development, taking into account the material, social, and spiritual well-being of people. In an effort to avoid techno–bureaucratic top–down solutions, COMPAS-ED seeks to make local peoples' worldviews and livelihood strategies the starting point for development. The work of its partners

---

and resources that fit the local context. It leads to increased biocultural diversity, reduced environmental degradation, and a self-sustaining local and regional exchange of goods and services. *See* http://www.compasnet.org/?page_id=22 (accessed 14 March 2012).

[18] Jorge Ishizawa, 'Affirmation of Cultural Diversity' (2009), p. 111.

[19] Ibid., quote from Terre des homes-Germany, *Children and Biodiversity in the Andes* (Lima, 2001), p. 23.

in Guatemala, India, and Ghana[20] is evidence that these worldviews and livelihood strategies promote sustainable development as a balance between material, social, and spiritual well-being.[21]

Post-development as a discipline that valorized community ecological practices arose as a result of political ecology's critique of techno–bureaucratic solutions to development and conservation. In this sense it broke from sections of the established environmental thinking by insisting on an integral link between environmental conservation and community rights to manage their lands and waters.

(UN) COMMON WISDOM OF THE COMMONERS

The post-development movement found a natural ally in the movement for the commons. The latter had, through empirical data, begun to turn the 'tragedy of the commons' argument on its head.[22] The theory of the 'tragedy of the commons' was based on an assumption that, where consequences regarding commonly held resources are borne by the community as a whole, individuals would seek to maximize self-interest to the detriment of the community and sustainability of the resource. Therefore, the 'tragedy of the commons' is an argument that long-term sustainability of common-pool resources is best ensured when such resources are privatized or state controlled.[23]

Extensive research on governance of the commons by political scientists and economists such as Elinor Ostrom[24] and Arun Agrawal[25] unequivocally established that state control or privatization of common-pool resources are not necessarily the best solutions to ensure conservation, and in many cases are counter-productive. Contrary to the 'tragedy of the commons' assertion of the destruction of common-pool resources due to mismanagement by communities

[20] *Community Well-being and Biocultural Diversity through Endogenous Development, COMPAS Network: Outcomes, Impact and New Initiatives*, by request www.compasnet.org (accessed 13 September 2011).

[21] *See generally*, www.compasnet.org (accessed 13 September 2011).

[22] John Tierny, 'The Non-Tragedy of the Commons' (2009).

[23] Garrett Hardin, 'The Tragedy of the Commons', *Science* 162 (3859), pp. 1243–8.

[24] Elinor Ostrom, *Governing the Commons: The Evolution of Institutions for Collective Action* (New York: Cambridge University Press, 1990).

and the free-rider problem,[26] researchers working on the commons established that under certain conditions[27] communities are best able to conserve ecosystems.

Recent research evaluating the effectiveness of protected areas under different kinds of management regimes traced forest change in three diverse landscapes: the Chitwan District of Nepal, the Mahananda Wildlife Sanctuary in West Bengal, India, and the Tadoba-Andhari Tiger Reserve in Maharashtra, India. The research found that a protectionist approach that excludes local communities is likely to fail without expensive government inputs. Conservation is also likely to fail in cases where outsiders or dominant insiders impose rules on the community for use of resources. However, the research also proved that effective management of forest resources occurs when community members are genuinely involved in decision-making and in developing rules for the use of these resources.[28]

[25] Ashwini Chhatre and Arun Agrawal, 'Forest Commons and Local Enforcement', *Proceedings of the National Academy of Sciences* 105(36) (2008), pp. 13286–91.

[26] The problem of the 'free-rider' in economic theory arises when individuals who do not contribute to its maintenance consume public goods/resources thereby free riding on the contributions of the rest of the community for the upkeep of the goods/resources. See also Russell Hardin, 'The Free-Rider Problem', *The Stanford Encyclopedia of Philosophy* (2003), http://plato.stanford.edu/entries/free-rider/ (accessed 13 September 2011).

[27] These conditions are what Ostrom terms as the eight design principles for effective common-pool resource management. They are: 1) define clear group boundaries; 2) match rules governing use of common goods to local needs and conditions; 3) ensure that those affected by the rules can participate in modifying the rules; 4) make sure the rulemaking rights of community members are respected by outside authorities; 5) develop a system, carried out by community members, for monitoring members' behaviour; 6) use graduated sanctions for rule violators; 7) provide accessible, low-cost means for dispute resolution; 8) build responsibility for governing the common resource in nested tiers from the lowest level up to the entire interconnected system. Ostrom, *Governing the Commons: The Evolution of Institutions for Collective Action* (1990), p. 90.

[28] Elinor Ostrom and Harini Nagendra, 'Insights on Linking Forests, Trees, and People from the Air, on the Ground, and in the Laboratory',

The intersection of the post-development with the commons movement, the latter empirically validating the postulates of post-development theorists, further highlighted the role that communities played in the conservation of ecosystems. This was a politically significant marriage of strengths, and represented a new certainty that could no longer be ignored by policy makers in the face of the ecological catastrophe surrounding them. Ostrom best summed up this certainty when she responded to a question that asked her advice to state actors who influence natural resource policy:

> No panaceas! We (policy makers) tend to want simple formulas. We have two main prescriptions: privatize the resource or make it state property with uniform rules. But sometimes the people who are living on the resource are in the best position to figure out how to manage it as a commons.[29]

Indigenous Peoples and the Right to Ecological Stewardship

International efforts for indigenous peoples' rights go back to 1923. It began with the efforts of Levi General Deskaheh, chief of the Younger Bear Clan of the Cayuga Nation, a spokesperson of the six nations of the Grand River Land near Brantford, Ontario. He obtained a hearing at the League of Nations regarding a dispute with Canada over tribal self-government.[30] Since the 1980s, however, a global movement for indigenous peoples' rights and the increasing use of supranational forums by indigenous peoples' groups to claim their rights have grown.[31]

Proceedings of the National Academy of Sciences 103(51) (2006), pp. 19224–31; *see also* 'Elinor Ostrom: Taking Sustainability Research Mainstream', FES, *Common Voices*, Issue 1 (2010), pp. 6–9.

[29] Fran Korten, 'Elinor Ostrom wins Nobel for Common(s) Sense', *Yes! Magazine* 26 February 2010, http://www.yesmagazine.org/issues/america-the-remix/elinor-ostrom-wins-nobel-for-common-s-sense (accessed 13 September 2011).

[30] Brian E. Titley, *A Narrow Vision: Duncan Campbell Scott and the Administration of Indian Affairs in Canada* (Vancouver: University of British Columbia Press, 1986), p. 122

[31] As a result of persistent lobbying at the UN by indigenous peoples, the Working Group on Indigenous Populations (WGIP) was established pursuant to Economic and Social Council Resolution 1982/34 (7 May

This global movement, though a distinctly modern phenomenon, represents itself as a primordial identity that unifies the estimated 300 million indigenous peoples from 4,000 distinct societies.[32] Unlike the 1960s' movements for the recognition of ethnicity, the indigenous peoples' movement asserts itself not as a legal category or an analytical concept but as a paradoxical expression of a global identity. This global identity of 'indigenous' harks to a unity amidst diversity and has, with remarkable success, used the United Nations as the key site of struggle for indigenous peoples' rights.[33]

While there is no universally agreed definition of who is indigenous, the definition around which there is a broad consensus was given by Jose R. Martinez Cobo, the Special Rapporteur of the Sub-Commission on Prevention of Discrimination and Protection of Minorities, in his seminal *Study on the Problem of Discrimination against Indigenous Populations*:

> Indigenous communities, peoples and nations are those which, having a historical continuity with pre-invasion and pre-colonial societies that developed on their territories, consider themselves distinct from other sectors of the societies now prevailing on those territories, or parts of them. They form at present non-dominant sectors of society and are determined to preserve, develop and transmit to future generations their ancestral territories, and their ethnic identity, as the basis of their continued existence as peoples, in accordance with their own cultural patterns, social institutions and legal system.[34]

1982) as a subsidiary body of the Sub-Commission on the Promotion and Protection of Human Rights. The work of the WGIP finally led to the Declaration on the Rights of Indigenous Peoples, adopted by the UN General Assembly in 2007. Since then the WGIP has been discontinued and replaced with the Expert Mechanism on the Rights of Indigenous Peoples (EMRIP) through Resolution 6/36 of the UN Human Rights Council (14 December 2007). See http://www2.ohchr.org/english/issues/indigenous/groups/wgip.htm (accessed 14 March 2012).

32 Ronald Niezen, *The Origins of Indigenism* (2003), p. 4.

33 *See generally*, Introduction; ibid.

34 UN Doc. E/CN.4/Sub.2/1986/7 and Add. 1-4. The report further states that 'On an individual basis, an indigenous person is one who belongs to these indigenous populations through self-identification as indigenous (group consciousness) and is recognized and accepted by these populations as one of its members (acceptance by the group),' paragraphs 379–82.

At the heart of the struggle for the rights of indigenous peoples is the 'right to self-determination'. As James Anaya, the UN Special Rapporteur on the Situation of Human Rights and Fundamental Freedoms of Indigenous Peoples notes, self-determination here is not a claim for separate statehood but a self-determination that is grounded in international human rights. Such self-determination has certain core values which are: non-discrimination, protection of cultural integrity, rights over lands and natural resources, social welfare for economic well-being, and self-government.[35]

Since the coming into force of the Convention on Biological Diversity (CBD)[36] in 1993 the nature of the indigenous 'self' that seeks the right to determine or actualize itself has extended beyond Martinez Cobo's 1987 definition. The definition of indigenous that has now captured the public imagination includes the role of indigenous peoples as the original trustees of the earth. Strategically and steadfastly, indigenous peoples have begun to uphold their role as guardians of the ecosystem and demand the rights to ecological stewardship in negotiations towards multilateral environmental agreements, programs of work, decisions, and guidelines under the CBD.[37] Riding on the momentum of the commons and post-development movements, indigenous peoples present recognition

[35] James Anaya, *Indigenous Peoples in International Law*, 2nd ed. (New York: Oxford University Press, 2004), p. 6.

[36] The CBD entered into force in 1993. It has 193 state parties and aims to ensure the conservation and sustainable use of biological diversity and the fair and equitable sharing of benefits arising from its commercial and research utilization. Many developing countries view the CBD as a way to redefine historical benefit flows from the use of genetic resources. *See generally*, Lyle Glowka Françoise Burhenne-Guilmin and Hugh Synge, *A Guide to the Convention on Biological Diversity* (Gland: IUCN, 1994). *See also* Lyle Glowka, 'Emerging Legislative Approaches to Implement Article 15 of the Convention on Biological Diversity', *RECIEL* 6 (3) (1997), pp. 249–62.

[37] The Akwé: Kon Guidelines (www.cbd.int/doc/publications/akwe-brochure-en.pdf, accessed 13 September 2011) and *Tkarihwaié:ri* Code of Ethical Conduct (http://www.cbd.int/decision/cop/?id=12308, accessed 13 September 2011) are some examples of the discourse of stewardship in international environmental law.

of their rights to self-determination as both a practical and moral solution to the ecological crisis.

Discourses around the strong cultural and spiritual links between indigenous peoples and their lands are not new. They stretch back to the beliefs of some of the oldest aboriginal peoples of the world such as the San of southern Africa. The common theme among the different San groups was:

> [T]he existence of a primal time, a mythic age in which beings and states were ontologically fluid and a certain state of inchoate amorphousness prevailed .... The majority of the beings of primal time were beings, in which animal and human traits co-mingled .... These therianthropic variants of the 'Early Race' bore animal names - Anteater, Lion, Hyena, Jackal, Springbok, Blue Crane, Tortoise .... Yet they were also human, and were married, in a riotous mix of cross-species alliances, including with humans of the 'Early Race' .... They behaved in all ways like humans; however now and again their actions took an animal twist, in line with the protagonist's specific faunal trait.[38]

The origins of the CBD had much to do with the emergence of the *homo economicus* and the consequent desacralizing of Nature.[39] An alarming report issued by the Secretariat of the CBD states that species are now disappearing at 50–100 times the natural rate, and this is predicted to continue to rise exponentially. An estimated 34,000 plant and 5,200 animal species, including one in eight of the world's bird species, face extinction. About 45 per cent of the Earth's original forests are gone and continue to shrink. Up to 10 per cent of coral reefs, which are among the most biologically diverse ecosystems, have been destroyed and one third of those remaining face collapse over the next 10 to 20 years. Coastal

[38] Mathias Guenther, 'On /Xam San Folklore', in Miklos Szalay (ed.), *The Moon as Shoe: Drawings of the San* (Zurich: Scheidegger and Spiess, 2002), p. 92.

[39] S.H. Bragdon, 'The Evolution and the Future of Law of Sustainable Development: Lessons from the Convention on Biological Diversity', *Georgetown International Environmental Law Review* VIII (3) (1996), pp. 389–513.

mangroves, a vital nursery habitat for countless species, are also vulnerable, with half already gone.[40]

In a political climate where grand top–down development theories have been discredited and local systems of resource management affirmed, the indigenous peoples' movement has begun to make a critical link between their right to self-determination and environmental conservation. To do so, they have begun to highlight their role as guardians of ecosystems and the significance of their cultural and spiritual bonds with Nature.

Indigenous peoples also point out that their territories are some of the most biodiversity rich, and the collapse of local ecosystems began with the dispossession of communities from the lands and waters they traditionally occupied.[41] The natural corollary that follows from this view is that biodiversity conservation is integrally linked to securing the rights of indigenous peoples to their territories, their way of life, their culture, and customary ways of decision-making.

The Genesis of Biocultural Rights: At the Confluence of Three Streams

Biocultural rights arise at the confluence of the movements for post-development, the commons, and the rights of indigenous peoples. Despite their differences, the overlap between these three movements is their common goal to protect local ecosystems and an understanding that these ecosystems are best protected by securing the rights of communities who live in them. Biocultural rights therefore denote all the rights required to secure the stewardship role of communities over their lands and waters. This role represents a way of life where the identity of a community, its culture, spirituality, systems of governance, and traditional occupations are inseparable from its lands and waters. The relationship of the community to its

[40] Secretariat of the Convention on Biological Diversity. *Sustaining Life on Earth: How the Convention on Biological Diversity Promotes Nature and Well-Being* (Montreal: Secretariat of the Convention on Biological Diversity, 2000), p. 5.

[41] *See generally*, 'Bio-cultural Diversity Conserved by Indigenous Peoples and Local Communities' (2010).

territory is akin to a fiduciary duty of care and protection, rather than an exercise of dominion.[42]

The CBD was the first international treaty that explicitly recognized the link between traditional ways of life of communities and biodiversity conservation. More importantly, in Articles 8(j)[43] and 10(c)[44] the CBD obliged its 193 state parties to safeguard these traditional ways of life by ensuring the integrity of their cultures, encouraging customary use of biological resources, and upholding local decision-making structures. These CBD rights have been underscored by various indigenous peoples' declarations and statements that have called for the recognition of the right of indigenous peoples to maintain and strengthen their distinctive spiritual relationship with their traditionally owned or occupied territories in accordance with Article 25 of the *United Nations Declaration on the Rights of Indigenous Peoples* (UNDRIP).[45]

Examples of indigenous peoples' declarations include the May 2007, *Declaration on Indigenous Peoples' Rights to Genetic Resources and Indigenous Knowledge* which was issued by 44 indigenous peoples' groups. The document reaffirmed their spiritual and cultural relationship with all life forms existing in their traditional

[42] *See generally,* Chapter IX for a further elaboration of biocultural rights and the discourse of stewardship.

[43] Article 8(j) of the Convention on Biological Diversity (CBD) reads 'Each Contracting Party shall, as far as possible and appropriate (chapeau) subject to its national legislation, respect, preserve and maintain knowledge, innovations and practices of indigenous and local communities embodying traditional lifestyles relevant for the conservation and sustainable use of biological diversity and promote their wider application with the approval and involvement of the holders of such knowledge, innovations and practices and encourage the equitable sharing of the benefits arising from the utilization of such knowledge, innovations and practices'. *See* http://www.cbd.int/convention/text/ (accessed 13 September 2011).

[44] Article 10(c) of the CBD reads 'Each Contracting Party shall, as far as possible and appropriate protect and encourage customary use of biological resources in accordance with traditional cultural practices that are compatible with conservation or sustainable use requirements'. [http://www.cbd.int/convention/text/ (accessed 13 September 2011)]

[45] On 14 September 2007, the United Nations General Assembly adopted the '*Declaration on the Rights of Indigenous Peoples*'. Article 25 of

territories, and their fundamental role and responsibility as the guardians of their territories, lands, and natural resources. Other examples are the August 1997 *Heart of the People Declaration* and the February 1995 *Declaration of Indigenous Peoples of the Western Hemisphere Regarding the Human Genome Diversity Project.* The *Heart of the People Declaration* best captures the sentiment of the stewardship role of indigenous peoples vis-à-vis their territories by stating:

> Mother Earth and all human, plant and animal relatives are sacred, sovereign, respected, unique living beings with their own right to survive, and each plays an essential role in the survival and health of the natural world. Human beings are not separate from the rest of the natural world, but are created to live in relationship and harmony with it and with all life. The Creator has given us a sacred responsibility to protect and care for the land and all of life, as well as to safeguard its well being for future generations to come.[46]

The CBD has, therefore, engendered a new legal landscape where biocultural rights are being developed as a people-led alternative to state-led technocratic solutions to the environmental crisis.[47] Nearly every CBD body, including the Working Group on Article 8(j); the Working Group on Access and Benefit Sharing (ABS); the Working Group on Protected Areas; and the Subsidiary Body on Scientific, Technical and Technological Advice (SBSTTA) has become a fertile ground for conceptualizing and realizing biocultural rights. In many

---

the Declaration states: 'Indigenous peoples have the right to maintain and strengthen their distinctive spiritual relationship with their traditionally owned or otherwise occupied and used lands, territories, waters and coastal seas and other resources and to uphold their responsibilities to future generations in this regard'. *See* http://www.un.org/esa/socdev/unpfii/en/drip.html (accessed 13 September 2011).

[46] *See* http://www.ienearth.org/docs/declare.html for full texts of these declarations (accessed 13 September 2011).

[47] *See generally*, Brendan Tobin, '"Law Giveth and the Law Taketh Away": The Case for Recognition of Customary Law in International ABS and Traditional Knowledge Governance', *Policy Matters*, Issue 17 (October 2010), pp. 16–24.

ways these rights have begun to crystallize as a subset of the third generation group or solidarity rights.[48]

The discourse on biocultural rights is spilling over from the CBD to other UN and international fora and other environmental conventions such as the World Intellectual Property Organization-Intergovernmental Committee on Intellectual Property and Genetic Resources, Traditional Knowledge and Folklore (WIPO-IGC),[49] the Commission on Genetic Resources for Food and Agriculture (CGRFA),[50] the UN Convention on Combating Desertification

[48] Under international law, first generation rights are commonly understood as civil and political rights attributed to the Universal Declaration on Human Rights (UDHR) and the International Covenant on Civil and Political Rights (ICCPR). Second generation rights are socio-economic and cultural rights covered to some extent by the UDHR but enshrined in the International Covenant on Economic, Social and Cultural Rights (ICESR). Solidarity rights or group rights which are considered third generation rights have begun to gain increasing momentum through the Declaration on the Rights of Indigenous Peoples adopted by the UN General Assembly in 2007.

[49] Established by the World Intellectual Property Organization (WIPO) General Assembly in October 2000 (document WO/GA/26/6), the WIPO Intergovernmental Committee on Intellectual Property and Genetic Resources, Traditional Knowledge and Folklore (WIPO-IGC) is undertaking text-based negotiations with the objective of reaching agreement on a text of an international legal instrument (or instruments) which will ensure the effective protection of traditional knowledge (TK), traditional cultural expressions (TCEs)/folklore and genetic resources. *See* http://www.wipo.int/tk/en/igc/ (accessed 13 September 2011). For a spillover of biocultural rights into the WIPO-IGC negotiations, *see generally, Intellectual Property and Traditional Knowledge*, Booklet no.2 (New York: WIPO Publication No.920 (E).

[50] The Commission on Genetic Resources for Food and Agriculture (CGRFA) is a permanent forum where governments discuss and negotiate matters relevant to biodiversity for food and agriculture. The main objectives of the Commission are to ensure the conservation and sustainable utilization of genetic resources for food and agriculture, as well as the fair and equitable sharing of benefits derived from their use, for present and future generations. The CGRFA was established in 1983 to deal with issues related to plant genetic resources. In 1995, the Food and Agriculture Organization (FAO) Conference broadened the Commission's mandate to cover all components of biodiversity of relevance to food and agriculture. Since its establishment, the Commission

(UNCCD),[51] and the UN Framework Convention on Climate Change (UNFCCC).[52]

has overseen global assessments of the state of the world's plant and animal genetic resources for food and agriculture and negotiated major international instruments, including the International Treaty on Plant Genetic Resources for Food and Agriculture (ITPGRFA), 2001. *See, Biodiversity for a World without Hunger: The Commission on Genetic Resources for Food and Agriculture*, Rome: FAO, www.fao.org/nr/cgrfa (accessed 11 September 2011). *See also* Ilse Köhler-Rollefson and Evelyn Mathias 'Livestock Keepers' Rights: A Rights-Based Approach to Invoking Justice for Pastoralists and Biodiversity Conserving Livestock Keepers', *Policy Matters*, Issue 17 (October 2010), pp. 113–15.

[51] The UNCCD was adopted in 1994 and has 194 parties. The objective of the Convention is to combat desertification and mitigate the effects of drought in countries experiencing serious drought and/or desertification, particularly in Africa, through effective action at all levels, with a view to contributing to the achievement of sustainable development in affectted areas. *See* Article 2 of the Convention for the objectives of the UNCCD. For a spillover of biocultural rights into the UNCCD, *see generally*, Jean Zeigler, Grégoire de Kalbermatten, Liliane Ortega, Christophe Golay, Claire Mahon, Sally-Anne Way, and Michaela Büschi, 'Human Rights and Desertification: Exploring the Complementarity of International Human Rights Law and the United Nations Convention to Combat Desertification', Issue paper 1, *Desertification, Land Degradation and Drought* (Bonn: UNCCD, 2008).

[52] In 1992, the UNFCCC was adopted as the basis for a global response to the problem of climate change. With 194 Parties, the ultimate objective of the Convention is to stabilize greenhouse gas concentrations in the atmosphere at a level that will prevent dangerous human interference with the climate system. The Convention is complemented by the 1997 Kyoto Protocol, which has 192 Parties. Under this treaty, 37 industrialized countries and the European Community have committed to reducing their emissions by an average of 5 per cent by 2012 against 1990 levels. Industrialized countries must first and foremost take domestic action against climate change. But the Protocol also allows them to meet their emission reduction commitments abroad through so-called 'market-based mechanisms'. *See,* UNFCC, *An Introduction to the United Nations Framework Convention on Climate Change (UNFCCC) and its Kyoto Protocol,* Fact Sheet, UNFCC (February 2011). For a spillover on biocultural rights into the UNFCCC, *see generally,* Peter Wood Olivier Rukundo and Johanna von Braun., 'REDD Community Protocols: A Community Approach to Ensuring the Local Integrity of REDD', *Outreach,* Special Post-COP 15 Issue (2010), p. 7.

Biocultural Rights: Future Trajectories

Biocultural rights denoting the rights of communities to fulfil their role as trustees of their cultures, lands, waters, and resources are increasingly being recognized in international environmental law. These rights include the rights of communities, in accordance with their customary laws, to regulate access to their cultures and territories by parties outside their traditional circle. It is critical to distinguish biocultural rights from a pure property claim by a hitherto excluded group in the typical market sense of property being universally commensurable, commodifiable, and alienable. On the contrary, biocultural rights are collective rights of communities to carry out traditional stewardship roles vis-à-vis Nature.

Mounting evidence of sophisticated systems of conservation and sustainable use of ecosystems by communities in accordance with their customary laws and values has laid a firm foundation for biocultural rights. Examples include action-research projects by the International Institute for Environment and Development (IIED) since 2005. These projects compared conservation practices of indigenous peoples and local communities in India, China, Peru, Panama, and Kenya.[53] One of the most interesting findings of these projects has been the discovery of a set of ecological ethics common to all these communities despite their diverse cultures and vastly different terrains. These ethics that resonated with communities internationally were initially identified as Quechua customary norms through the pioneering work of Alejandro Argumedo of Asociación ANDES with the Quechua communities of Peru who had set up a Potato Park as an *in situ* gene bank and a biocultural territory to conserve their traditional potato varieties. The IIED has summed up these ethics as: reciprocity (what is taken from Nature is given back in equal measure), duality (everything in Nature has a complementary opposite, and these opposites must be balanced),

[53] Krystyna Swiderska, Alejandro Argumedo, Yiching Song, Jingsong Li, Ruchi Pant, Heraclio Herrera, Doris Mutta, Peter Munyi, S Vedavathy, 'Protecting Community Rights over Traditional Knowledge: Implications of Customary Laws and Practices: Key Findings and Recommendations 2005–2009' (London: IIED, 2009), http://pubs.iied.org/14591IIED.html?c=biocon (accessed 13 September 2011).

and equilibrium (everything in Nature is in a state of dynamic equilibrium or harmony and this harmony must not be disrupted).[54]

Further evidence of intergenerational conservation by indigenous peoples of their territories has been marshalled by studies conducted by the Forest Peoples Programme (FPP) in Bangladesh, Suriname, Guyana, Cameroon, and Thailand.[55] Much of this evidence has played a key role in the emerging discourse around Indigenous Peoples' and Community Conserved Areas (ICCAs) under Element 2 (Governance, Participation, Equity and Benefit Sharing) of the Program of Work on Protected Areas (PoWPA) within the CBD framework.[56] The discourse around the ICCAs is emblematic of the battle lines between a state-led technocratic approach of fencing off 'protected areas' for conservation purposes and the response

[54] Swiderska et al. 'Protecting Community Rights' (2009). *See also* IIED, ANDES (Peru) and the Potato Park Communities, 'Community Biocultural Protocols: Building Mechanisms for Access and Benefit Sharing Amongst the Communities of the Potato Park Based on Quechua Customary Norms' (London: IIED, 2011).

[55] Forest Peoples Programme (FPP), Organization of Kaliña and Lokono in Marowijne (KLIM), South Central People's Development Association (SCPDA), Inter Mountain Peoples Education and Culture in Thailand (IMPECT), Association Okani (OKANI), Centre pour l'Environnement et le Développement (CED), and Unnayan Onneshan, 'Customary Sustainable Use of Biodiversity by Indigenous Peoples and Local Communities: Examples, Challenges, Community Initiatives and Recommendations Relating to CBD Article 10(c)', A Synthesis Paper by the FPP and Partner Organizations (October 2010), http://www.forestpeoples.org/topics/convention-biological-diversity-cbd/publication/2010/synthesis-paper-10c-case-studies (accessed 13 September 2011).

[56] The Programme of Work on Protected Areas (PoWPA) of the CBD was adopted in 2004 at the Seventh Conference of the Parties. It enshrines the development of participatory, ecologically representative, and effectively managed national and regional systems of protected areas, where necessary, stretching across national boundaries. PoWPA consists of four interlinked elements: **Element 1:** Direct Actions for Planning, Selecting, Establishing, Strengthening, and Managing, Protected Area Systems and Sites; **Element 2:** Governance, Participation, Equity and Benefit Sharing; **Element 3:** Enabling Activities; **Element 4:** Standards, Assessment, and Monitoring. See also, Stan Stevens, 'Implementing the UN Declaration on the Rights of Indigenous

by the ICCA Consortium[57] demanding legal recognition of local conservation practices in the tradition of political ecology.[58]

Pastoralists and livestock keepers across the world are also advocating biocultural rights by seeking legal recognition of their role as creators of livestock breeds and custodians of local ecosystems.[59] To this end the LIFE (Local Livestock for Empowerment) Network[60] is advocating biocultural rights in the form of rights of livestock keepers and pastoralists both under the CBD and the FAO.[61] These rights outlined in the LIFE Network facilitated *2009 Declaration on Livestock Keepers Rights*[62] is endorsed by a number of pastoralists' and livestock keepers' organizations. The principles underlying livestock keepers' rights are based on recognition of the integral links between the livestock keepers, their breeds and the ecosystem, and the conservation cycles that these links engender.

The emergence of farmers' rights under Article 9 of the ITPGRFA is a further example of biocultural rights. The ITPGRFA came into force in June 2004 and currently has 130 state parties, including the EU, who are obliged under Article 9 to recognize farmers' rights.

Peoples and the International Human Rights Law through the Recognition of ICCAs', *Policy Matters*, Issue 17 (October 2010), pp. 181–94.

57 The ICCA Consortium is a global network of CBOs and NGOs working towards securing the rights of indigenous peoples and local communities to govern and maintain their community conserved areas. *See* http://www.iccaworld.com/ (accessed 13 September 2011).

58 *See generally*, Holly Shrumm et al., 'Exploring the Right to Diversity in Conservation Law, Policy and Practice', *Policy Matters*, Issue 17 (October 2010), pp. 10–14.

59 *See generally*, the declarations and decisions of pastoral peoples at www.pastoralpeoples.org (accessed 13 September 2011).

60 The LIFE Network is a global network of organizations and individuals who support community conservation of livestock breeds.

61 The FAO is an intergovernmental organization with 191 Member Nations, two associate members and one member organization—the European Union (EU). The FAO was set up with the mandate to raise levels of nutrition, improve agricultural productivity, better the lives of rural populations, and contribute to the growth of the world economy. *See* www.fao.org (accessed 14 March 2012).

62 *See* http://www.pastoralpeoples.org/ (accessed 13 September 2011).

The ITPGRFA recognizes contributions of farmers in conserving and developing crop genetic resources. According to Article 9, governments are to protect and promote farmers' rights, but can choose a variety of locally relevant measures towards this aim. While the modalities for the implementation of farmers' rights are still nebulous, the Governing Body of the ITPGRFA is making efforts towards the realization of these rights. While the ITPGRFA does not define these rights, the generally agreed definition underscores their biocultural nature. Farmers' rights are said to consist of the customary rights of farmers to save, use, exchange, and sell farm-saved seed and propagating material; their rights to be recognized, rewarded, and supported for their contribution to the global pool of genetic resources as well as to the development of commercial varieties of plants; and to participate in decision-making on issues related to crop genetic resources.[63]

[63] *See* http://www.farmersrights.org/about/index.html (accessed 13 September 2011) for discussions on interpreting farmers' rights under the ITPGRFA. The website is an excellent resource on farmers' rights maintained by the Fridtj of Nansen Institute. Article 9 of the ITPGRFA dealing with farmers' rights states: 9.1

> Thc Contracting Parties recognize the enormous contribution that the local and indigenous communities and farmers of all regions of the world, particularly those in the centers of origin and crop diversity, have made and will continue to make for the conservation and development of plant genetic resources which constitute the basis of food and agriculture production throughout the world; 9.2 The Contracting Parties agree that the responsibility for realizing Farmers Rights, as they relate to plant genetic resources for food and agriculture, rests with national governments. In accordance with their needs and priorities, each Contracting Party should, as appropriate, and subject to its national legislation, take measures to protect and promote Farmers' Rights, including: (a) protection of traditional knowledge relevant to plant genetic resources for food and agriculture; (b) the right to equitably participate in sharing benefits arising from the utilization of plant genetic resources for food and agriculture; and (c) the right to participate in making decisions, at the national level, on matters related to the conservation and sustainable use of plant genetic resources for food and agriculture; 9.3 Nothing in this Article shall be interpreted to limit any rights that farmers have to save, use, exchange and sell farm-saved seed/propagating material, subject to national law and as appropriate.

Significant gains regarding biocultural rights have been made within the CBD through the Working Group on Article 8(j)[64] and other related provisions. Article 8(j), which in 1993 seemed an anodyne provision, has been transformed into the cutting edge of political ecology and indigenous peoples and local communities' rights. Examples of this include *the Akwé: Kon Guidelines on the conduct of social, cultural and environmental impact assessments on developments on the lands of indigenous and local communities*[65] and the recent *Tkarihwaié:ri Code of Ethical Conduct to ensure respect for the cultural and intellectual heritage of indigenous and local communities.*[66]

[64] *See* www.cbd.int for information about the Working Group on Article 8(j) and its work.

[65] The Akwé: Kon Guidelines were developed pursuant to task 9 of the programme of work on Article 8(j) and adopted by the Conference of the Parties of the CBD at its 5th meeting 2000. The Guidelines state their purpose as providing a collaborative framework within which Governments, indigenous and local communities, decision makers, and managers of developments can: (a) support the full and effective participation and involvement of indigenous and local communities in screening, scoping, and development planning exercises; (b) properly take into account the cultural, environmental and social concerns and interests of indigenous and local communities, especially of women who often bear a disproportionately large share of negative development impacts; (c) take into account the traditional knowledge, innovations, and practices of indigenous and local communities as part of environmental, social and cultural impact-assessment processes, with due regard to the ownership of and the need for the protection and safeguarding of traditional knowledge, innovations, and practices; (d) promote the use of appropriate technologies; (e) identify and implement appropriate measures to prevent or mitigate any negative impacts of proposed developments; (f) take into consideration the interrelationships among cultural, environmental, and social elements. *See* www.cbd.int/doc/publications/akwe-brochure-en.pdf (accessed 13 September 2011).

[66] The 10th meeting of the Conference of Parties (CoP) to the CBD in 2010 adopted the *Tkarihwaié:ri* Code of Ethical Conduct in its decision X/42. Section 2 of the Code identifies one of its main aims as the promotion of respect for the cultural and intellectual heritage of indigenous and local communities relevant for the conservation and sustainable use of biological diversity as a way of contributing to the achievement of the objectives of Article 8(j) of the CBD. One of the main elements of the Code relevant

The most recent, and high profile victory for biocultural rights is the *Nagoya Protocol on Access and Benefit Sharing,*[67] which was adopted in October 2010 by 193 state parties to the CBD. Four pivotal biocultural rights are established which significantly

---

for biocultural rights is Principle 20 dealing with traditional guardianship/custodianship. It states that

> Traditional guardianship/custodianship recognizes the holistic interconnectedness of humanity with ecosystems and obligations and responsibilities of indigenous and local communities, to preserve and maintain their traditional role as traditional guardians and custodians of these ecosystems through the maintenance of their cultures, spiritual beliefs and customary practices. Because of this, cultural diversity, including linguistic diversity, ought to be recognized as keys to the conservation and sustainable use of biological diversity. Therefore, indigenous and local communities should, where relevant, be actively involved in the management of lands and waters traditionally occupied or used by them, including sacred sites and protected areas. Indigenous and local communities may also view certain species of plants and animals as sacred and, as custodians of biological diversity, have responsibilities for their well-being and sustainability, and this should be respected and taken into account in all activities/interactions.

[*See* http://www.cbd.int/decision/cop/?id=12308 (accessed 13 September 2011)]

[67] *See* http://www.cbd.int/abs/text/ (accessed 13 September 2011). In the African context, biocultural rights preceded the Nagoya Protocol through the African Model Law for the Protection of the Rights of Local Communities, Farmers and Breeders and for the Regulation of Access to Biological Resources prepared in 1997 by an Organization of African Unity (OAU) Task Force. The OAU Ministerial Session, followed by the OAU Summit of Heads of State and Government, adopted this Model Law in Ouagadougou in 1998, and recommended that it be the basis of African national law. Article 16 of the African Model Law states: The state recognizes the rights of communities over the following:

i) their biological resources;
ii) the right to collectively benefit from the use of their biological resources;
iii) their innovations, practices, knowledge, and technologies acquired through generations;

affirm the self-determination of indigenous peoples and local communities. They are the right to:

i. Traditional knowledge
ii. Genetic resources
iii. Self-governance through own laws and community protocols
iv. Benefit from the utilization of traditional knowledge and genetic resources by third parties outside the traditional circle[68]

While none of these rights are unqualified and all allow for limited state involvement, they should be seen as substantial gains in the direction of a political ecology.

TOWARDS A BIOCULTURAL JURISPRUDENCE

Biocultural rights have been an unsung arrival on the international legal stage. This is primarily due to three important reasons:

1. The justificatory premise of biocultural rights has less to do with the third generation 'group or solidarity rights'[69] and more to do with the crisis of biodiversity loss and its ramifications for food, health, and economic security. As a result of intensive lobbying by environmental groups and a growing mountain of empirical evidence, states have had to make a policy U-turn from the disastrous 'fines and fences' approach[70] to conservation—an

---

iv) the right to collectively benefit from the utilization of their innovations, practices, knowledge, and technologies;
v) their rights to use their innovations, practices, knowledge, and technologies in the conservation and sustainable use of biological diversity; and
vi) the exercise of collective rights as legitimate custodians and users of their biological resources.

68 These conclusions have been drawn from my interpretation of specific articles of the Nagoya Protocol on ABS, the rationale for which will be elaborated in Chapter 5.

69 *See* fn. 48.

70 *See generally*, Child, Brian, Helen Suich, and Spenceley Anna (eds) *Evolution and Innovation in Wildlife Conservation: Parks and Game Ranches to Transfrontier Conservation Areas* (London: Earthscan, 2009).

approach that involved disenfranchising communities who had historically occupied common lands in favour of state control or private ownership. This policy U-turn meant, in essence, that to ensure conservation and sustainable use of biodiversity, states needed to affirm and secure the rights of communities who were the custodians of ecosystems for generations.

2. Biocultural rights were born as the shadow twin of third generation 'group rights'. But unlike these rights, which carried the undertone of self-determination, and made states nervous, biocultural rights were predominantly lobbied for under the Rio Conventions as 'environmental rights' of communities to ensure biodiversity conservation. They initially appeared in non-threatening forms such as 'farmers' rights', 'livestock keepers' rights' and rights to traditional knowledge, which, though hard won, were not seen as a threat to state sovereignty. Biocultural rights also differed significantly from group rights in that the nature of group rights they sought to assert was not only based on ethnicity or religion or minority status but primarily on a history of stewardship of ecosystems. So the nature of self-determination that was asserted was one around community governance and management of natural resources with evidence of an excellent track record of conservation that in most cases was more effective than state-centred approaches to ecosystem management.
3. Biocultural rights were advocated in international environmental negotiations as a defence against 'biopiracy'. Communities, in essence, demanded state protection against corporate theft of their knowledge and resources. With the politically fraught legal landscape of the Trade Related Aspects of Intellectual Property Rights Agreement (TRIPS) negotiations, developing countries supported biocultural rights as state assertions, using communities as proxies of the same kind of intellectual property rights that companies and individuals claimed, albeit in a *sui generis* form.[71]

[71] *See Intellectual Property and Traditional Knowledge* (WIPO Publications No.920 [E]).

As a subset of third generation rights, biocultural rights have elements of group rights but differ from the latter in their explicit commitment to conservation and the sustainable use of biodiversity. In many ways, biocultural rights have achieved greater recognition than group rights because their unobjectionable nature thereby acts as a bulwark for the more difficult claims of third generation rights such as self-determination.

Currently there is no research comprehensively describing the development of the nature and content of the 'biocultural rights' that have emerged through international environmental law. The lack of an effective description of the biocultural tendency in international law has led to an issue-based fragmentation of rights with similar content. For example, despite the seeming differences between livestock keepers' rights; farmers' rights; and rights of communities over their forests, genetic resources and traditional knowledge, they all have the same pith and substance—that is, they seek to secure the stewardship role of communities over their cultures, lands, and waters.

From a rights' perspective, the failure to trace the development of biocultural rights is a crisis of significant proportions. Little or no effort has been made to consolidate this biocultural jurisprudence into a body of knowledge that can be used by the very communities who struggled for it. There are a number of reasons for this lack of description and consolidation of biocultural rights and they all involve a dominant political, economic, and social imagination, which is unable to reconfigure itself to embrace the notion of stewardship ethics. This inability has much to do with the very foundations of market economy, dominant discourses on private property, and the assumptions about the nature and role of human beings in this context. It is to deconstruct these assumptions along with making the case for biocultural rights that we will turn in the following chapters.

CHAPTER TWO

Homo Economicus on Trial

Towards an Ethic of Stewardship

Political economy proceeds from the fact of private property. It does not explain it. It grasps the material process of private property, the process through which it actually passes, in general and abstract formulae, which it then takes as laws. It does not comprehend these laws; that is it does not show how they arise out of nature of private property.

—*Karl Marx,* 'Economic and Philosophical Manuscripts'[1]

Biocultural rights, as mentioned in the previous chapter, stem from the confluence of three movements. It is indigenous peoples, farmers, pastoralists, and traditional communities, however, who are at the forefront of the struggle for biocultural rights. For these groups, the fight for biocultural rights is a campaign for their very survival. The relationship communities have with their ecosystems is for the most part based on what they understand to be their role as guardians of their ecosystems.

Biocultural rights are therefore collective rights with a specific aim of affirming the right of stewardship of communities over their lands and waters. These rights differ from private property rights in that they refuse to conceive of Nature as solely a fungible and alienable commodity with exchange value. Rather they seek to safeguard the stewarding relation between a community and its ecosystem. While for the most part biocultural rights are asserted by communities that have traditionally had strong cultural and spiritual ties to their lands, there is no reason why they should not also be claimed by urban communities aspiring

[1] Karl Marx, 'Economic and Philosophical Manuscripts', in *Early Writings* (London: Penguin Books, 1975), p. 322.

to prevent the destruction of their local parks, wetlands, lakes, and trees in the name of development. Nevertheless, further research needs to be done to establish whether urban communities are able to develop and assert the same kinds of strong biocultural relationships to their lands as traditional communities have.

This chapter will lay the theoretical foundations of biocultural rights by making the case that the widespread belief in the naturalness and universality of market values lacks the rigour of proper historical analysis. The chapter will then go on to establish that it is the ethic of stewardship or care that is widespread amongst traditional communities across the world while the predominance of market values is a symptom of late capitalism. An argument will be made here that the contemporary global movement of indigenous peoples and traditional communities is a strategic assertion of a set of pre-capitalist values in an unprecedented political space created due to the ecological crisis caused by capitalism.

The dominant legal paradigm based on the market economy presents private property rights and the consequent commodification of Nature as ahistorical and therefore 'natural'. This approach is rooted in the American absolute 'castle or ownership' conception of property that views any legally imposed restrictions on the ability to act freely on one's own land as limitations on the rights of the owner and presumptively illegitimate. The use of one's property in such an approach is considered to be a 'self-regarding act' which means that as long as one's actions on one's land do not harm others in any tangible way, one is free to do what one pleases. The changes in law and morals over the years with the rise of the market economy meant that the ownership conception of property allowed owners to interpret their self-regarding acts as including the liberty to impose harm on others in the exercise of their property rights. Harm to others in the enjoyment of one's property became a policy question that was answered not on the basis of public morals but on the basis of whether certain limitations on absoluteness of property rights would adversely affect the market economy (which was deemed to be the greatest good).[2]

[2] Joseph Singer, 'How Property Norms Construct the Externalities of Ownership', *Harvard Law School Public Law Research* Paper No. 08–06 (2007), p. 2, http://ssrn.com/abstract=1093341 (accessed 28 February 2012);

This private property discourse arising out of the market economy makes absurd the questions put by communities, who ask 'how did land become property, trees become lumber, knowledge become intellectual property, and life become genetic resources?' The dismissal of questions such as these and the near omnipotence of the discourse that understands Nature in market terms is what we will deconstruct here.

Private property rights are portrayed in classical economics as mirroring a psychosocial reality where the assumption about the character of human beings is one of the *homo economicus* (a narrowly self-interested human) and the character of communities is a collection of commodity owners and consumers coming together for mutual self-interest.[3] The dominance of the private property rights discourse is taken as a given and remains unquestioned in societies where market relations override all other forms of social relations. It is this dominance, as we shall see later, that spawns a legal system requiring biocultural rights to justify themselves, whereas private property rights that perceive Nature in purely economic terms and communities as commodity producers are viewed as natural and timeless. It is therefore pertinent to interrogate the 'naturalness' of the *homo economicus* and to historicize private property rights — in effect to question the truth of Adam Smith's understanding of human nature, when he asserts in his work *The Wealth of Nations* that 'it is not from the benevolence of the butcher, the brewer or the baker that we expect our dinner, but from their regard to their self-interest'.[4]

The hypothesis here is that evidence from history and anthropology suggest that, far from being natural, the *homo economicus* is a social construction resulting from (and affirming) capitalist systems

---

See also, Joseph Singer, 'The Ownership Society and Takings of Property: Castles, Investments and Just Obligations', *Harvard Environmental Law Review,* Vol. 30 (2006), pp. 314–22.

[3] Regarding the origins of the *homo economicus, see generally,* Irene Ng and Lu-Ming Tseng 'Learning to be Sociable: The Evolution of Homo Economicus', *The American Journal of Economics and Sociology* 67(2) (April 2008), pp. 265–86.

[4] Adam Smith, 'On the Division of Labour', in *The Wealth of Nations,* Books I–III (New York: Penguin Classics, 1986), p. 119.

of production. It is at best a reification of a dimension of human life, presented as natural and timeless, thereby reinforcing the ideology of capitalism through a circular logic. The market economy is presented as the social flowering of 'human nature,' a euphemism for *homo economicus*, thereby presenting its logic as a biological imperative. The market economy then successfully closes this circle by forcing individuals to behave like the *homo economicus* by meticulously eliminating all other social opportunities where people may behave otherwise. Social relations are steadily replaced with market relations, thereby ensuring that the *homo economicus* becomes a self-fulfilling prophecy. It is only by understanding the atypical character of the predominance of the market economy that we will understand the naturalness of biocultural rights.

It is to validate this hypothesis that we shall now turn.

The Unnaturalness of Market Values

> *Homo economicus is not behind us, but before, like the moral man, the man of duty, the scientific man and the reasonable man. For a long time man was something quite different; and it is not so long now since he became a machine—a calculating machine.*
>
> —*Marcel Mauss, The Gift: Forms and Functions of Exchange in Archaic Societies*[5]

Adam Smith's *The Wealth of Nations*[6] was published in England in 1776. The impact of this text cannot be overestimated since it laid the foundations of the market economy, and its ramifications are felt to this day. The market economy is rooted in the idea of a self-regulating system or, in Adam Smith's terms, 'the invisible hand of the market',[7] which is the synergistic outcome of the interplay of individual self-interest. This person or the *homo economicus,* is the philosophical cornerstone of the theory of the market economy, and is based on a twofold assumption that human beings are fundamentally

[5] Marcel Mauss, *The Gift: Forms and Functions of Exchange in Archaic Societies* (New York: Norton Library, 1967), p. 74.

[6] Smith, *The Wealth of Nations* (1986).

[7] Adam Smith, *The Theory of Moral Sentiments* (New York: Prometheus Books, 2000), p. 240.

motivated by self-gain and that they behave in a manner to maximize this self-gain.

Adam Smith saw the market economy as a spontaneous and self-regulating manifestation of the self-interested activities of human beings. Based on this understanding of human nature, the only rational economic system of production and distribution we could envisage is one where all activities are motivated by private gain. As Smith says, it is the human being's natural propensity to 'truck, barter and exchange one thing for another'[8] that leads to the development of the market economy.

It was only in 1944 that the assumptions of the *homo economicus* and the 'naturalness' of the market economy were fundamentally challenged by the economic historian Karl Polanyi in his groundbreaking work *The Great Transformation.*[9] While Polanyi did not challenge the existence of an economy in all societies, he disagreed with the assertion of a number of economists that gain or profit seeking made through commodity exchanges predominated in every society. Polanyi noted that historically the production and distribution of goods in societies was rooted in maintaining social relations and affirming community rather than in generating surplus for individual profit. He says:

> The outstanding discovery of recent historical and anthropological research is that man's economy, as a rule, is submerged in his social relationships. He does not act so as to safeguard his individual interest in the possession of material goods; he acts so as to safeguard his social standing, his social claims, his social assets. He values material goods only in so far as they serve this end. Neither the process of production nor that of distribution is linked to specific economic interests attached to the possession of goods; but every single step in that process is geared to a number of social interests which eventually ensure that the required step is taken ... the economic system will be run on noneconomic motives.[10]

[8] *See* Chapter 2, 'Of the Principle which gives Occasion to the Division of Labour', in Smith, *The Wealth of Nations* (1986).

[9] Karl Polanyi, *The Great Transformation: The Political and Economic Origins of Our Time* (Boston: Beacon Press, 2001).

[10] Ibid., p. 44.

Marshall Sahlins in his seminal work *Stone Age Economics*[11] restates this point by noting that the notion of 'economy' should not be understood as something separate from society but rather as:

> [T]he process of provisioning society (or the 'socio-cultural system'). No social relation, institution, or set of institutions is of itself 'economic'. Any institution, say a family or a lineage order, if it has material consequence for provisioning society can be placed in an economic context and considered part of the economic process. The same institution may be equally or more involved in the political process, thus profitably considered as well in a political context. This way of looking at economics or politics— or for that matter, religion, education and any number of other cultural processes— is dictated by the nature of primitive culture. Here we find no socially distinct 'economy' or 'government,' merely social groups and relations with multiple functions, which we distinguish as economic, political and so forth.[12]

The crucial point made by both Polanyi and Sahlins is that, until the nineteenth century, contrary to popular myth, the economy was embedded in social relations. The modern phenomena of social relations being embedded in or defined by the economy were strongly resisted by communities in the past.[13]

Production and distribution were not based on the need to create surplus for the purposes of trade and individual gain, but were designed to meet the needs of the community.[14] Hence for Polanyi, the *homo economicus* is a fiction of relatively recent vintage. Ethnographic accounts of production and distribution in traditional societies show that the economy was not based on exchange but on the principles of householding, reciprocity, and redistribution.

Householding was production for one's own use, and was predominant in agricultural rather than hunter-gatherer societies. Householding meant that what one used was not procured through the exchange of surplus for goods that one needed to survive. On the

[11] Marshall Sahlins, *Stone Age Economics* (London: Tavistock Publications, 1972).

[12] Ibid., pp. 185–6.

[13] *See generally*, Polanyi, *The Great Transformation* (2001).

[14] *See generally*, Sahlins, *Stone Age Economics* (1972).

contrary, one produced to meet one's essential needs first, and, only if there was any surplus, was it exchanged. The primary motivation for householding was subsistence, not gain. Sufficiency and not profit or accumulation was the ethic.[15]

Redistribution was based on the ethic of sharing, and was grounded in a pattern Polanyi calls 'centricity'. A portion of what was produced by the community members was given to a central political authority, such as the chief, who in turn ensured its redistribution—again belying the myth of trucking or haggling for self-gain.[16] Reciprocity organized around the pattern of 'symmetry' is based on the ethic of caring in the 'gift economy' where things were gifted away to the community, the giver secure in the knowledge that the community would at some point in the future reciprocate in equal measure.[17]

The ethics of sufficiency, sharing, and caring are all interlinked. They reject avarice, self-interest, and opportunism, the values that undergird the *homo economicus,* as unnatural. On the contrary, these ethics indicate that the glorification of free markets disembodied from social relations is a reality peculiar to capitalist societies. Polanyi highlights the dangers of sacrificing the ethics of care at the altar of accumulation by noting:

> To allow the market mechanism to be sole director of the fate of human beings and their natural environment ... would result in the demolition of society .... Robbed of the protective covering of cultural institutions, human beings would perish from the effects of social exposure .... Nature would be reduced its elements neighbourhoods and landscapes defiled, rivers polluted ... no society could stand the effects of such a system of crude fictions even for the shortest stretch of time unless its human and natural substance as well as its business organization was protected against the ravages of this satanic mill.[18]

The transformation of pre-capitalist cultures to cultures where the market economy predominates involves the transformation of

[15] Polanyi, *The Great Transformation* (2001), pp. 55–9.

[16] Ibid., pp. 59–60.

[17] Isaac Balbus, *Governing Subjects* (New York: Routledge, 2009), e-book location 1801–11.

[18] Polanyi, *The Great Transformation* (2001), p. 77.

the *homo socialis*[19] to the *homo economicus.* These transformations were not without resistance, and the anthropologist Michael Taussig, in his important work *The Devil and Commodity Fetishism in South America,*[20] has carefully documented the cultural resistance of peasants inexorably being drawn into wage labour. Taussig documented rituals invoking the Devil by displaced Afro-American peasants employed as wage labour in the sugarcane plantations of the Cauca valley in Colombia, and by the dislocated Amerindian peasantry working as tin miners in the Bolivian highlands.

These neophyte proletarians in Taussig's work make sense of and resist their growing proletarianization by interpreting this turn of events using pre-capitalist imagery. The Devil in these cultures represents a rapacious being with which a pact can be made for short-term monetary gain, the price of which is a long march down the road to perdition. Taussig notes that these beliefs will erode once capitalism becomes firmly established in the cultural consciousness of these peasant turned proletarians. In the meantime, capitalism will be subjected to pre-capitalist worldviews that see it as the 'beginning of the end,' whereby these communities begin to lose control over their means of production, the social relations that underlie such production, and therefore a lifeworld itself.[21]

Such resistance carries over all the way into the twenty first century despite the near hegemony of the trope of the *homo economicus.* The continuing call for biocultural rights of indigenous peoples, small farmers, and pastoralists across the world is evidence of this. Taussig cites Malinowski, who noted that the white traders in the Trobriands had great difficulties with the native labour force that they used as pearl-divers. No amount of rewards could motivate them to work beyond what the natives thought was absolutely necessary to exchange pearls for the tobacco that the traders bartered.

[19] I use the term *homo socialis* to refer to the self in pre-capitalist societies that is construed as a locus of social relations where social obligations override self-interest.

[20] Michael Taussig, *The Devil and Commodity Fetishism in South America* (Chapel Hill: University of North Carolina Press, 2010).

[21] *See generally,* ibid.

Malinowski noted that the Trobriander was contemptuous of the trader's infantile obsession with pearls and he says that:

> [T]he greatest bribery and economic lures, the personal pressures of the White trader and competitive keenness of wealth, [could not] make the native give up his own pursuits for those foisted upon him. 'When the gardens are in full swing the god-damn niggers won't swim even if you stuff them with *kaloma* and tobacco', as it was pointed out to me by one of my trader friends.[22]

Taussig provides further examples of pre-capitalist meaning systems interpreting the capitalist turn by highlighting the resistance of the Bakweri of western Cameroon to German and British banana plantations. Those Bakweri who ended up becoming financially better off by working as wage labour in the plantations were suspected by their kinsmen of witchcraft. They were accused of killing their relatives and children, and turning them into zombies that were made to work in distant mountains.[23]

Polanyi's conclusions about the ahistorical nature of the *homo economicus* and Taussig's evidence of the active resistance of pre-capitalist cultures to this trope are summed up by Max Weber in *The Protestant Ethic and the Spirit of Capitalism*.[24] Highlighting the difficulty of substituting the *homo socialis* with the *homo economicus*, Weber comments:

> Labour must ... be performed as if it were an absolute end in itself, a calling. But such an attitude is by no means a product of nature. It cannot be evoked by low wages or high ones alone, but can only be the product of a long and arduous process of education. Today, capitalism once in the saddle, can recruit its labouring force in all industrial countries with comparative ease. In the past this was in every case an extremely difficult problem.[25]

[22] Bronislaw Malinowski, *The Coral Gardens and Their Magic*, Vol. 1 (Bloomington: University of Indiana Press, 1965), pp. 19–20 cited in ibid., at 19.

[23] Ibid., p. 20; Taussig notes that the word 'zombie' comes from the word *sombi* meaning to pledge or pawn, implying that people themselves became pledges or pawns in exchange for wealth.

[24] Max Weber, *The Protestant Ethic and the Spirit of Capitalism* (New York: Charles Scribner's Sons, 1950).

[25] Ibid., p. 62.

THE ETHICS OF STEWARDSHIP

For it is in giving that we receive.

—*Prayer of St. Francis of Assisi*[26]

Environmental educationist, Chet Bowers, notes that our relationship with Nature informs our 'root metaphors' and vice versa. Root metaphors in language constitute our worldview and become the furrows through which our thoughts flow — creating thought patterns or mindsets. While the central 'root metaphor' of biocultural rights is that of a 'web of life', the root metaphor of private property rights is one of the '*homo economicus*' where Nature is understood as 'resources'. On this metaphor are based other secondary, or what Bowers terms 'iconic' metaphors, such as the 'gain' that contributes to a market worldview, where Nature is seen as a 'commodity' that must be 'traded' and used 'profitably'.[27]

The principle of stewardship that forms the content of biocultural rights is based on the root metaphor of the 'web of life'. Ethics of sufficiency, sharing, and caring alluded to by Polanyi are at their core the glue that bind a community together and direct their relationship with Nature.

The *Gunis*, who are traditional healers in central and western India, name themselves after the word '*guna*', which means both healing and virtue. They believe that the efficacy of their healing practices is linked to their spiritual bond with the plant kingdom. In their biocultural community protocol, they stress their kinship with the plant world where plants appear in their dreams offering themselves as antidotes to ailments the Gunis intend to treat. The Gunis then offer prayers to the plant requesting its healing power and seeking permission to harvest a portion of it, promising not to hurt the plant. Selfless service to the community is integral to the Guni

[26] Kirby Page, *Living Courageously* (New York: Farrar & Rinehart, Inc., 1936).

[27] Chet Bowers, *The Culture of Denial: Why the Environmental Movement Needs a Strategy for Reforming Universities and Public Schools* (New York: State University of New York Press, 1997), pp. 204–6. *See also*, Chet Bowers, 2001. 'Towards an Eco-Justice Pedagogy', http://www.cabowers.net/CAbookarticle.php (accessed on 13 September 2011).

dharma (ethical duty), and the Gunis see themselves as guardians of both the physical and spiritual wellbeing of all.[28]

The Gunis have an aphorism in Hindi that sums up the Guni *dharma: Daya dharam ka mool hai, paap ka mool abhiman.* This is translated as 'compassion is the root of virtue, and the root of wrongdoing is self-centeredness'. This aphorism goes to the heart of stewardship ethics of sufficiency, sharing, and caring, and connects the Gunis to other groups of traditional healers like the Vaidyas[29] of the Malayalee hills in South India and the healers of Bushbuckridge[30] in South Africa: groups with similar ethics that radically break from the values of the *homo economicus* notwithstanding the diversity of their contexts and cultures, and have nurtured their ecosystems as an extension of themselves. The Vaidyas for example pick leaves of medicinal herbs only with their thumb and little finger so as to minimize pain to the plant. Every time they harvest a plant, they sprinkle its seeds upstream so the water would carry the seeds downstream spreading them along its banks.[31]

The 'gift economy' of communities has been highlighted by ethnographers as perhaps one of the most resounding arguments against the paradigm of the *homo economicus.* Amongst the most written about examples, are those that have been studied by Bronislaw Malinowski. He observes the Kula gift tradition of the Massim peoples of the South Sea Islands near the eastern tip of New Guinea, as embodying some of the most significant values of community.[32]

[28] From the biocultural community protocol of the Gunis on the resources page of naturaljustice.org (http://www.unep.org/communityprotocols/PDF/GuniMedical_BCP.pdf 2009, accessed 13 September 2011). Biocultural community protocols are discussed in greater detail in Chapter IX of this work.

[29] From the community protocol of the Vaidyas, on the resources page of naturaljustice.org (http://www.abs-initiative.info/uploads/media/Nairobi-0909-Makhubela_02.pdf. 2010, accessed 13 September 2011).

[30] From the community protocol of the traditional healers of Bushbuckridge, on the resources page of naturaljustice.org (accessed 13 September 2011).

[31] Community protocol of the Vaidyas, naturaljustice.org

[32] Bronislaw Malinowski, *Argonauts of the Western Pacific* (London: Routledge and Sons, 1922).

The continual movement of Kula gifts, as armbands or necklaces, around the Massim archipelago affirmed the leitmotif of the ethic of stewardship through the circle of gift exchange.

Malinowski makes a careful distinction between the Kula gift exchange and barter by arguing:

> The main principle underlying the regulations of actual exchange is that the Kula consists in bestowing of a ceremonial gift that must be repaid by an equivalent counter-gift .... The natives sharply distinguish it from barter which they practice extensively .... Often, when criticizing an incorrect, too hasty, or indecorous procedure of Kula, they will say—'He conducts his Kula as if it were *gimwali* (barter)' ... the equivalence of the counter-gift is left to the giver, and it cannot be enforced by any kind of coercion.[33]

Making a sharp break from the myth of the *homo economicus*, Malinowski asks what is it amongst the culture of the Massim people that ensured the counter-gift? To this question he responds:

> The great misconception of attributing to the savage a pure economic nature, might lead us to reason incorrectly thus—The passion of acquiring, the loathing to lose or give away is the fundamental and most primitive element in man's attitude to wealth .... The fundamental error in this reasoning is that it assumes that 'primitive man,' as represented by the present day savage, lives, at least in economic matters untrammeled by conventions and social restrictions. Quite the reverse is the case.[34]

Malinowski concludes by emphasizing the strong social obligation to 'give' that overrides the economic imperative to 'take or keep':

> This (Kula) social code ... lays down that to possess is to be great, and that wealth is the indispensable appanage of social rank and attribute of personal virtue. But the important point is that with them (the Massim) *to possess is to give* (emphasis mine)—here the natives differ from us notably.[35]

[33] Bronislaw Malinowski, 'The Kula', in Margaret Mead and Nicolas Calas (eds), *Primitive Heritage: An Anthropological Anthology* (London: Victor Gollancz, 1954), p. 373.

[34] Ibid., p. 374.

[35] Ibid.

Every individual who receives a Kula gift is a recipient of an act of generosity and he is therefore a steward of this ethic and must bestow generosity in equal measure on another person. The gift cannot be used as capital nor is it based on a bargain. On the contrary it is the vehicle through which the individual–self expands into the communal-self.

Lewis Hyde in his extraordinary work *The Gift: How the Creative Spirit Transforms the World*,[36] analyses the ethos of stewardship that is developed through gift exchange between the Maori and Nature. The Maori word *hau* is translated as 'spirit'— which is the 'spirit' of the gift and of the forest that gives food. When hunters return with birds that they have hunted, they give some of the kill to the priests, who cook it over the sacred fire in a ceremony called *whangai hau*, which means nourishing the *hau* or feeding the spirit. They then eat some of it and prepare a talisman, which is called the *mauri*, the physical embodiment of *hau* of the forest. The *mauri* is then given back to the forest, which is believed to cause the birds to be abundant.[37]

Hyde emphasizes the point that the movement of the gift has to go beyond the mutual reciprocity of two for it to become an ethic of giving. This ethic is born only when what is valued is shared or given without an immediate expectation of equivalent return. The value of the gift lies in its movement, and the movement of the gift from the forest to the hunters to the priests and back to the forest, expands the tribe to include Nature as a part of the widening ethical circle. Hyde says:

> Every gift calls for a return gift, and so, by placing the gift back in the forest, the priests treat the birds as a gift of nature. We now understand this to be ecological .... Widening the study of ecology to include man means to look at ourselves as a part of nature again, not its lord ... So the circle is a sign of an ecological insight as much as of gift exchange. We come to feel ourselves as one part of a large self-regulating system. The return gift, the 'nourishing *hau*', is literally feedback, as they say in cybernetics. Without it, that is to say, with the exercise of any greed or arrogance of will, the cycle is broken .... The forest's abundance is in fact a consequence of man's treating its wealth as a gift.[38]

[36] Lewis Hyde, *The Gift: How the Creative Spirit Transforms the World* (Edinburgh: Canongate, 1983).

[37] Ibid., p. 19.

[38] Ibid.

Redistribution and reciprocity is not restricted to the Massim or the Maori. Among the /Xam San of the Northern Cape, if three hunters tracked and killed a springbok, the division of the meat would be made by the other two hunters whose arrows did not make the kill. Lorna Marshall records that with the !Xun-speaking- San of the Nyae Nyae, the hunter was obliged to share the meat with the one who gave him the arrow that secured the kill, who in turn shared the meat with another from whom he received the arrow. She notes that the system of sharing meat and exchanging of arrows ensured that the hunter who made the kill received less meat than those further down the line of distribution, thus affirming the ethic of sharing and caring on which the clan depended. As was pointed out by the missionary, Robert Moffat, amongst the /Xam, the one who received food gifts from the Dutch farmers, retained the least for himself and redistributed the rest.[39]

The struggle by communities for biocultural rights should be seen as a struggle against the dominance of the market economy and the erosion of an ethical universe that accompanies such a mode of production. The ethics of stewardship asserted by these communities have found unprecedented traction in emerging international environmental law at a time when capitalism's Achilles heel has been exposed: the environmental crisis caused by the *homo economicus*. The call for biocultural rights no longer seems an anachronistic claim of 'primitive traditionalism' but a fight for our collective future. In fact, these pre-capitalist values in the form of stewardship ethics appear as a clarion call for a world where our obligations to the planet are no longer the epiphenomenon of market relations.

In their biocultural community protocol, the Maldhari pastoralists of Kachchh in western India[40] describe their stewardship duties towards the Banni (the grasslands) and their unique buffalo breeds, as being entrusted to them by Nature itself. Nature here is the guardian

39 Roger Hewitt, 'An Ethnographic Sketch of the /Xam', in Miklos Szalay (ed.), *The Moon as Shoe: Drawings of the San* (Zurich: Scheidegger and Spiess, 2002), p. 44.

40 The Maldhari community protocol is on file with the author. Copies of it can be requested from the *Banni Pashu Uccherak Maldhari Sangathan*, c/o Sahjeevan 2010., www.sahjeevan.org (accessed 13 September 2011).

of the Maldhari way of life, and the Maldharis have seen themselves as its stewards for the last 450 years. The fragile Banni ecosystem and the harsh droughts of Kachchh are the very conditions that hold the Maldhari communities together, and bind them to Nature. Unaided, the *homo economicus* will not survive the fierceness of Kachchh, but sufficiency, sharing, and caring have seen the Maldhari through for nearly half a millennium.

THE PHILOSOPHY OF PRAXIS

> *Ethnographic reports speak of 'the transpersonal self' (Native Americans), of the self as 'a locus of shared social relations or shared biographies' (Caroline Islands), of persons as 'the plural and composite site of the relationships that produced them' (New Guinea Highlands) .... Clearly the self in these societies is not synonymous with the bounded, unitary and autonomous individual .... Rather, the individual is the locus of multiple other selves with whom he or she is joined in mutual relations of being; even as, for the same reason, any person's self is more or less widely distributed among others.*
>
> —*Marshall Sahlins, The Western Illusion of Human Nature*[41]

Historicizing the *homo economicus* and challenging its apparent universality with examples of stewardship necessarily begs the question of the 'essential' nature of human beings. Is the human essence best represented by the *homo economicus* or the *homo socialis*? Hitherto, efforts at providing ethnographic and historical evidence of stewardship ethics amongst pre-capitalist communities aimed to refute the universality of the paradigm of *homo economicus*. The argument so far has attempted to destabilize assertions by market economists from Adam Smith onwards, that the essence of human beings is 'self interest', together with claims by political philosophers of the 'social contract' variety (which echo the Hobbesian view that in the state of nature, the life of man is 'solitary, poor, nasty, brutish and short').[42]

[41] Marshall Sahlins, *The Western Illusion of Human Nature* (Chicago: Prickly Paradigm Press, 2008), p. 48.

[42] Thomas Hobbes, *Leviathan or the Matter, Form and Power of the Commonwealth* (London: Printed for Andrew Crooke at the Green Dragon in St. Paul's Churchyard, 1651), p. 99.

Any question regarding the 'essential nature' of human beings is moot since it spawns an inconclusive debate, which presumes an immutable human essence that stands outside history and the material conditions of life. Every example of human altruism is presented with a counter example of human covetousness. Our understanding of the struggle for biocultural rights disengages from this question by presenting the struggle of communities as a 'philosophy of praxis'.[43]

The 'philosophy of praxis' implies a unity between theory and practice, and suggests that the essence of human beings is not a question that can be answered outside history and social context, but, on the contrary, needs to be worked out in practice or action. Such an understanding facilitates an analysis of the political mobilization of communities for biocultural rights as progressive action towards the ethics of stewardship rather than merely romanticizing a pre-capitalist way of life. It is imperative to bear in mind that the call for biocultural rights is not a call for cultural relativism or for supporting everything traditional, but specifically a call for rejecting the hegemony of market values and affirming the ethics of stewardship towards Nature.

Among the most significant challenges to the notion of an immutable human nature was the one posed by Marx who stated:

> It is not the consciousness of men that determines their existence, but their social existence that determines their consciousness.[44]

[43] The 'philosophy of praxis' is a term used by the Italian Marxist Antonio Gramsci in his *Prison Notebooks* to indicate 'absolute historicism and the absolute bringing down to earth and worldliness of thought', *See* David Forgacs (ed.), *The Gramsci Reader: Selected Writings 1916–1935* (New York: New York University Press, 2000), p. 429.

[44] Karl Marx, 'Preface to A Contribution to the Critique of Political Economy', in *Early Writings* (1975), p. 425; Marx's statement here reflects the early disagreements that Marx and Engels had with the Young Hegelians especially Ludwig Feuerbach, Bruno Bauer, and Max Stirner. The Young Hegelians were Left-leaning followers of Hegel who after his death, used aspects of his thought to reclaim for humanity its *essence*, which they argued had been projected onto Christianity and the Prussian state, leaving human beings empty. If the *homo economicus* is one universal model of the essence of humanity, the Young Hegelians in their efforts to reclaim human essence

In his *Theses on Feuerbach*[45] written in 1845, Marx criticizes Ludwig Feuerbach for his views that human beings alienate themselves from their essence by attributing to God qualities that are the basis of humanity. The basis of Marx's criticism was that despite Feuerbach's best intentions, he was calling for reclamation of a human essence, which was presented as unhistorical and theoretical. Marx makes his disagreement clear by stating that:

> Feuerbach resolves the religious essence into the human essence. But the human essence is no abstraction inherent in each single individual. *In its reality it is the ensemble of the social relations* (emphasis mine).[46]

Marx further goes on to state that this attempt of Feuerbach's to seek a universal human essence forces him to:

> Abstract from the historical process and to fix the religious sentiment as something by itself and to presuppose an abstract—*isolated*—human individual .... Feuerbach, consequently, does not see that the religious sentiment is itself a social product, and that the abstract individual whom he analyses belongs to a particular form of society.[47]

For Marx, therefore, human essence is relational or what he terms as the 'ensemble of social relations'. French Marxist philosopher, Etienne Balibar, refers to this understanding of 'human essence' as *transindividuality*.

> The only true subject (for Marx) is the practical subject or the subject of practice or better still, that *the subject is nothing other than practice* which has always already begun and continues indefinitely.[48]

Marx and Engels elaborate on this practice in their work *The German Ideology* that was also written in 1845, after the initial notes

---

from religion and the state were developing another universal model of human essence. Marx's criticism of the Young Hegelians stemmed from his fundamental disagreement with the very quest for a universal human essence separate from the material conditions of life.

[45] Karl Marx, 'Concerning Feuerbach' Ibid., at 421.

[46] Ibid., p. 423.

[47] Ibid.

[48] Etienne Balibar, *The Philosophy of Marx* (London: Verso, 2007), p. 25.

that Marx made in the *Thesis on Feuerbach*.[49] In *The German Ideology*,[50] Marx develops the thesis that there is no human essence standing outside history, and human history begins with the production of means of subsistence. Hence for Marx, 'the nature of individuals thus depends on the material conditions determining their production'.[51]

Marx disagrees with philosophers who argue that 'liberation' of humankind is achieved by developing true 'self-consciousness'. He emphasizes that real liberation can only be achieved in the 'real world' using 'real means'.[52] 'Consciousness' then for Marx is a social product; it is always a consciousness of something. Marx affirms that: 'The production of ideas, of conceptions, of consciousness, is at first directly interwoven with the material activity and the material intercourse of men, the language of real life'[53] and 'Life is not determined by consciousness, but consciousness by life'.[54] In essence, Marx's argument is that human essence is not a 'noun' but a 'verb'. It is the result of a continual dialectic between consciousness and the world. Hence, our real nature or essence cannot be determined outside of practice. We are or rather we become what we do.

Nearly 60 years after Marx's polemic against the Young Hegelians, the eminent American psychologist and philosopher William James corroborated these insights into the nature of consciousness. James argued that the only thing that exists is pure experience, which is split into the experiencing subject and the experienced object, or knower and known. James concluded that:

> *Experience ... has no such inner duplicity; and the separation of it into consciousness and content comes, not by way of subtraction, but by way of addition*—the addition, to a given concrete piece of it (experience), other sets of experiences, in connection with which severally its use or function may be of two different kinds .... Just so, I maintain,

[49] Marx, 'Concerning Fuerbach' (1975).

[50] Karl Marx and Friedrich Engels, *The German Ideology* (1932) http://faculty.rcc.edu/sellick/The German Ideology.pdf (accessed 13 September 2011).

[51] Ibid., p. 5.

[52] Ibid., p. 14.

[53] Ibid., p. 7.

[54] Ibid.

does a given undivided portion of experience, taken in one context of associates, play the part of a knower, of a state of mind, of 'consciousness'; while in a different context the same undivided bit of experience plays the part of a thing known, of an objective 'content'. In a word, in one group it figures as a thought, in another group as a thing.[55]

The endeavour towards biocultural rights then is not about establishing an enduring 'indigenous self' onto which the ecological movement can project its vision of an 'ideal' humanity. Much of this has already happened with indigenous peoples and traditional communities having to bear the burden of living up to stereotypes of the 'natural man' created by idealists disaffected by the market economy's ravaging of Nature. On the contrary, biocultural rights call for the reinforcing and, where necessary, a restoration, of stewardship ethics prevalent in cultures still shielded from the cultural defoliation of full-blown capitalism.

The political struggle for biocultural rights is neither the swansong of a fast disappearing way of life nor a battle that can only be won by turning back the clock on the means of production in capitalist societies. In fact, it embodies Gramsci's argument that the means and relations of production and the cultural and political institutions in any society are inextricably intertwined, each interpenetrating and reinforcing the other and forming a 'historical bloc'.[56]

Biocultural rights are an effort to challenge the hegemony of the values of *homo economicus.* The term 'hegemony'[57] here is used in the Gramscian sense as a relation that manufactures consent not merely by coercion but also by means of a political and ideological leadership. The hegemony of the *homo economicus* is a result of the reinforcing of market values through a range of institutions and alliances. Indigenous peoples have begun to challenge this hegemony by forming alliances with farmers' groups, the environmental

[55] William James, 'Does Consciousness Exist?', *Journal of Philosophy, Psychology, and Scientific Methods*, 1 (1904), pp. 477–91.

[56] Antonio Gramsci, 'Hegemony, Relations of Force, Historical Bloc', in Forgacs (ed.), *The Gramsci Reader* (2000), p. 193.

[57] Roger Simon, *Gramsci's Political Thought—An Introduction* (London: Lawrence and Wishart, 1991), p. 26.

movement, livestock keepers, and anti-capitalist forces. They counter this hegemony with intellectual reform[58] rooted in the ethics of stewardship. They are not calling for a return to innocence but for a broad based struggle to protect the Earth. Their struggle is one of praxis, and embodies Marx's famous statement: '*Philosophers have only interpreted the world in various ways; the point is to change it*'.[59]

The persistence of the presumption of the *homo economicus* despite being belied by anthropology and economic history is a curious phenomenon. Such persistence in the face of overwhelming evidence to the contrary can only be understood by viewing the *homo economicus* as symptomatic of something much deeper. It is the pursuit of this first cause that we shall embark upon in the next chapter.

58 Ibid., p. 28.

59 Karl Marx, 'Concerning Feuerbach' (1975), p. 423; this famous statement is also carved as an epitaph on Marx's tombstone.

CHAPTER THREE

Fighting Fetishism

Biocultural Readings of Social Hieroglyphs

To be radical is to grasp things by the root; but for man the root is man himself.

—*Karl Marx,* 'A Contribution to Hegel's Philosophy of Rights'[1]

The neoliberal turn towards the end of the twentieth century ensured that the market economy would reach its zenith.[2] It is during such a ubiquity of market values that questions regarding well-being and our relationship with Nature are being asked with unprecedented urgency. The values of pre-capitalist cultures are presented as a moral compass that will deliver us from the ecological crisis to a post-capitalist future. While many of these values are being reconfigured using market terminology like the 'green economy'[3] or

[1] Karl Marx, 'A Contribution to Hegel's Philosophy of Rights' (1844), http://www.marxists.org/archive/marx/works/1843/critique-hpr/intro.htm (accessed 13 September 2011).

[2] *See generally*, David Harvey, *A Brief History of Neoliberalism* (New York: Oxford University Press, 2005).

[3] The United Nations Environment Program (UNEP) launched the Green Economy Initiative in late 2008. The Initiative consists of several components whose collective overall objective is to provide the analysis and policy support for investing in green sectors and in greening environmentally unfriendly sectors. For the purposes of the Green Economy Initiative, UNEP has developed a working definition of a green economy as 'one that results in **improved human well-being and social equity, while significantly reducing environmental risks and ecological scarcities**. In its simplest expression, a green economy can be thought of as one which is **low carbon, resource efficient** and **socially inclusive**'. UNEP further

'payment for ecosystem services'[4] or 'the economics of ecosystems and biodiversity,'[5] these still do not fundamentally challenge the paradigm of the *homo economicus*.

---

explains the green economy as an economy 'whose growth in income and employment is driven by public and private investments that reduce carbon emissions and pollution, enhance energy and resource efficiency, and prevent the loss of biodiversity and ecosystem services. These investments need to be catalyzed and supported by targeted public expenditure, policy reforms and regulation changes. This development path should maintain, enhance and, where necessary, rebuild natural capital as a critical economic asset and source of public benefits, especially for poor people whose livelihoods and security depend strongly on nature'. In July 2011, UNEP released the Green Economy Report titled *Towards a Green Economy: Pathways towards Sustainable Development and Poverty Eradication.* The report according to UNEP seeks to demonstrate that the greening of economies is not generally a drag on growth but rather a new engine of growth; that it is a net generator of decent jobs, and that it is also a vital strategy for the elimination of persistent poverty. *See* http://www.unep.org/greeneconomy/Home/tabid/29770/Default.aspx (accessed 13 September 2011).

[4] A definition for payment for ecosystem services (PES) that has become fairly well accepted has been put forward by Sven Wunder, in which he explains, '"[a] payment for environmental services scheme" is a voluntary transaction in which a well defined environmental service (ES), or a form of land use likely to secure that service is bought by at least one ES buyer from a minimum of one ES provider if and only if the provider continues to supply that service (conditionality)'. Wunder, Sven, Payments for Environmental Services, CIFOR, Occasional Paper No.42, Jakarta: CIFOR, 2005,, quoted on the CIFOR website: http://www.cifor.cgiar.org/pes/_ref/about/index.htm (accessed 13 September 2011). The key characteristic of PES deals is that the focus is on maintaining a flow of a specified ecosystem 'service'—such as clean water, biodiversity habitat, or carbon sequestration capabilities—in exchange for something of economic value. The critical, defining factor of what constitutes a PES transaction, however, is not just that money changes hands and an environmental service is either delivered or maintained. Rather, the key is that the payment causes the benefit to occur where it would not have otherwise. That is, the service is 'additional' to 'business as usual,' or at the very least, the service can be quantified and tied to the payment. *See, Payment for Ecosystem Services- Getting Started: A Primer* (Nairobi: UNEP, Forest Trends and the Katoomba Group, 2008), p. 3.

[5] The Economics of Ecosystems and Biodiversity (TEEB) study is an international initiative to draw attention to the global economic benefits of

This call for a discursive shift should not be caricatured as a call for a 'return to innocence' or a rejection of markets. Rather it should be understood as a call for reclaiming social values that have been eclipsed by the values of the market. The campaign for biocultural rights is an effort to realize this call. At its core this campaign seeks to transfer control of ecosystems from distant markets and techno–bureaucrats to communities whose stewardship ethics have for generations protected these ecosystems.

Perhaps the greatest challenge for biocultural rights is what Gramsci refers to as a 'passive revolution',[6] which is a top–down restructuring that occurs once the powerful market interests are widely threatened. Popular uprisings and calls for self-determination and greater recognition by indigenous peoples or farmers' groups are met with state controlled techno–bureaucratic solutions designed to take the edge off these demands and restate them as anodyne claims for conservation and wider redistribution of market benefits. At the end of such a process, these top–down solutions ensure that the values of the *homo economicus* still remain sacrosanct, and reconciliatory discourses like 'sustainable growth' and 'green incentives' are deployed. Once again 'business as usual' is restored with the primacy of the market ordering our social and moral universe being unequivocally affirmed.

It is, therefore, pertinent to ask ourselves the question: how has the model of the *homo economicus* maintained its cultural hegemony despite its being unsubstantiated by history and unfounded by

---

biodiversity. Its objective is to highlight the growing cost of biodiversity loss and ecosystem degradation and to draw together expertise from the fields of science, economics, and policy to enable practical actions. The lack of market prices for ecosystem services and biodiversity means that the benefits derived from these goods (often public in nature) are usually neglected or undervalued in decision-making. This in turn leads to actions that not only result in biodiversity loss, but also impact human well-being. TEEB, therefore, seeks to economically value Nature as natural capital with the aim of ensuring that costs of ecosystem services are incorporated rather than externalized in all policy and business decision-making. *See, The Economics of Ecosystems and Biodiversity: TEEB for Policy Makers, Summary: Responding to the Value of Nature* (Wesseling: UNEP, 2009).

[6] *See* Forgacs (ed.), *The Gramsci Reader* (2000) p. 428.

ethnography? From where does it derive its enormous strength? Communities have long puzzled over the way it has captured popular imagination in capitalist societies, especially when support for market values comes from across the class spectrum.

The *homo economicus* is a secondary symptom whose first cause is the fetishism of commodities in capitalist societies. It is the dominance of the commodity form that gives rise to the *homo economicus,* not the other way round. By understanding the true nature of commodities as the core of capitalism we can answer the question indigenous peoples and traditional communities have often posed: 'How did land become property, trees become lumber, traditional knowledge become intellectual property and life become genetic resources?' Fetishism of commodities is not restricted to markets but profoundly influences both law and policy. If the aim of the proponents of biocultural rights is to mount a foundational critique of the existing legal system, then an understanding of the fetishism of commodities is imperative. Hence it is towards an analysis of the commodity form and its consequences for law and policy to which we shall now turn.

FETISHES, PHANTOMS, AND HIEROGLYPHICS

> *It is absolutely clear that, by its activity humanity changes the form of the materials of nature in such a way as to make them useful to it. The form of wood, for instance, is altered if a table is made out of it. Nevertheless the table continues to be wood, an ordinary, sensible thing. But as soon as it emerges as a commodity, it changes into a thing that transcends sensuousness. It not only stands with its feet on the ground, but, in relation to all other commodities, it stands on its head, and evolves out of its wooden brain grotesque ideas, far more wonderful than if it were to begin dancing of its own free will.*
>
> —*Karl Marx,* 'The Fetish Character of the Commodity and Its Secret'[7]

[7] Karl Marx, 'The Fetish Character of the Commodity and its Secret', in Karl Marx (trans. by B. Fowkes), *Capital: A Critique of Political Economy,* Vol. 1 (London: Penguin, 1976), p. 163.

Contemporary analyses on 'commodification' in market economies owe a significant debt to the work of Karl Marx. Marx's analysis was groundbreaking; it created a blueprint for understanding the mysterious nature of commodities. Marx himself referred to commodities as 'fetishes', 'social hieroglyphics', and 'phantasmagorical', terms that alluded to their cryptic nature, and the title of the chapter in his work *Capital* that deals with nature of commodities is mysteriously titled 'The Fetish Character of the Commodity and its Secret'.[8] In the above example of the wooden table, Marx indicates the supernatural powers it acquires when it becomes a commodity and every metaphor that Marx uses to describe commodities hints at their paranormal nature.

The term hieroglyphic, though most commonly used in the context of Egyptology originated in the late sixteenth century and traces its roots to the Greek word '*heirogluphikos*', with *heiro* meaning 'sacred' and *gluphe* meaning 'carving'.[9] 'Phantasmagoric', is an early nineteenth century word which refers to ghostly optical illusions produced through the use of a magic lantern (an image projector) in theatrical exhibitions and séances.[10] 'Fetish' or 'fetishism' is a word coined in 1757 by Charles de Brosses in his work comparing the religion of ancient Egypt and west Africa. The term derives from the pidgin term *fetisso* used along the coast of West Africa around that time, originating from the medieval Portuguese word *fetico*, meaning charm or sorcery. The Portuguese traders used the term to make sense of the unfathomable attachment that some west African tribes had for certain objects.[11]

By using these terms, Marx attempted to describe a phenomenon whereby commodities are treated with reverence and given mysterious powers greater than the abilities of the very humans that created them. These commodities then have a double meaning: they are functional and have use value for humans, while at the same time they take on a life of their own, extending far beyond their functionality. For Marx,

[8] Marx, 'The Fetish Character of the Commodity and Its Secret', p. 163.

[9] Peter Osborne, *How to Read Marx* (New York: W. W. Norton and Co., 2005), p. 15.

[10] Ibid., p. 16.

[11] Ibid., pp. 17–18.

the fetishism of commodities in capitalist societies was not an obsession with commodities per se, but rather an inability to see them for what they really are: products of human labour created to meet specific human needs. We shall focus here on understanding this amnesia regarding the origin of commodities peculiar to market economies.

Marx began his quest by seeking to understand how things humans produce that embody the richness of their experience, the skill of their hands, the depth of their cultures, become commodities or objects whose value is measured in terms of money? Marx in many ways pre-empted the incredulity of indigenous peoples when they are asked to quantify in terms of cash the value of their forests or traditional knowledge. This incredulity is commonly misunderstood as an inability of 'primitive cultures' to engage the market, rather than analysing the basic building blocks of the market economy itself.

For Marx, like Polanyi after him, markets and commodities play a role in every society, and the problem is not markets or even commodities themselves. The real problem is the eclipsing of all social relations by market relations. Marx argued that everything humans produce has 'use value', for example traditional knowledge or the art works of indigenous peoples has value for them. They are the result of unique skill, cultural exchanges, spiritual norms, and interactions with the ecosystem. In an economy of householding, redistribution, or reciprocity, these things are valued for themselves rather than as compared to something else. For example, corn is valued for its use value rather than the quantity of meat that can be exchanged for it. In fact, the corn is shared and so is the meat, with the tacit understanding of the mutual interdependence of individuals within the community.[12]

'Use value' becomes 'exchange value' in situations where barter comes in, that is, when meat is exchanged or traded for corn. Marx makes the point that it is with exchange value that markets and commodities come into existence, and, while all societies have an aspect of their economy that is based on exchange value, its omnipresence is a unique feature of our times. Use value is converted

[12] Karl Marx (ed. by Maurice Dobb), *A Contribution to the Critique of Political Economy* (New York: International Publishers, 1979), pp. 19–55.

to exchange value when the question of equivalence is posed. Ultimately according to Marx, the equivalence would be established, based on the amount of labour it would take to produce a kilogram of meat versus the amount of labour it would take to produce the same quantity of corn.[13]

The labour that is referred to here is a social average, that is, based on the average time taken by a skilled worker. Of course things become more complicated when we speak, for example, of computers where the social average of labour has to include the labour of not just the hardware engineer who is assembling the computer but also the labour it takes to build the technology and the parts required to produce the computer. An hour of an engineer's labour is also valued more than an hour of an unskilled labourer because of the need to account for the labour that went into producing the engineer in the first place. Technology also changes the social average of labour; for example the invention of the electric loom reduced the amount of labour it took to produce fabric from a handloom.[14]

Therefore, according to Marx, the basic unit of measurement to establish equivalence for the purposes of exchange value is human labour. But here we are already getting into the notion of 'abstract labour', wherein human effort has become a unit of measurement that is oriented towards generating exchange value. It is effectively divorced from the real conditions, skills, and needs of the producers. Abstract labour then begins to appear as an impersonal force separate from the real labouring humans who are its source. One can see how in a market economy, where exchange value predominates, the exchange value (which is an abstraction) becomes more real than use value (which is concrete). Here, there is a paradigm shift from pre-capitalist economies of householding, redistribution, and reciprocity, where use value predominates, to market economies where all production is necessarily the production of commodities geared towards generating exchange value.

[13] Stephen Shapiro, *How to Read Marx's Capital* (London: Pluto Press, 2008), pp. 7–15.

[14] Karl Marx, 'The Buying and Selling of Labour-Power', (Chapter 6) in *Capital*, Vol.1 (1867), http://www.marxists.org/archive/marx/works/1867-c1/ch06.htm (accessed 13 September 2011).

This level of abstraction is taken to its extreme with the concept of money, which is the ultimate symbol of exchange value. Money has no use value in itself; it is pure exchange value. For example, one cannot eat or drink money. According to Marx, it represents abstract labour and therefore becomes a symbol of another symbol, thereby the ultimate abstraction in a market economy. This ultimate abstraction then becomes the ultimate reality in all capitalist societies.[15]

Money and commodities are abstractions that stand for each other. In market economies the human labour that produces things for use value, becomes abstract labour that produces commodities for exchange value, and money is the fundamental symbol of exchange value. To decode the social hieroglyphic of a commodity is to comprehend it as essentially a product of human labour valued for the purposes of market exchange through abstract labour represented by money.

Exchange value establishes equivalence between things that are fundamentally different. Even though the effort, skill, and the cultural context of corn growing (use value) is very different from the effort, skill, and the cultural context of hunting for meat, equivalence is established between them by the market, based on abstract labour represented by money. So we have the conclusion: 5 bushels of corn equal a kilogram of meat or rather 5 bushels of corn costs 20 rands and a kilogram of meat costs 20 rands.

Exchange value therefore is purely conceptual and has nothing to do with the intrinsic properties of the commodity or its use value. For instance, a numeral like the number '5' does not have any use value; it does not have any concrete 'fiveness'. As Marxist scholar Stephen Shapiro notes:

> 'Fiveness' belongs to the collection of five actual objects, let's say apples. The number '5' is only a conceptual device, an abstract marker that erases the concrete differences between the individual apples, such as their particular shape, colour, or taste.[16]

Through the creation of exchange value, use value is masked or erased. Exchange value has very little to do with the 'sensory

[15] Shapiro, *How to Read Marx's Capital* (2008), pp. 41–5.
[16] Ibid., p. 11.

experience' of production and consumption that is so prevalent in use value. Exchange value on the contrary has a 'ghostly objectivity' (phantasmagoria), which accompanies the product of labour. Money is the ultimate means of exchange value and becomes the universal economic equivalent through which the value of every other commodity can be expressed. As Marx notes:

> The memory of use value, as distinct from exchange value, has become entirely extinguished in this incarnation of pure exchange value.[17]

Exchange value or 'commodification' is in itself unavoidable in situations of 'trucking, bartering or exchange'. As observed previously, many communities through history have always had some form of market and conception of money. Even Malinowski highlights that among the Massim peoples, the existence of the Kula gift economy did not mean that there was no barter or trade for other essentials.[18] The Maldharis of Kachchh are another classic example: they are renowned in the region for the high price their Banni buffaloes fetch in the trade fairs.[19] But, as Marx points out, the total eclipsing of all use value at the altar of exchange value is the hallmark of capitalism: 'all that is solid, melts into air, all that is holy is profaned'.[20]

The discussion above shows that it is the ubiquity of exchange value in market economies that gives rise to the fetishism of commodities. Unlike pre-capitalist economies, individuals within a market economy lose the ability to see commodities as products of the labour of real people within specific contexts, that is, they are unable to see the social relations behind the production of goods and services. Instead, they perceive commodities as 'things in themselves', divorced from the people who produced them, and valued purely in terms of money. Social relations between people are replaced by relationships between commodities, and commodities acquire a

[17] Karl Marx, *Grundrisse: Foundation of the Critique of Political Economy* (Harmondsworth: Penguin Books, 1973), pp. 239–40.

[18] Malinowski, 'The Kula' (1954).

[19] The Maldhari community protocol [Copies available, www.sahjeevan.org (accessed 13 September 2011)].

[20] Karl Marx and Friedrich Engels, *The Communist Manifesto* (1848), http://www.gutenberg.org/ebooks/61 (accessed 13 September 2011).

transcendent power, which they invest in those who possess them, rather than those who produce them.

In market economies, commodities and money, which are abstractions of exchange value, become the overriding reality that erase the memory of use value, human labour, and the context of production: social relations are eclipsed by market relations. As Marx observes:

> [T]he commodity-form, and the value-relation of the products of labour within which it appears, have absolutely no connection with the physical nature of the commodity and the material relations arising out of this. It (the commodity) is nothing but the determinate social relation between people themselves that assumes here, for them, the fantastic (phantasmagorical) form of a relation between things .... I call this the fetishism that attaches itself to the products of labour as soon as they are produced as commodities ...[21]

To answer the question posed at the start: the transformation of land to property, trees to lumber, etc. occurs through the fetishism of commodities. When all aspects of life begin to be articulated purely in terms of exchange value, land, trees, traditional knowledge, and life begin to be viewed primarily as property, lumber, intellectual property, and genetic resources. The memory of use value that pre-capitalist communities have with Nature is erased once Nature enters the market economy. Everything begins to be viewed in terms of exchange value, giving birth to the *homo economicus*.

The memory of use value, however, is too strong for these communities to start immediately viewing everything in terms of exchange value. Indigenous people who, for example, protest against the conversion of a sacred site into a golf estate are branded as superstitious, and real estate developers, who buy into the phantasmagoria of commodities by viewing all land as property, are hailed as pragmatic.

ESTRANGEMENT: RUPTURING BIOCULTURAL RELATIONS

> *Money, in as much as it possesses the property of being able to buy everything and appropriate all objects, is the object most worth possessing. The universality of this property is the basis of money's omnipotence; hence it is*

[21] Marx, 'The Fetish Character of the Commodity and its Secret' (1976).

> *regarded as an omnipotent being .... Money is the pimp between need and object, between life and man's means of life. But that which mediates my life also mediates the existence of other men for me. It is for me the other person.*[22]
>
> *That which exists for me through the medium of money, that which I can pay for, i.e. which money can buy, that am I, the possessor of money. The stronger the power of my money, the stronger am I. The properties of money are my, the possessor's properties and essential powers. Therefore what I am and what I can do is by no means determined by my individuality. I am ugly but I can buy the most beautiful woman ... I am lame, but money procures me twenty-four legs ... I am a wicked, dishonest ... but money is respected, and so also is its owner. Money is the highest good, and consequently its owner is also good ... I am mindless, but if money is the true mind of all things, how can its owner be mindless .... Do I not possess all human abilities? Does not money therefore transform all my incapacities into their opposite? If money is the bond, which ties me to human life and society to me, which links me to nature and to man, is money not the bond of all bonds? .... It is the true agent of separation and the true cementing agent, it is the chemical power of society.*
>
> —*Karl Marx, 'Economic and Philosophical Manuscripts'*[23]

In a culture that celebrates the *homo economicus* it may be difficult to see a problem with the fetishism of commodities and the omnipotence of money. For Marx, however, the real problem with commodity fetishism is one of estrangement or alienation of human beings from themselves, from others, and therefore from their common humanity. Marx can be read as arguing that in capitalist societies commodities and money mediate peoples' lives and their relations with each other and Nature. Their inability to see beyond the commodity form and their ability to realize themselves only through purchasing other people's labour blinds them to the reality of social relations that underlie all production. They become two-dimensional, estranged from the richness of social relations, their own abilities, and those of others.

As Marx notes, we are an 'ensemble of social relations,'[24] and our individuality is a transindividuality[25] or an intersubjectivity that

[22] Marx, 'Economic and Philosophical Manuscripts' in *Early Writings* (London: Penguin, 1975), p. 375.

[23] Ibid., p. 377.

[24] Ibid., p. 423.

[25] Balibar, *The Philosophy of Marx* (2007).

knows itself through practice, that is, the things we create and the relationships we form. To be human, then, is to realize the fullness of our existence in its most concrete form. The fetishism of commodities or money is the belief in an illusion that estranges us from our real potential, other people, and the richness of life itself. While the truth is that commodities and money are abstractions and therefore not concrete, we believe them to be so. This belief in turn makes us treat what is real—our abilities, other people, and our relationship with Nature—as means to an end. We are tricked into becoming prisoners of our own doing.

In a capitalist society, people in general and workers in particular, according to Marx, are triply alienated. First, they are alienated from the products of their labour, because what they produce is purely for exchange value, so the manifestation of their labour or life force becomes a marketable commodity which is valued in terms of abstract labour, divorced from the specific context or experience of the workers. Secondly, the very process of production in market economies is alienating, since production processes are geared only to generate exchange value and not to realize the fullness of one's being. When 'work' is reduced to 'labour', and 'worth' is reduced to 'value', the alienation of activity becomes the activity of alienation.[26] The more we produce, the more alienated we become, because work no longer has anything to do with human fulfilment, but aims purely to generate exchange value.

Thirdly, people in a capitalist society are alienated from their generic humanity. Without attempting to define an essential humanity, if we understand humanity as practice, then our practice is manifested through our relations with Nature and community. Humanity is represented by what we create through Nature and each other, and goes beyond merely fulfilling our primary needs. The books we write, the buildings we build, the cultures we inhabit, the music we create, the relationships we have, are all humanity in practice. When this richness of human life is boiled down to pure exchange value, and the trope of *homo economicus* is paraded as the 'essence of humanity', then people become alienated from each other

[26] Marx, 'Economic and Philosophical Manuscripts' (1975), p. 326.

and Nature. In fact, Marx lists the alienation of people from other people as a fourth kind of alienation separate from the alienation of people from Nature. When a person is self-estranged, then the relationship s/he sets up with other people is also one of estrangement, where people relate to each other through commodities: as within, so without.[27]

In 1844, at the age of 26, Marx in his notes (posthumously discovered and published as *Economic and Philosophical Manuscripts*) had pre-empted the contemporary concerns of indigenous peoples and traditional communities. He had shown the denial by the state and the market of the depth of their relationship with Nature. The humanism in early Marx that forms the basis of his later writing is clear when he says:

> The universality of man manifests itself in practice in that universality which makes the whole of nature his inorganic body, (1) as a direct means of life and (2) as the matter, the object and the tool of his life activity. Nature is man's *inorganic body*, that is to say nature in so far as it is not the human body. Man *lives* from nature, i.e. nature is his *body*, and he must maintain a continuing dialogue with it if he is not to die. To say man's physical and mental life is linked to nature simply means that nature is linked to itself, for man is a part of nature'[28].

Marx goes on to add:

> 'estranged labour turns man's species being (his generic humanity) both nature and his intellectual species-powers into a being *alien* to him and a *means* of his *individual existence*. It estranges man from his own body, from nature, as it exists outside him, from his spiritual essence (*Wesen*), his *human* essence'.[29]

The 'human essence' that Marx refers to here is not something innate, universal, and discovered outside history. On the contrary, we come to know who we are through our works: life informs consciousness. The 'personhood' that Marx advocates is one that embraces its inter subjectivity and rebels against any kind

[27] Marx, 'Estranged Labour', in *Economic and Philosophical Manuscripts* (1975) at 322.

[28] Ibid., p. 328.

[29] Ibid., p. 329.

of reductionism. Similar to Kitaro Nishida's[30] philosophy of Zen Buddhism (which does not advocate a human essence but rather the blade of 'pure experience' cutting through the ossified concepts of subject/object (fetishes) and affirming interconnectedness), Marx too advocates breaking free from estrangement by destroying our fetishes. Such liberation from estrangement can come from a consciousness of the fullness of our relational selves (we are formed through our relations with others and Nature) and through political action that contests the hegemony of exchange value and the fetishism of commodities it engenders.

Fetishizing Traditional Knowledge

Current efforts in law to protect the traditional knowledge of communities are a case in point of how the articulation of rights in the language of the market economy may deny a way of life. The CBD seeks to protect traditional knowledge as a way of combating the current environmental crisis. The measures for traditional knowledge protection within the CBD are based on three cornerstones: (1) the emerging evidence of the role that traditional knowledge plays in the conservation of biodiversity; (2) the need to conserve biodiversity through protecting the way of life of communities embodying such traditional knowledge; and (3) the importance of affirming this way of life through requiring the consent of these communities prior to the commercial or research use of their traditional knowledge and the fair and equitable sharing of benefits arising from such use.[31]

Article 8(j) is progressive to the extent that it is an unprecedented acknowledgement in an international treaty ratified by 193 countries that conservation of biodiversity is integrally linked to a way of life. Nature, according to the way of life of communities, is not perceived purely as a commodity but rather as an extension of the communal body constituted through the community's biocultural relations

[30] Kitaro Nishida, *An Enquiry into the Good* (New Haven: Yale University Press, 1990).

[31] Glowka et al.,1994 *A Guide to the Convention on Biological Diversity* (1994).

with the ecosystem. These relations override market relations, and any interface between the two is regulated by their customary norms and values. Biocultural relations reject estrangement by a practice of stewardship ethics, which affirm the intersubjectivity between the community and Nature.

The dominant interpretation of Article 8(j) by states, however, fetishizes traditional knowledge by limiting enforcement measures to allowing communities to control their traditional knowledge, rather than by affirming a way of life.[32] Thus the legal emphasis is on ensuring that communities provide prior informed consent for the commercial and research utilization of their traditional knowledge, and ensuring that they receive a fair share of the benefits that arise from such utilization.[33] It is important to note that recognition of community rights to traditional knowledge is a significant achievement and should not be underestimated. Nevertheless, the subtext of the measures employed by states towards the protection of traditional knowledge misconstrues it as a commodity and assumes that biodiversity can be conserved by incentivizing communities through profits generated from the exclusive rights to trade in traditional knowledge. What is ignored here is that community conservation practices have less to do with market benefits and more to do with a way of life, where biocultural relations and not exchange values predominate.

The recognition of community rights to traditional knowledge must go hand in hand with recognition of the biocultural rights of communities to their territories and cultures. Instead fetishization of

[32] Brendan Tobin and Emily Taylor , 'Across the Great Divide: A Case Study of Complementarity and Conflict between Customary Law and TK Protection Legislation in Peru', Initiative for the Prevention of Biopiracy, Research Documents, Year IV, No.11, (May 2009), p. 4.

[33] The interpretation of Article 8(j) of the CBD as requiring the informed consent of indigenous and local communities prior to accessing their traditional knowledge by non-traditional users was first articulated in the Program of Work on the Implementation of Article 8(j) and Related Provisions of the CBD, adopted by the 5th Conference of Parties (CoP) to the CBD in Decision V/16. (2005; available at http://www.cbd.int/decision/cop/default.shtml?id=7148).

traditional knowledge is apparent in the negotiations both under the CBD and the WIPO-IGC, where states in the name of sovereignty suppress in-depth discussions around recognition of rights of communities to their lands and waters and to government of their territories in accordance with their customary laws. For the most part, the negotiations focus on ways to extend intellectual property rights protection to traditional knowledge and preventive measures, such as creating traditional knowledge databases.

THE HOODIA FETISH: ESTRANGING THE SAN

The traditional knowledge of the San relating to the hunger staving qualities of the Hoodia plant is an interesting example of commodity fetishism and the estrangement it causes. The South African Council for Scientific and Industrial Research (CSIR) extracted a bioactive compound relating to the Hoodia's hunger staving properties based on San traditional knowledge. The process of extraction and the use of the bioactive compound for appetite suppressant purposes were patented by the CSIR. This patent was then licensed to a UK based company, Phytopharm, which, in turn, sublicensed it, first, to Pfizer and then, later, Unilever to develop food supplements for the diet industry.[34]

Recently Phytopharm returned the patent to the CSIR, since both Pfizer and Unilever were for various reasons unable to develop products based on the Hoodia patent. After initial concerns raised by the San that the CSIR had commercially used San traditional knowledge without their consent, the CSIR in 2003 negotiated an ABS agreement with the San that involved payment to them of a percentage of royalties received by the CSIR from Phytopharm.[35]

[34] Roger Chennells, 'Ethics and Practice in Ethnobiology: The Experience of the San Peoples of Southern Africa', in Charles McManis (ed.), *Biodiversity and the Law: Intellectual Property, Biotechnology and Traditional Knowledge* (London: Earthscan, 2010), p. 413.

[35] Ben Bouckley, 'Phytopharm CEO Insists Hoodia Still "Interesting" Despite Patent Disposal' (8 December 2010), http://www.nutraingredients.com/Industry/Phytopharm-CEO-insists-Hoodia-still-interesting-despite-patent-disposal (accessed 23 March 2011).

The significance of the San Hoodia agreement cannot be overestimated. It was one of the world's first ABS agreements, and it was definitely the first such agreement in Africa between a historically marginalized indigenous community and a commercial entity. Nevertheless, it is critical to note that, despite the San receiving some milestone payments from the CSIR at specific stages of the clinical trials and product development, the fetishizing of the San traditional knowledge brought with it a unique set of problems.[36]

The South African San Council, which negotiated the ABS agreement with the CSIR, sought to represent the San of South Africa, Namibia, Angola, and Botswana, since it felt that all the San of the region collectively held the knowledge relating to the Hoodia. However, the urgency of responding to the fact that the CSIR had already registered a patent based on San traditional knowledge meant that the ABS agreement negotiations had to be hurried by the South African San Council without the necessary consultations with the larger San community.[37]

The negotiations between the San and the CSIR opened with the incontrovertibility of the CSIR patent on the Hoodia. The patent had already been registered and the San Council was informed that any commercial interest in the Hoodia and potential financial benefits for the San were possible only if the San did not challenge the patent. This meant that the San who had, until then, relied on their knowledge of the Hoodia as use value were asked to engage in a negotiation, which regarded their traditional knowledge as pure exchange value. The moment this transformation of use value to absolute exchange value occurred, all other discussions around the context in which knowledge about the Hoodia had been historically developed, used, and shared by the San were abandoned. Negotiations from thereon focused on market potential; investment in research and development by the CSIR and its licensees; and the share of benefits that the San could realistically expect from the ABS agreement.

36 Kabir Bavikatte et al., 'Shifting Sands of ABS Best Practice', resources page, naturaljustice.org, (accessed 13 September 2011).

37 Saskia Vermeylen, 'From Life Force to Slimming Aid: Exploring Views on the Commodification of Traditional Medicinal Knowledge', *Applied Geography* 28 (2008), pp. 224–35.

This was the first step towards estrangement, whereby the Hoodia traditional knowledge was approached as a commodity delinked from the way of life of the San and their history of discrimination. The discussions became less about the real needs of the San, the breakdown of traditional leadership, and the limited representational mandate of the hurriedly constituted South African San Council, and more about traditional knowledge itself and its commercial potential. The time required for substantial consultation within the San community based on their customary values about the kind of benefits needed and how they would be collectively shared was unavailable.[38] Like all commercial negotiations, this too had to take place in 'market time', with an emphasis on quick and efficient drawing up of an agreement to utilize the traditional knowledge and capitalizing on the 'first mover advantage'.

The second step towards estrangement came when the Hoodia traditional knowledge became more real than the San themselves. The San were used as a part of a marketing campaign around the appetite-suppressant qualities of the Hoodia to combat overeating. Pictures were beamed across the world of lithe San people, in their traditional clothes, hunting with bows and arrows and set against the Kalahari landscape. This bore no semblance to the reality of San life, of a people who are chronic victims of discrimination and dispossession. The San's fast disappearing way of life was no longer viewed on its own terms, with necessary attention to its insurmountable challenges, but merely as a means to an end, the end being profits from Hoodia diet supplements.[39]

The third form of estrangement was an alienation from Nature itself. The growing demand for Hoodia resulting from the extensive media coverage of the San-Hoodia case sparked off widespread illegal harvesting of the plant. This harvest put Hoodia on the endangered plants list in South Africa. At the same time, a number of commercial farmers began to cultivate Hoodia for the export market. Significant profits were made due to a spike in demand. Both the illegal

[38] Saskia Vermeylen, 'Contextualizing "Fair" and "Equitable": The San's Reflections on the Hoodia Benefit-Sharing Agreement', *Local Environment* 12(4) (August, 2007), pp. 423–36.

[39] *See generally,* ibid.

harvesting and commercial cultivation of Hoodia viewed the San traditional knowledge as primarily exchange value.[40]

For the San, this unprecedented interest in Hoodia by the anti-obesity market obscured the way of life from which this traditional knowledge arose. The ethics of stewardship that underlies the San interactions with their ecosystem, and the context within which the Hoodia is used, were never mentioned in the market rhetoric around the traditional knowledge. The fetishism of Hoodia and the emergent market interest in it had the paradoxical effect of reinforcing an approach to Nature as exchange value rather than an appreciation of the biocultural relations that the San historically had with the Kalahari.

Finally, the ABS agreement resulted in the CSIR gaining exclusive use rights to traditional knowledge relating to Hoodia through the San acceptance of the CSIR's patent in exchange for benefits. This caused the fourth kind of estrangement, one between the San and the Nama (another indigenous group that shared with the San the knowledge about the Hoodia).[41] When this knowledge functioned within the realm of use value, the San, the Nama, and other communities in the region all freely shared and exchanged it. However, the moment these social relations were overridden by market relations through the CSIR patent, the result was an estrangement between two communities that had lived in harmony for centuries.[42]

The Nama felt that the San did not have the authority to grant exclusive rights to the CSIR, and that they (the Nama) should also

[40] Based on interviews conducted by the author with Robbie Gass, a Hoodia commercial farmer in South Africa.

[41] Rachel Wynberg and Roger Chennells, 'Green Diamonds of the South: An Overview of the San Hoodia Case', in Rachel Wynberg et al. (eds), *Indigenous Peoples, Consent and Benefit Sharing* (New York: Springer, 2009), p. 115.

[42] The author was actively involved between 2007 and 2009 as a lawyer supporting the South African San Council and the Hoodia Trust in implementing the benefit sharing aspects of the ABS agreement that had been entered into with the CSIR. The views expressed in this section are predominantly based on the author's personal experience in working with the San communities in South Africa in implementing their ABS agreement.

have been included as beneficiaries to the ABS agreement. The San, however, argued that they (the San) were 'primary rights holders' since they were the original inhabitants of the region, the Nama having arrived later. The entire debate was ironic as both these communities had coexisted for several hundred years in South Africa and Namibia, and their ancient social relations were now precipitously punctuated with market terminology, such as 'primary rights holders' and 'profit percentages'. The San and the Nama have since entered into an agreement amongst themselves to share in the benefits arising from the San-CSIR ABS agreement. Divorcing traditional knowledge from the cultural context in which it was communally used and shared, however, has the paradoxical effect of temporarily disrupting intercommunity relations, which have played a crucial role in conserving the ecosystem of the region.

This analysis of the Hoodia case is not performed through the condescending gaze of posterity nor is it a tirade against the commodification of traditional knowledge. Roger Chennells, the lawyer representing the San did pioneering work in what is considered one of the earliest ABS agreements between an indigenous group and a commercial interest. It is also clear that the ABS agreement between the CSIR and the San was an important forerunner to the establishment of rights of communities to their traditional knowledge and the right to benefit from the commercial uses of such knowledge. During the negotiations many San leaders held a considered view that the desperately poor community would clearly benefit from monies that would arise from the agreement.

The Hoodia case, however, is an example of how market forces deepened the sense of estrangement in an already alienated community by overriding the San's biocultural values, and failing to deliberate on the consequences thereof. The very rights to peoplehood that the San had been fighting for, which had been denied to them through state discrimination, were undercut through the fetishization of their traditional knowledge. Once again, the peoplehood of the San and their biocultural relations with the Kalahari were reduced to a caricature of gaunt Bushmen peddling diet pills to consumers who couldn't stop overeating. The traditional knowledge relating to the Hoodia became more real than the San from whom it came. The pith of the problem is not commodities per se, but their phantasmagoric power within market economies to delegitimize and erase all other ways of being and knowing that do not adhere to the image of the *homo economicus*.

The legal system does not only reinforce the fetishism of commodities but the latter in many situations constitutes the very basis of certain laws and judicial decisions. The next chapter will explore how the law both structures and is structured by the commodity form.

CHAPTER FOUR

Reification

The Law as a Collective Conspiracy

Communism as the positive supersession of private property as human self-estrangement, and hence the true appropriation of the human essence through and for humankind; hence as the complete return of humankind to itself as a social, i.e. human humankind .... This communism, as fully developed naturalism equals humanism, and as fully developed humanism equals naturalism; it is the genuine resolution of the conflict between humankind and nature, and within humankind, the true resolution of the conflict between existence and essence, between objectification and self-affirmation ...
Karl Marx, 'Economic and Philosophical Manuscripts'[1]

The fetishism of commodities is a result of an erasure of the memory of their 'use value' and their 'exchange value' exercising a monopoly on social consciousness. This causes an inversion of the relationship between human beings and commodities. The human - and -natural origins of commodities are erased; commodities take on a life of their own, mediating the relations between the very humans whose labour created them. The outcome of this divorce between commodities and their human roots is a sense of estrangement.

Estrangement or alienation is a palpable sense of a lack of wholeness or an incompleteness of personhood, whereby aspects of ourselves, which we know from experience as real, are denied. The Latin origin of the English term 'alienation' comes from *alius* meaning 'other' and *alienus* meaning 'belonging to another person or place'.[2]

[1] Karl Marx, 'Economic and Philosophical Manuscripts' in *Early Writings* (London: Penguin 1975). p. 348.

[2] *See* 'Alienation in Social Science', http://what-when-how.com/social-sciences/alienation-social-science/ (accessed 23 March 2012).

Alienation or estrangement should not be crudely equated with buying or selling, or markets per se. If we extend our personhood to include everything we produce, then the very act of giving, whether it is for the purpose of redistribution or reciprocity is also a kind of alienation. Alienation in its real sense should be understood as the antithesis between labour and capital. As Marx notes: 'labour, the subjective essence of private property as exclusion of property, and capital, objective labour, as exclusion of labour, constitute private property'.[3]

It is critical here to understand the nuance that has been ignored in the crude forms of state socialism. The 'fetishism of commodities' or the 'fetishism of private property' is one and the same thing. Private property is a kind of commodity since it signifies pure exchange value. The key point here is that human labour or effort is what creates value.

The traditional knowledge of the San, for example, is a manifestation of the San way of life, their labour, and their biocultural relations with their land. This 'way of life' is the subjective essence of private property; in this case the San's way of life is the subjective essence of their traditional knowledge. But this way of life is paradoxically excluded when traditional knowledge is fetishized as pure exchange value. So it is 'private property as exclusion of property', since the real property here is the San way of life and their labour, but this is denied by converting traditional knowledge to capital or objective labour, as exclusion of labour. This implies that, while the rights of the San to their traditional knowledge are upheld, their right to their way of life—the subjective essence of property is denied. Private property, then, is both the cause and consequence of alienation.

'Objective labour' is dead labour. It is human labour congealed into commodities.[4] Thus, when traditional knowledge is viewed purely as a commodity, we do not see that it was developed through living labour or a way of life. Instead we fetishize it as a tradable commodity. The consequence is a lack of attention to the importance of ownership or rights over the 'means of production'. In capitalist societies, this appears in the form of a worker, whose labour produces

[3] Marx, 'Economic and Philosophical Manuscripts' (1975), p. 345.

[4] Chris Harman, *Zombie Capitalism: The Global Crisis and the Relevance of Marx* (Chicago: Haymarket Books, 2010), pp. 51–2.

the commodity (which is objectified human labour) having no control over the production processes. S/he is reduced to a mere cog in the wheel, and the real power is vested in the commodity. In the context of indigenous peoples, the lack of attention to their biocultural relations with their territories at the expense of fetishization of their traditional knowledge (which is a result of such relations) results in a denial of their rights over the means of production (their territories and cultures).

The current legal focus on traditional knowledge and genetic resources of communities as a tradable commodity, without the concomitant respect for a way of life or rights to territory and systems of governance, leads to estrangement. This term refers to a loss of wholeness, where the part (traditional knowledge) is misunderstood as the whole, and the memory of the whole is erased. It is the kind of estrangement that results in the conflict between humankind and Nature.

To resolve this conflict a vital question must now be posed: Despite the alienation or estrangement that fetishism of commodities causes, why do we find it so difficult to challenge this estrangement within the law? Or rather: What is it about the law that makes us believe that the way things are, is the way they ought to be? It is to answer this question that we shall now turn.

THE JURIDICAL SUBJECT AS *HOMO ECONOMICUS*[5]

> *The law, in its majestic equality, forbids the rich as well as the poor to sleep under bridges, to beg in the streets, and to steal bread.*
>
> *—Anatole France, Le Lys Rouge (The Red Lily) 1894*[6]

As we have seen previously, in market economies or capitalist societies, there is an inversion of the relationship between commodities

[5] *See generally*, Isaac Balbus, 'Commodity Form and Legal Form: An Essay on the Relative Autonomy of the Law', *Law and Society* 11(Winter 1977), pp. 571–88, and Evgeny Pashukanis, *Law and Marxism: A General Theory* (London: Ink Links, 1978). Balbus and Pashukanis originally worked out the link between the commodity form and the legal form and the relative autonomy of the law.

[6] Anatole France, *The Red Lily* (e-book, 2006), http://www.gutenberg.org/ebooks/3922 (accessed on 13 September 2011).

and humans. Commodities become real and humans merely shadows of their former selves, leading to a sense of estrangement.[7] In the context of communities, for example, their 'genetic resources' or 'intellectual property' become real, and become 'objects' to be purchased. Their way of life and their plural and composite relationships with Nature that give rise to such knowledge and biodiversity, however, become mere footnotes to the language of markets.

The law in market economies works to normalize estrangement. Simplistic 'instrumentalist' approaches to law, as the handmaid of the rich and the powerful, will not work here. Every example of case law or legislation that is antithetical to the interests of indigenous peoples and traditional communities can be countered by case law or legislation that countenances their interests. On the other hand, 'formalist' approaches to law that speak of law as an autonomous neutral system with its own internal rules that are not biased towards any particular class or interest group, are equally simplistic. Any hard-bitten lawyer based on his/her courtroom experience will tell us otherwise: the law is politics.[8] A useful way to understand the law is by comprehending its 'relative autonomy'. This goes beyond the simplistic binary of the formalists versus the instrumentalists. The relative autonomy of the law requires us to look at the deep structure of the law—the rules of the game so to speak. In the present case, it asks us to look at the construction of the 'juridical subject' itself.[9]

[7] *See* Georg Lukacs, *History and Class Consciousness: Studies in Marxist Dialectics* (Cambridge: MIT Press, 1971); providing a rigorous analysis of commodity fetishism and the alienation it causes.

[8] *See generally*, Mark Kelman, *A Guide to Critical Legal Studies* (Boston: Harvard University Press, 1987).

[9] Balbus, 'Commodity Form and Legal Form' (1977), p. 575; Here Balbus explains the 'legal form' as: If, in a capitalist mode of production, products take on the form of individual commodities, people take on the form of individual citizens; the exchange of commodities is paralleled by the exchange of citizens .... An individual citizen, to begin with, is a qualitatively distinct, concrete subject with qualitatively distinct human needs or interests .... At the same time, however, individual citizens are not only, and not immediately, subjects with needs but also and rather objects of exchange who exist in order to represent, and be represented by other individual citizens. The existence of political exchange or representation thus requires

The skeleton around which the juridical subject is fleshed out is based on the institution of private property, or more specifically the 'commodity form'. The impact of the commodity form on the legal form was initially introduced by Marx but more substantially worked out by Isaac Balbus[10] and Evgeny Pashukanis in his work *Law and Marxism*.[11] Anatole France's ironic remark above, about the formal equality of the law is a useful point of reference when we analyse here the impact of the commodity form on the construction of the juridical subject.

In 2008, the US Ninth Circuit Court in *Navajo Nation* v. *US Forest Service*[12] passed a telling decision. In this case, the Navajo Nation along with several other Native American tribes who hold the San Francisco Peaks of Northern Arizona as a sacred site for their religious ceremonies (like the Navajo Blessingway Ceremony), challenged a permit given by the U.S. Forest Service. The permit allowed the use of recycled water containing traces of human waste from the Snowbowl ski area to make artificial snow to use for recreational activities, such as skiing on the San Francisco Peaks. The land on which the San Francisco Peaks stood was public land belonging to the Federal Government. The Navajo Nation and its co-plaintiffs argued that the use of recycled water desecrated one of their most sacred sites and would violate the U.S. Religious Freedom Restoration Act of 1993.[13]

The Ninth Circuit Court, relying on the 1988 Supreme Court decision in *Lyng* v. *Northwest Indian Cemetery Protective Association,*[14] found that the Navajo Nation had no legal standing. The Court rationalized its decision by arguing that, if it upheld the religious claims of every citizen over state-owned land, then it would establish a *de facto* beneficial ownership that would destabilize the property right itself.

---

that qualitatively distinct individuals with otherwise incommensurable interests enter into a formal relationship of equivalence with one another.

[10] Ibid.

[11] Pashukanis, *Law and Marxism* (1978).

[12] 535 F.3d 1058 (9th Cir. 2008).

[13] Ibid.

[14] 485 US 439 (1988).

In *Lyng*, Native American tribes had challenged the approval given by the Forest Service for the construction of a logging road in the Chimney Rock area of the Six Rivers National Forest in California. The tribes contended that the construction would interfere with their free exercise of religion by disturbing a sacred area. The area was an integral and indispensible part of the tribes' religious practices, and a Forest Service study concluded that the construction 'would cause serious and irreparable damage to the sacred areas'. The Supreme Court held that:

> However much we might wish that it were otherwise, government simply could not operate if it were required to satisfy every citizen's religious needs and desires .... No disrespect for these practices is implied when one notes that such beliefs could easily require *de facto* beneficial ownership of some rather spacious tracts of public property .... *Whatever rights the Indians may have to the use of the area, however, those rights do not divest the Government of its right to use what is, after all, its land.*[15]

Despite the elaborate reasoning of the courts, both *Navajo Nation* and *Lyng* turned on one important question: should the spiritual and cultural beliefs of the tribes be allowed to make inroads into the institution of private property? Another way of posing the same question would be to ask 'should "use value" in certain cases be allowed to trump "exchange value"?' or simply put, 'should the richness of the tribes relationship with the land be allowed to override the property rights of the federal government?'

The fetishization of private property that occurred in the court's reasoning is a telling reminder on the influence of the commodity form in the development of the legal form: private property rights are presented almost as if they are natural and the desire of the tribes to protect their sacred site as unreasonable. Land as a commodity is fetishized, whereby the commodity is more real than the relationships that tribes have with their sacred site. From the perspective of property rights, justice has been done, and the decision of the Ninth Circuit Court will have precedent value that can be used in other situations

[15] *Navajo Nation* v. *US Forest* Service 535 F.3d 1058 (9th Cir. 2008), quoting *Lyng*, ibid., at 1057–8.

to uphold the sanctity of private property. From the biocultural rights approach, however, the stewardship ethic has been violated, and the law has no auditory space for a discourse of stewardship, which, from the perspective of the tribes is a grave injustice.

If one observes the reasoning of the courts in both these cases, it is plain to see that the 'commodity form' has given rise to a legal form, that of a particular type of juridical subject. It is germane at this juncture to ask the question: how can the Native American tribes feel a palpable sense of injustice when the courts have upheld the right to property? One could hypothesize that the feeling of being 'hard done by' has to do with the right to property accommodating the fullness of the tribes' relationship with the land.

Land as private property is, in essence, land as a commodity, and, as noted earlier, when use value is turned into exchange value it erases the memory of use thereby flattening lifeworlds; land becomes property, trees become lumber, traditional knowledge becomes intellectual property, life becomes genetic resources, and human beings become property owners. No other kind of relationship, be it social or spiritual, can be entertained outside the bounds of the commodity relationship. The relationship between human beings has now become a relationship between commodities, and humans can only interact with each other as commodity owners. In Marx's words:

> In order that these objects may enter into relations with each other as commodities, their guardians must place themselves in relation to one another as persons whose will resides in these objects, and must behave in such a way that each does not appropriate the commodity of the other, and alienate his own except through an act to which both parties consent. The guardians must therefore recognize each other as owners of private property.[16]

If the commodity is formed when use value is turned into pure exchange value, then, similarly, the juridical subject is born when human beings with their diverse contexts and cultures are flattened into uniform, interchangeable, atomistic bearers of rights. There

[16] Karl Marx, *Capital*, Vol. 1 (New York: International Publishers, 1967), p. 178.

is a two-step process at play here. In the first step, individuals and communities with their complex histories and different interests are turned into abstract citizens. What is unequal or different is made equal, just as the incommensurable nature of use value is equalized through exchange value.

In the second step, these abstract citizens who in effect are 'unequal' are made 'equal', and this formal equality is presented as the reality. To paraphrase Anatole France: *The law, in its majestic equality, forbids the Navajo as well as the banker to worship on federal property, to hunt in the forests, and to harvest medicinal plants on private land.* The law, like money, as the universal political equivalent has, through its creation of the abstract juridical subject, in effect, extinguished the memory of the different cosmovisions. As Marx says:

> The state abolishes after its fashion, the distinctions established by birth, social rank, education, occupation, when it decrees that birth, social rank, education, occupation are *non-political* distinctions; when it proclaims, without regard to these distinctions that every member is an *equal* partner in popular sovereignty.[17]

The juridical subject then is a hollow individual, with real rights but an artificial life, alienated from his/her social existence, equal in theory, and unequal in practice. The experience of the Navajo Nation in the Ninth Circuit Court is one where their lifeworld is denied in the name of equal rights to property to which all juridical subjects are entitled.

Legal Order as the Superego of the Public Self

> *People 'believe in' the legal order because the legal order substitutes a harmonious abstract world for the concrete alienation that characterizes their lived experience. Thus, while legal thought represses, it also reassures; it is, so to speak, the superego of the public self at the level of social interpretation. The character of this repressive thought is accurately described by the word 'reification' which is properly understood as a certain sort of distortion of meaning that occurs within communication. This distortion is sometimes called 'the fallacy of misplaced concreteness'*

[17] Karl Marx, 'On the Jewish Question', in Robert C. Tucker (ed.), *The Marx and Engels Reader* (New York: Norton, 1972), p. 31.

> *because when we 'reify,' we draw an abstraction from a concrete milieu and then mistake the abstraction for: the concrete.*
>
> —*Peter Gabel,* 'Reification in Legal Reasoning'[18]

The mere argument that the legal form through the juridical subject mirrors the commodity form is insufficient to explain the persistence of the legal form. As noted previously, we have to plumb the depths of the 'relative autonomy of the law'. We must ask ourselves, how do we end up consenting to a palpable sense of estrangement? Or, rather, how is it that the decisions of the courts in the *Navajo Nation* and *Lyng* appear as the way things ought to be rather than militating against our basic sense of what it means to be human.

Critical legal studies theorist, Peter Gabel, points out in the passage above that the belief in the legal order is a result of the substitution of a harmonious abstract world for the concrete sense of alienation that people experience every day. The law both represses and reassures: it represses through legal forms that create and legitimize estrangement, and it reassures by creating the impression that the abstract legal system is both realistic (it takes into account how things really are) and normative (it aspires towards how things ought to be). This simultaneous repression and reassurance is carried out through a process of reification.[19]

In many ways reification is what sustains the juridical subject in capitalist societies. It is the transformer that converts the commodity form into a legal form. As Gabel notes, reification occurs when we draw an abstraction from a concrete milieu and mistake the abstraction for the concrete. The fetishization of commodities in market economies is a result of reification. The creation of exchange value for the purposes of the market is an aspect of all complex societies. To abstract exchange value as a dimension of the economy, however, and then to argue that it is the only form of value, is to engage in reification. Another example of reification is the *homo economicus*, which is clearly an abstraction of an aspect of human

[18] Peter Gabel, 'Reification in Legal Reasoning', *Research in Law and Sociology*, Vol. 3 (1980), pp. 25–6.

[19] Ibid.

behaviour that is generalized as human nature itself, and therefore the basis of the juridical subject.

For Gabel, reified communication is a three-step process: 1) speakers misunderstand by asserting that the abstract is concrete; 2) speakers know that they misunderstand; 3) speakers deny to both themselves and their listeners their knowledge of this misunderstanding, thereby affirming that the communication is true.[20] In reified communication, one has a sense that what is being said does not entirely correspond with the reality of experience and yet simultaneously denies that one is communicating a false concrete. For example, when the law speaks of traditional knowledge or genetic resources of indigenous peoples as commodities, it is not unaware that this knowledge is an aspect of a way of life. Yet, it unconsciously denies to the listeners, and to itself, this deeper truth.

In fact, reification is what sustains estrangement. We would never know that we were estranged, if we didn't feel unease at some deep level. For example, we know subconsciously that the universality of the *homo economicus* is a false concrete, since it does not bear out in all our experiences. Yet, we behave as if it is universal, and thereby actively make it universal. We are both victims and agents of reification, and we constantly 'other' ourselves. We participate in a collective conspiracy, like a truth that dare not speak its name, for the fear of derailing society from the well-grooved tracks of social communication. The law as reified communication reassures by its denial of our collective feeling of estrangement. It fuses both the concrete and the normative, by stating that what 'is', 'ought' to be; the purpose of the law, as we saw in both *Navajo* and *Lyng,* is legitimation.

Reification in legal processes necessarily involves restoring a systemic equilibrium. The judge for the most part unconsciously plays the part of legitimating the market economy, or, rather, the market economy legitimizes itself through the judge. In the case of indigenous peoples the institution of private property is legitimized to the exclusion of all other possible biocultural relations.

The first step in this process of legitimation is to take a set of facts that has caused disequilibrium in the reified system, and fit them

[20] Gabel, 'Reification in Legal Reasoning' (1980), p. 26.

into neat legal categories, such as owner, property, occupier, etc. The facts are then restated in a way that allows for these legal categories to play out their interlocking functions. In this way, the 'is' of life is fused with the 'ought' of the law, ensuring that the law is a true representation of life. Private property is no longer a legal category, but a fact of life.

The next step in the process of judicial legitimation is to fit the individuals to a dispute into one of the avatars of the juridical subject. Thus, just as a commodity is a generic category that signifies pure exchange value, but allows for the existence of different types of commodities, the juridical subject too is a generic category that spawns a variety of different types of actors, such as sellers, buyers, owners, tenants, etc. All these actors have different interlocking rights and duties, which constitute variations of the rights and duties of the universal juridical subject. The roles, rights, and duties of the different actors are presented as both a norm and a practice.

Reification in legal reasoning then presents itself both as an accurate representation of life and how life ought to be lived. Property owners behave as property owners because, according to the law, they ought to, and because they behave so, the 'ought' is justified as a representation of reality. Reification is a result of people being 'passivized' into particular variations of the juridical subject, and this passivity is both the cause and consequence of estrangement.[21]

The final step in judicial decision-making is then to apply the law to a set of facts that have already been pre-moulded to fit the law. The relative autonomy of the law in market economies ensures that we do not have uniformity in decision-making. Sometimes property owners win and at other times tenants. But in general, an equilibrium is maintained that does not disrupt the internal logic of capitalism, that is, the institution of private property and the trope of the *homo economicus* remains unchallenged.

This is not to say that the dice are always loaded or that the fight is always fixed, and that there is no hope for biocultural rights or stewardship ethics. On the contrary, the point is that communities should be aware that their call for biocultural rights challenges the

[21] Ibid.

very cell structure of the market economy: the commodity form. The self-adjusting response of the system in such a case will be to include within the commodity form these community claims; for example, the right of communities to sell their traditional knowledge and genetic resources. It is, therefore, critical for communities to hold fast to the position that the call for biocultural rights should not be misunderstood as a demand for pre-capitalist communities to be included in the market economy. It is, instead, a call for a foundational rethink of our relationship with Nature.

Reification in Practice: *Nkosi* v. *Bührmann*[22]

The 2001 decision of the South African Supreme Court of Appeal in the case of *Nkosi* v. *Bührmann*[23] is a good example of reification in practice. The facts of the case are as follows: Grace Nkosi wanted to bury her son Petros Nkosi on a farm that belonged to Gideon Bührmann. He refused to allow it. Grace had moved to the Bührmann farm in 1966 with her husband and family as farm labourers. As was the practice then, Grace and her family were in return for their services allowed to live on the farm and graze their few livestock and raise some crops. While Grace's husband worked as a general labourer and tractor driver, she worked as domestic help in the Bührmann household. Petros was born on the farm in 1968. Grace informed the court that Gideon's father, the elder Bührmann, had previously allowed her to bury her grandchild on an area in the farm. Thereafter seven other family members including her mother-in-law and brother-in-law were also buried in this area.

Grace communicated to the court the significance of her relationship with the land, one that went beyond viewing it purely as private property. She explained, that prior to the first burial:

> Consistent with our tradition and cultural beliefs, my husband and his mother performed the rituals necessary to declare and introduce that piece of ground as an official home for our ancestors. I must state that it is our custom and religious belief that when a member of our family passes away, he/she gets only physically separated from us but

[22] *Nkosi* v. *Bührmann* (1/2000) [2001] ZASCA 98.
[23] Ibid.

> spiritually that person will always be with us and is capable of sharing a day to day life with us though in a different form. It is against this background that a graveyard to us is not only a place to bury our deceased, but a second home for those of us who live in the world of spirits. Once a certain piece of ground is declared a home to our ancestors, it remains so until another ritual is accordingly performed by the elders clothed with the necessary ability ...[24]

Except for a period of six intervening years, from 1981–86, the Nkosis lived as labourers on the Bührmann farm for a total of 29 years. The farm was not simply their home. The area had become the abode of their dear departed. It was for this reason that Grace had wanted to bury her son Petros on the site where he could join his kin in the spirit world and yet stay close to Grace. The five judges of the South African Supreme Court of Appeal were unanimous in concurring that the Bührmann right to private property trumped any possible relation Grace may have to the spiritual home of her deceased family.

The three step legitimizing process of legal reification highlighted in the previous section was applied. These three steps, however, are not necessarily sequential; they occur simultaneously. In his judgment, Judge Craig Howie reinterpreted and slotted the facts into legal categories.

At the outset the facts had to be restated as a conflict between Grace Nkosi's right to practise her 'religion' versus Bührmann's right to private property. Relying on an interpretation of the South African Constitution[25] and the Extension of Security of Tenure Act,[26] Judge Howie distinguished the current case from two other previous Constitutional Court decisions by stating that: 'in neither case was it said or suggested that for the practice of one's religion one may demand assistance, whether financial or patrimonial from another, much less that one may actively diminish another's patrimony by way of appropriation'.[27]

[24] Ibid., at paragraph 6.
[25] Constitution of the Republic of South Africa, Act 108 of 1996.
[26] Act 62 of 1997, South Africa.
[27] [2001] ZASCA 98, paragraph 45.

An interesting judicial sleight of hand took place in this case. The Judge reduced Grace Nkosi's claim to one of freedom of religion. By doing this, he masked what Marx points out as the conflict between labour and capital or use and ownership. The fact that Grace's family had lived laboured and died on the land over a period 29 years did not provide them with any ownership rights. Their labour had been estranged from them and converted to capital, and Bührmann owned the capital. Capital or the means of production was vested in Bührmann through the right to private property. For Grace Nkosi, her living labour and the relations she had developed with the land through the life that she had built around and through her labour were estranged from her. She was paid her wages, and that was that. As we can see, the facts were tamed by sidestepping the heart of the matter. Now it was a question of balancing the right to practise religion versus the right to private property. The unruly facts that spelt disequilibrium had been massaged back into the system, where they could be neatly categorized.

When Grace Nkosi's claim had been reduced to her desire to practise her faith, the facts were again interpreted to show that her freedom of religion had not been restricted. The Judge noted:

> What the evidence in this case shows is that the appellant's beliefs are that the existing family graves constitute a spiritual home for her ancestors and therefore the site where subsequent family dead should be buried. What renders this particular land appropriate for the burial (apart from its convenience) is that it has been consecrated for family burials. She does not, and cannot, claim that this gravesite comprises the only place where her religious burial dictates could possibly be satisfied. Obviously that was not the position before she lived on the farm or when her residence there was interrupted for some six years. Nor does she allege, as I have said, that burial of Petros's body anywhere else would pose problems from the point of view of expense or logistics. In other words she is able to bury her son.[28]

When the Judge severed the connection between Grace Nkosi's way of life, or living labour and the land, it was quite possible for him to reduce the problem to 'expense, logistics and choice'. He made the

[28] [2001] ZASCA 98, at paragraph 46.

point that, clearly, not everyone in the history of the Nkosi family had been buried on the Bührmann land, nor did they bury kinsfolk there during the six years when the Nkosis did not live on the farm. Hence Grace had other options, and her link to the land was not strong enough to override Bührmann's right to private property. The internal logic of the system had been satisfied through ensuring the coexistence of competing rights. Grace still had the right to practise her religion, but not on Bührmann's land, and Bührmann's right to private property was affirmed.

The next phase of legitimation was one of reconciliation and affirmation, where necessary exceptions to the absolute right to private property were created as an assurance that private property was not the taproot of South African society. By allowing for other kinds of relations to the land to be recognized under exceptional circumstances, however, this phase affirmed the normalcy of private property as the very cell structure of society. The Judge pointed out:

> [T]his does not exclude the possibility, however, that where religious or cultural beliefs are so inherently attached to particular land that the right to hold and practice them would be denied if the rights of ownership are asserted, the latter rights might be required to give way. That does not arise in the present case.[29]

The crux of this statement symbolized a fetish of private property to the extent that it no longer needed to justify itself, irrespective of whether it was an inheritance by an individual, who had little or no connection to the land, or a purchase validated by a title deed on a piece of paper. Private property was an *a priori* given. All other right-claimants, if challenging this fetish, would have the burden of establishing their claim—one that would be entertained only in the most extreme of cases.

In addition to highlighting these exceptional circumstances, the Judge seemed to issue a caveat, that too many exceptions would undermine the abstract universality of the juridical subject. Exceptions, which represented lived experience, and went against the grain of abstraction of the commodity form, were a threat that needed to be contained. The limitation on too many exceptions was presented as

[29] Ibid.

the state's duty to treat all its citizens equally, since all juridical subjects (in abstraction) were necessarily equal. The Judge presented the caveat as follows:

> Outside the jurisdiction of a local authority one is necessarily dependent on the consent of the landowner, be it the state a juristic person or an individual. These are legal constraints that bind everyone. No religion can demand more than another. Although the Act (The Extension of Security of Tenure Act) aims to treat occupiers specially, the right of religious freedom is the right of all.[30]

Shrinking Grace Nkosi's challenge to the internal coherence of the system to a minor misunderstanding completed the process of legitimation. The Judge therefore concluded:

> (T)hat the right to freedom of religion and religious practice has internal limits. It does not confer unfettered liberty to choose a grave site nor does it include the right to take a grave site without the consent of the owner of the land concerned.[31]

FIGHTING ESTRANGEMENT: THE CASE FOR BIOCULTURAL RIGHTS

The juridical subject, as we have seen, is both the cause and consequence of reification of the commodity form into the legal form. The case for biocultural rights therefore is not merely one that asks for recognition of stewardship relations that indigenous peoples and traditional communities have with Nature. On the contrary, it makes the case that stewardship of Nature is impossible without deconstructing our understanding of human nature, a euphemism for the *homo economicus* in capitalist societies. Going further, the fight for biocultural rights is a fight against the estrangement that is experienced when market relations eclipse all social relations.

This fight is not an easy one, since it has to confront the fetishism of commodities or the predominance of exchange value at every turn. Indigenous peoples and traditional communities bear a grave

[30] [2001] ZASCA 98, paragraph 47.
[31] Ibid., at paragraph 49.

responsibility to help us remember pre-capitalist stewardship values, and to use them to navigate our way towards a post-capitalist world.

With the growing momentum around biocultural rights in international law, communities, whose life world is one where exchange value has not yet eclipsed the memory of use value, have begun to provide us with a lens to help address our collective estrangement from Nature. The language these communities rely upon is distinctly pre-capitalist—they use terms such as 'Mother Earth', and rely on narratives of kinship with animals and value systems that say everything is not for sale. But it is precisely this language that is able to identify our estrangement and turn on the lights in a phantasmagoria of commodities.

Indigenous peoples and traditional communities certainly understand exchange value, as they too participate in markets. They also know, however, that a world hidden by exchange value, where all social relations are embedded in market relations, estranges us from the richness of our daily experience and the fullness of our humanity. Such a world has no place for stewardship. Stewardship at its core resists alienation by requiring the expansion of the self to include one's community and Nature. It is the contention of this book, that it is stewardship and not private property that is natural.

The fight for biocultural rights is a fight against the dominant reification of our times. It says that we are more than just abstract juridical subjects, interchangeable and alienated. On the contrary, our lives are lived through dense relationships with our communities and our lands. At the core of biocultural rights, is a challenge to the fetishism of the law. It refuses to accept that we are creations of the law. Rather it insists that the law is our creation.

Many communities have now opened up a new front against the *homo economicus*. Their struggle says that we are more than owners of real estate; we are stewards of the earth. Sahlins sums this sentiment in his critique of the *homo economicus* when he says:

> Natural self-interest? For the greater part of humanity, self-interest as we know it is unnatural in the normative sense: it is considered madness ... Rather than expressing a pre-social human nature, such avarice is generally taken for a loss of humanity. It puts in abeyance the mutual relationships of being that define a human existence. Yet if the self, the body, experience, pleasure, pain, agency and intentionality,

> even death itself, are transpersonal relationships in so many societies and in all likelihood through so many eons of human history, it follows that the native Western concept of man's self-regarding animal nature is an illusion of world-anthropological proportions.[32]

So how have communities begun to address legal reification and the estrangement that it causes? What are their methods and how successful are they? We shall attempt to answer these questions in the next chapter by exploring the strategic role played by communities in the negotiations towards the Nagoya Protocol on ABS.

[32] Sahlins, *The Western Illusion of Human Nature* (2008), p. 51.

CHAPTER FIVE

Fighting Reification

Towards a Peoples' History of the Law*

So advance but do not use your feet
Seize but do not use your arms
Cut but do not use your sword
Fight but do not use your own power

—*Lao Tzu, Tao Te Ching, verse 69*[1]

Legal reification is not without its challengers. The struggle for biocultural rights is emblematic of the agency of indigenous peoples and traditional communities to re-member their wholeness from the dismembering or estrangement wreaked by capitalism and the juridical subject it spawns. It is to understand the dynamics of this struggle that we shall now turn.

The English Marxist historian, E.P. Thompson, in his classic work *The Making of the English Working Class*,[2] marshals rich evidence of a history from below, which challenges the history that is written as if it were a result of great figures or global forces. According to Thompson, history is not made by the forces of the market alone but also by the struggles, aspirations, and hopes of ordinary people

* Parts of this chapter have been published in Kabir Bavikatte and Daniel F. Robinson, 'Towards a People's History of the Law: Biocultural Jurisprudence and the Nagoya Protocol on Access and Benefit Sharing', *The Law, Environment & Development Journal*, 7(1): 37–51; http://www.lead-journal.org/content/11035.pdf (accessed 13 September 2011).

[1] Lao Tzu (trans. by Jonathan Star), *Tao Te Ching* (New York: Tarcher Cornerstone Editions, 2001), p. 90.

[2] Edward Palmer Thompson, *The Making of the English Working Class* (London: Gollancz, 1963).

striving to influence the condition of their lives. For Thompson, people, by making history, also make themselves. To perceive the struggles of communities for biocultural rights, we must move away from an understanding of the law as purely repressive to an understanding of the law as a 'site of struggle'—where the structure of the law is frequently challenged by the agency of the subaltern.

In his effort to interrogate a functionalist approach to history, Thompson writes: 'I am seeking to rescue the poor stockinger, the Luddite cropper, the "obsolete" handloom weaver, the "utopian" artisan .... from the enormous condescension of posterity'.[3] This 'enormous condescension of posterity' becomes obvious when, for example, we speak of multilateral environmental agreements like the CBD.

We refer to the CBD as an international treaty between 193 state parties to conserve the environment, thereby conveying the sense that it is the result of state action stemming from enlightened politicians reacting responsibly to crisis warnings by scientists. Such an understanding hides as much as it reveals. While it is true that the negotiations leading up to the CBD did involve enlightened politicians and knowledgeable scientists, what is hidden is an understanding of the negotiations and the years preceding them as a terrain of struggle, one in which communities and civil society organizations deployed strategies, formed alliances, occupied and expanded legal space, and made significant rights advances.

On the face of it, multilateral environmental negotiations in supranational forums seem like the typical UN model of negotiations between sovereign states. This impression is reinforced by a doctrinaire approach to public international law commonly taught in law schools. Here the sources of international law are typically understood as those listed in Article 38 of the Statute of the International Court of Justice. This states that:

1. The Court, whose function is to decide in accordance with international law such disputes as are submitted to it, shall apply:
   a. international conventions, whether general or particular, establishing rules expressly recognized by the contesting states;
   b. international custom, as evidence of a general practice accepted as law;
   c. the general principles of law recognized by civilized nations;

[3] Ibid., p. 12.

d. subject to the provisions of Article 59, judicial decisions and the teachings of the most highly qualified publicists of the various nations, as subsidiary means for the determination of rules of law.[4]

Anyone seasoned in international negotiations, however, would argue that there is more to international law making than Article 38. The last six years of negotiations towards the Nagoya Protocol on ABS under the framework of the CBD was a typical example of the role played by highly organized indigenous peoples' groups to advance the discourse on biocultural rights and to secure specific rights gains. Reports on the Nagoya Protocol, that hailed its successes or decried its limitations, were unaware of the ethnography of subaltern strategies in the negotiations. Instead, the reports present the Protocol as a *fait accompli* that exemplifies either the wisdom of state parties or the lack of it. Reporting of this nature is typically guilty of the 'enormous condescension of posterity', and misses what political scientist and anthropologist James Scott refers to as 'infrapolitics' and the 'hidden transcripts' that underlie such politics.[5]

In his work *Domination and the Arts of Resistance*,[6] Scott seeks to show how 'each realm of open resistance to domination is shadowed by an infrapolitical twin sister who aims at the same strategic goals but whose low profile is better adapted to resisting an opponent who could probably win any open confrontation'.[7] Speaking of the hidden transcripts of infrapolitics, Scott points out that the 'hidden transcript is not just behind-the-scenes griping and grumbling; it is enacted in a host of down-to-earth, low profile stratagems designed to minimize appropriation'.[8] However, these hidden transcripts must 'largely be inferred by practice—a quiet practice at that'.[9]

[4] Statute of the International Court of Justice, http://www.icj-cij.org/documents/index.php?p1=4&p2=2&p3=0 (accessed 23 March 2012).

[5] James Scott, *Domination and the Arts of Resistance: Hidden Transcripts* (New Haven: Yale University Press, 1990).

[6] Ibid.

[7] James Scott, 'The Infrapolitics of Subordinate Groups', in Louise Amoore (ed.), *Global Resistance Reader* (London: Routledge, 2005), p. 66.

[8] Ibid., p. 68.

[9] Ibid., p. 69.

The strategic lobbying of communities for their biocultural rights in supranational forums like the CBD may seem small compared to massive on-the-ground popular protests, but under 'appropriate conditions, the accumulation of petty acts can, rather like snowflakes on a steep mountainside, set off an avalanche'.[10] Arguing that the art of understanding infrapolitics lies in cultivating a gaze that is able to read between the lines, Scott points out that:

> The strategic imperatives of infrapolitics make it not simply different in degree from the open politics of modern democracies; they impose a fundamentally different logic of political action. No public claims are made; no open symbolic lines are drawn. All political action takes forms that are designed to obscure their intentions or to take cover behind an apparent meaning. Virtually no one acts in his own name for avowed purposes, for that would be self-defeating. Precisely because such political action is studiously designed to be anonymous or to disclaim its purpose, infrapolitics requires more than a little interpretation. Things are not exactly as they seem.[11]

The emerging discourse on biocultural rights in international environmental law, and its challenges to the trope of the *homo economicus*, owe as much to open activism by communities on the streets and in the courts as it does to the painstaking, well-organized infrapolitical movements occurring amidst the well-ordered multilateral environmental treaty negotiations. A close examination of the negotiations leading up to the Nagoya Protocol on ABS will provide an insight into the profound ways in which communities have begun to secure their right to stewardship in international law.

The Nagoya Protocol on Access and Benefit Sharing: The Background

The Nagoya Protocol is an international treaty that was recently adopted by the 193 Parties to the CBD. The Protocol was intensely negotiated over six years under the framework of the CBD.

[10] Scott, 'The Infrapolitics of Subordinate Groups' (2005), p. 70.
[11] Ibid., p. 72.

To comprehend the success of the infrapolitics behind the community rights gains, the Protocol should be analysed with the aid of three guiding questions:

i. What was the *status quo* prior to the Protocol?
ii. What did communities seek to achieve through the Protocol and how did they go about doing this?
iii. What is the outcome of these community efforts in the Protocol?

The aim of the Nagoya Protocol on ABS was to give effect to the fair and equitable benefit sharing provisions of the CBD. Article 1 of the latter lists its three objectives as: i) the conservation of biological diversity; ii) the sustainable use of its components; and iii) the fair and equitable sharing of benefits arising from such use. While these objectives seem simple enough, the deep structure of the CBD seeks to straddle both a rights and an incentive based approach to biodiversity conservation. The CBD recognizes the sovereign rights of states over genetic resources found in *in situ* conditions within their territories. This is unprecedented in international law to the extent that it once and for all lays to rest the claim that genetic resources are the common heritage of humankind.[12] Instead the CBD, through its Article 15,[13] vests in states, absolute rights over naturally occurring genetic resources.

[12] Doris Schroeder and Balakrishna Pisupati, 'Justice and the Convention on Biological Diversity', *Ethics and International Affairs* 23(3), pp. 267–80.

[13] Article 15, Access to Genetic Resources

1. Recognizing the sovereign rights of states over their natural resources, the authority to determine access to genetic resources rests with the national governments and is subject to national legislation.
2. Each Contracting Party shall endeavour to create conditions to facilitate access to genetic resources for environmentally sound uses by other Contracting Parties and not to impose restrictions that run counter to the objectives of this Convention.
3. For the purpose of this Convention, the genetic resources being provided by a Contracting Party, as referred to in this Article and Articles 16 and 19, are only those that are provided by Contracting Parties that are countries of origin of such resources or by the

In many ways, Article 15 was a reaction by developing countries against the increasing number of patents taken out by research and commercial sectors from the developed world over pharmaceutical, agricultural, and other biotechnological innovations based on genetic resources freely accessed from developing countries.[14] Developing countries challenged the appropriation of genetic resources drawn from the common heritage of humankind through Article 15, which as we have seen gave states absolute rights over their naturally occurring genetic diversity.[15]

Parties that have acquired the genetic resources in accordance with this Convention.

4. Access, where granted, shall be on mutually agreed terms and subject to the provisions of this Article.
5. Access to genetic resources shall be subject to prior informed consent of the Contracting Party providing such resources, unless otherwise determined by that Party.
6. Each Contracting Party shall endeavour to develop and carry out scientific research based on genetic resources provided by other Contracting Parties with the full participation of, and where possible in, such Contracting Parties.
7. Each Contracting Party shall take legislative, administrative or policy measures, as appropriate, and in accordance with Articles 16 and 19 and, where necessary, through the financial mechanism established by Articles 20 and 21 with the aim of sharing in a fair and equitable way the results of research and development and the benefits arising from the commercial and other utilization of genetic resources with the Contracting Party providing such resources. Such sharing shall be upon mutually agreed terms.

[14] *See generally*, Gurdial Singh Nijar, *In Defence of Local Community Knowledge and Biodiversity: A Conceptual Framework and the Essential Elements of a Rights Regime* (Penang: Third World Network, 1996); P.R. Mooney, *Seeds of the Earth: A Private or Public Resource?* (London: International Coalition for Development Action, 1979); Tewolde Egziabher, 'The Convention on Biological Diversity, Intellectual Property Rights and the Interests of the South', in Vandana Shiva (ed.), *Biodiversity Conservation: Whose Resources? Whose Knowledge?* (New Delhi: Indian National Trust for Art and Cultural Heritage, 1994), pp. 198–215.

[15] *See*, J. Rifkin, *The Biotech Century: Harnessing the Gene and Remaking the World* (New York: Jeremy P. Tarcher/Putnam, 1998), p. 43.

Many developing countries saw the CBD as an effective vehicle to reclaim the political ground that had been lost under the World Trade Organization (WTO) and the TRIPS agreement.[16] The CBD went further to realize its third objective by declaring in Article 15 that any commercial or research use of genetic resources would require the consent of the state from within whose jurisdiction these resources were accessed and the fair and equitable sharing of benefits arising from such use with the state in question. The obligation to get prior informed consent and to share benefits extended beyond the use of genetic resources to include traditional knowledge.[17]

With respect to traditional knowledge, Article 8(j) of the CBD makes a critical link between the knowledge, innovations, and practices (traditional knowledge) of indigenous peoples and traditional communities[18] and conservation of biological diversity. It requires states to protect and promote such traditional knowledge by securing the rights of communities to consent to any non-traditional uses of their knowledge and the right to share in any benefits that may arise from the research or commercial uses of that knowledge. The CBD broke radically new ground in international treaty law by recognizing the significant role played by communities in biodiversity conservation, and by obliging states to secure the rights of these communities to their traditional knowledge relevant for biodiversity conservation.

In sum, the CBD in Articles 15 and 8(j) recognizes the rights of both states and communities to their genetic resources and traditional knowledge, respectively, and emphasizes the duty to share benefits arising from commercial and research use. Nearly 11 years after the

[16] Based on informal conversations between the author and the delegates from developing countries. *See generally*, Susan Bragdon, Kathryn Garforth, and John E. Haapala Jr, 'Safeguarding Biodiversity: The Convention on Biological Diversity (CBD)', in Geoff Tansey and Tasmin Rajotte (eds), *The Future Control of Food* (London: Earthscan, 2008), p. 82.

[17] Decision V/16 of the Conference of Parties to the CBD.

[18] The phrase that Article 8(j) uses is 'indigenous peoples and local communities'. However, for the purposes of specificity we will refer to local communities here as traditional communities.

CBD came into force in 1993, developing countries and communities began to push for an international regime on ABS to counteract the complete non-implementation of their CBD obligations by developed states, especially when it came to legally obliging research and commercial sectors based within their jurisdictions to seek consent prior to accessing genetic resources and traditional knowledge and sharing benefits arising from their utilization.

Initially the negotiations toward an international regime on ABS (which later took the form of the Nagoya Protocol) were driven by an imperative of 'justice in exchange'.[19] It was less about turning Nature and knowledge into commodities and more about ensuring fair and equitable sharing of benefits and challenging appropriation by the commercial and research sector of innovations based resources accessed from the 'commons'. Over the six years of negotiations that it took for Parties to agree on the Nagoya Protocol, however, there was a discursive shift from the environmental objectives of the CBD and the ideology of equitable benefit sharing to an incentive-based approach to conservation.

In the words of one of the key negotiators of the Nagoya Protocol, the negotiations seemed increasingly to resemble trade negotiations, a far cry from its loftier objectives.[20] Both developed and developing countries fought pitched battles for control over genetic resources. The talk was largely about monetary incentives to offset the opportunity costs incurred by developing countries in biodiversity conservation. Developed countries, on the other hand, constantly reiterated the position of their industry and research sectors: that the transaction costs incurred through onerous ABS requirements would affect efficiency and profitability. The history of appropriation of knowledge and resources through intellectual property rights

[19] *See generally*, Doris Schroeder and Balakrishna Pisupati, *Ethics, Justice and the Convention on Biological Diversity* (Nairobi: UNEP, 2010).

[20] Based on a conversation between the author (who acted as the legal advisor to the African Group of Countries in their negotiations towards the Nagoya Protocol) and one of the lead negotiators from another negotiating bloc.

was countered with the discourse of private property and exchange value.[21]

Amidst these heated discussions between states, the greatest causalities seemed to be the value of stewardship and the biocultural rights of indigenous peoples and traditional communities to their lands, waters, and cultures. There was little or no discussion about challenging market values and offering instead social values of sharing and exchange. Instead, the persistent theme seemed to be that the only way to save Nature would be to put a price on it or to speak of it in terms of exchange value. It is precisely in the wake of these fraught conditions, however, that indigenous peoples and traditional communities deployed the infrapolitics of resistance. It is the hidden transcripts of these infrapolitics that will now be analysed.

The Calm before the Storm: Status Quo Prior to the Nagoya Protocol

The decision of the 7th COP to the CBD in 2004 in Kuala Lumpur was a significant one. The specific paragraph of the COP 7 decision that sowed the seed of the Nagoya Protocol reads:

> Decides to mandate the Ad Hoc Open-ended Working Group on Access and Benefit-sharing with the collaboration of the Ad Hoc Open ended Inter-Sessional Working Group on Article 8(j) and Related Provisions, ensuring the participation of indigenous and local communities, non-governmental organizations, industry and scientific and academic institutions, as well as intergovernmental organizations, to elaborate and negotiate an international regime on access to genetic resources and benefit-sharing with the aim of

[21] From 2007 onwards the author has been first the rapporteur and later the legal adviser to the African Group of countries in its negotiations towards the Nagoya Protocol on ABS. The author actively participated in all the negotiations of the Working Group on ABS since 2007 and also worked as a legal drafter of the African Group's submissions to the Working Group. Many of the statements made in this chapter are based on the personal experience of the author as both a participant and an observer in the negotiations leading up to the Nagoya Protocol.

> adopting an instrument/instruments to effectively implement the provisions in Article 15 and Article 8(j) of the Convention and the three objectives of the Convention...[22]

The COP 7 decision was a result of intensive lobbying by developing countries that gathered momentum with the adoption of the Bonn Guidelines[23] by the 6th COP at The Hague in 2002. The primary concern of developing countries was that since the coming into force of the CBD in 1993, user countries[24] had done little to meet their compliance obligations under the CBD in effect nullifying its third objective, which is 'fair and equitable benefit sharing'. The inclusion of Article 8(j) as an article that would need to be implemented along with Article 15 is in itself testimony to the efforts of indigenous peoples and traditional communities.[25]

For these communities, Article 8(j) was a seemingly harmless Trojan Horse, which once introduced into the citadel of the Protocol negotiations would beget a range of biocultural rights to genetic resources and traditional knowledge. To get a sense of the status quo prior to the Nagoya Protocol is to comprehend the innocuous and limited nature of Article 8(j) of the CBD. It reads as follows:

> Each contracting Party shall as far as possible and as appropriate, subject to its national legislation, respect, preserve and maintain knowledge, innovations and practices of indigenous and local communities embodying traditional lifestyles relevant for the conservation and sustainable use of biological diversity and promote their wider application with the approval and involvement of the holders of such knowledge, innovations and practices and

[22] COP decision VII/19 (13 April 2004), http://www.cbd.int/decision/cop/?id=7756 (accessed 13 September 2011).

[23] The Bonn Guidelines on Access to Genetic Resources and the Fair and Equitable Sharing of Benefits Arising out of their Utilization, http://www.cbd.int/doc/publications/cbd-bonn-gdls-en.pdf (accessed 13 September 2011).

[24] Parties to the CBD in whose jurisdictions a predominant number of commercial users of genetic resources were located.

[25] Based on conversations between the author and a representative of the International Indigenous Forum on Biodiversity (IIFB).

> encourage the equitable sharing of the benefits arising from the utilization of such knowledge, innovations and practices.[26]

From a purely rights perspective Article 8(j) is not strong. It presents itself as an outcome of politically difficult negotiations, which states peppered with a number of 'exit clauses'. It begins with the words 'shall as far as possible and as appropriate, subject to its national legislation'. In negotiations-speak, words like this are hard fought, 'get out of jail free' passes, designed to weaken state obligation and to limit any inroads into national sovereignty. The modification of state obligations continues with the words 'promote their wider application with the approval and involvement of the holders of such knowledge, innovations and practices and encourage the equitable sharing of the benefits'. Note that nowhere does Article 8(j) speak of the mandatory nature of the 'prior informed consent' and 'benefit sharing' when it comes to the utilization of traditional knowledge (or what is referred to as knowledge, innovations and practices) of indigenous peoples and traditional communities.

Article 15, which is the main article, the implementation of which the 7th COP asked the Working Group on ABS to negotiate, makes no mention of any rights of indigenous peoples and local communities over genetic resources. It begins with an unassailable:

> Recognizing the sovereign rights of states over their natural resources, the authority to determine access to genetic resources rests with the national governments and is subject to national legislation.[27]

There are no 'exit clauses' here and, compared with Article 8(j), states wanted to eliminate any doubts and establish irrefutably their absolute rights over their genetic resources.

Jurisprudentially speaking, prior to the commencement of the negotiations of the Working Group on ABS, the rights of communities within the CBD system were enervated. This early state of play begs our second question: What did indigenous peoples and

[26] The full text of the CBD can be accessed at http://www.cbd.int/convention/text/ (accessed 13 September 2011).

[27] *See* Article 15, ibid.

local communities seek to achieve through the Nagoya Protocol, and how did they go about doing this?

THE ARTS OF RESISTANCE: NEGOTIATING THE NAGOYA PROTOCOL

James Scott, labels as 'masks of power' public performances that are designed to placate both the dominant and the subordinate groups.[28] But what goes on behind the scenes, or what Scott calls the 'hidden transcripts', reveal the real nature of resistance. From this perspective, the setting of the Working Group on ABS is a theatre, where an elaborate charade is enacted with diplomats referring to each other by the names of the states they represent, giving politely indignant speeches about the scope of the CBD and with indigenous peoples and traditional communities abiding by UN rules clearly biased towards states. But witnessing these negotiations tells us little about the hidden transcripts of feverish lobbying, threats, deal-making, and political sleight of hand that happens behind the scenes.

While the negotiations within the Working Group on ABS from 2004 onwards proceeded with regularity, they lacked direction, since there was very little agreement amongst Parties as to even the primary elements of an international agreement on ABS. Decision IX/12 of 9th CBD Conference of Parties (COP) in Bonn marked a radical departure from this state of affairs thanks to four significant points of convergence amongst Parties. They were:

i. The agreement on Annex 1 of Decision IX/12, which for the first time since 2004 provided the framework and elements of an 'international regime' on ABS. The elements were divided along a 'bricks' and 'bullets' formula, where 'bricks' were those elements of an 'international regime' whose inclusion in the regime Parties agreed upon but which still needed further elaboration. 'Bullets', on the other hand, were those possible elements which required further consideration because there was no consensus as to whether they should be included in the 'international regime'.

[28] Scott, *Domination and the Arts of Resistance* (1990) p. 9–10.

ii. An agreement to begin text-based negotiations through an invitation to Parties, intergovernmental organizations, indigenous peoples and local communities, and other relevant stakeholders to submit operational text and explanations based on the elements listed in Annex 1 of Decision IX/12.
iii. The establishment of three Groups of Technical and Legal Experts to advise the Working Group on ABS on: i) concepts, terms, working definitions, and sectoral approaches; ii) compliance; and iii) traditional knowledge associated with genetic resources.
iv. The agreement on escalating the pace and the intensity of the negotiations through the scheduling of three meetings of the Working Group on ABS, each for an extended period of seven days to ensure the completion of the negotiations towards an international regime on ABS in time for the deadline of the tenth COP in Nagoya.[29]

The first crucial opportunity for communities to substantially influence the negotiations of the Working Group on ABS presented itself in Hyderabad at the July 2009 meeting of the Group of Technical and Legal Experts (GTLE) on Traditional Knowledge associated with Genetic Resources. The Working Group on ABS set up this meeting at the 9th COP in Bonn. The 9th COP also set up two other GTLEs on 'Concepts, Terms and Definitions' and 'Compliance'. The establishment of the GTLE nearly broke the negotiations with the Like-Minded Megadiverse Countries (LMMC) grouping threatening to walkout of the negotiations on the argument that the GTLEs were a time-wasting tactic by the developed countries. The African Group, however, supported the establishment of GTLEs with the express intent of getting expert views on some of the issues that were deadlocked.[30]

The Secretariat of the CBD in its selection of country-nominated experts, chose individuals who were well-versed with community concerns. This was fortuitous since the experts who had a good grounding on community issues were also sympathetic to community

[29] UNEP/CBD/COP/DEC/IX/12 (accessed 13 September 2011).

[30] *See, Summary of the Ninth Conference of Parties to the CBD, Earth Negotiations Bulletin* 9(452).

concerns. Except for experts who represented Canada and industry, the remainder knew each other and tended to agree on virtually every issue. Furthermore, a sizeable number of chosen experts were from indigenous communities and some of them chaired various sessions of the GTLE, thereby palpably shifting the balance of power towards community interests.

The Working Group on ABS had provided the GTLE with a set of questions to be answered, and it was in answering these questions that the first cache of biocultural rights within the Trojan Horse of Article 8(j) emerged. The GTLE achieved a jurisprudential feat by expansively interpreting Article 8(j) in a way that had never been done before. Through the GTLE process, there were five critical victories for communities the fruits of which are seen in the Nagoya Protocol. They were:

i. An inseparable link between genetic resources and traditional knowledge was established thereby paving the way for a discourse on the rights of communities over genetics resources.
ii. The absolute requirement for prior informed consent and benefit sharing in relation to traditional knowledge of communities was read into Article 8(j) thereby closing the 'exit clauses' that states had given themselves.
iii. The need to comply with customary laws and community level procedures when accessing community resources and knowledge was affirmed, introducing an element of self-determination into Article 8(j).
iv. The 'subject to national law' component within Article 8(j) was substantially weakened by interpreting it as the duty of states to facilitate the rights of communities, that is, states had no discretion to decide whether or not to uphold these rights.
v. Clear reference was made to the importance of the UNDRIP in interpreting the provisions of the CBD for the purposes of the Protocol.[31]

[31] *See,* Report of the Meeting of the Group of Technical and Legal Experts on Traditional Knowledge Associated with Genetic Resources in the Context of the International Regime on Access and Benefit-Sharing, UNEP/CBD/WG-ABS/9/2 (July 2009).

In the 15 months from July 2009 to Nagoya in October 2010, there were a number of negotiations that ranged from the Working Group on ABS meetings to Friends of the Co-Chairs meetings to the Inter-regional Negotiating Group (ING) sessions to the Co-Chairs Informal Inter-regional Consultations. Communities strategically used every one of these negotiations to shore up the victories that resulted from the GTLE meeting on traditional knowledge. Their methods ranged from intensively lobbying delegates during the negotiations, to working closely with governments sympathetic to indigenous issues in the inter-sessional period, to networking with indigenous peoples' groups across the world in order convince them to lobby their governments.

At the 9th Meeting of the Working Group on ABS in Cali, the Co-Chairs provided the Parties with a Co-Chairs' text to break the stalemate that had plagued the negotiations until then. The Co-Chairs presented their text as a 'package deal' that balanced the interests of the different Parties and asked the Parties to begin their negotiations based on this text.[32] While the Co-Chairs' text was carefully drafted to cut the Gordian knot of the negotiations, for indigenous peoples and traditional communities it was the first step towards locking in the gains from the GLTE report.

The Co-Chairs' text was avowedly minimalist. It ensured prior informed consent and benefit sharing provisions vis-à-vis communities when their traditional knowledge was used. It also required Parties to ensure that such consent and benefit sharing was in accordance with the community's customary laws and community protocols. The text, however, was completely silent on compliance provisions obliging Parties to prevent the misappropriation of traditional knowledge. It also made no mention of rights of communities over genetic resources.[33] The first omission was in favour of the European

[32] *See*, Summary of the Ad-hoc Open Ended Working Group on Access and Benefit Sharing of the Convention on Biological Diversity, *Earth Negotiations Bulletin*, http://www.iisd.ca/biodiv/abs9/(accessed 23 March 2012).

[33] *See*, Annex 1 to the *Report of the First Part of the Ninth Meeting of the Ad-Hoc Open Ended Working Group on Access and Benefit Sharing*, UNEP/CBD/WG-ABS/9/3 (2010).

Union's (EU) position that the WIPO-IGC should deal with all compliance provisions relating to traditional knowledge. The second omission had to do with the absence of Party support for the rights of communities to genetic resources.

The Co-Chairs' text was intensely negotiated. When the second resumed session of the ING met on 13 October 2010 in Nagoya for the final round of negotiations, it had before it a heavily bracketed[34] draft Protocol that had come out of the ING meeting in Montreal a month before. India and China had reintroduced the term 'subject to national law' to the provision requiring prior informed consent of indigenous peoples and local communities. Furthermore, the EU bracketed references to customary laws and community protocols acting at the behest of France.

Indigenous peoples' groups reintroduced to the preamble section a reference to the UNDRIP, which was immediately bracketed by Canada. They also introduced a provision on the rights of communities over their genetic resources, which some Parties transformed into three possible text options all of which were promptly bracketed by other Parties. In fact, this provision was so heavily contested by the Group of Latin America and the Caribbean (GRULAC) in the September 2010 round of negotiations in Montreal that, after hours of discussion, the co-chairs to the small group negotiating the provision suggested dropping it altogether. This resulted in a walkout by the representatives of the IIFB. They stated that, as far as they were concerned, this was a non-negotiable issue. The outcome of these politically charged negotiations was that Parties in the small group agreed to keep these options and take them back to the ING for resolution.[35]

[34] Text-based negotiations between states of UN resolutions or treaties work on the principle of consensus. Bracketing of portions of text being negotiated indicates that a state party or a group of state parties do not agree to the wording of the text; *See*, Annex to the document, *Meeting of the Inter-Regional Negotiating Group*, UNEP/CBD/WG-ABS/9/ING/1 (10 September 2010).

[35] *See*, *Summary of the Interregional Negotiating Group on Access and Benefit Sharing*, 18–21 September 2010, *Earth Negotiations Bulletin*, http://www.iisd.ca/biodiv/absing/brief/absing_briefe.html (accessed 23 March 2012).

How did communities overcome these odds that were so heavily stacked against them? The odds were not simply relating to some Parties' white-knuckled reactions to what they perceived as a 'rights overreach' of the limited-scope Article 8(j). The most insurmountable of odds was the cold fact that communities as per UN rules could participate in the negotiations, but would require the explicit support of a Party for any text that they wanted to introduce or retain in the Protocol. As the COP 10 deadline loomed, the negotiations became increasingly frenetic and Parties began to make compromises, which exacerbated the danger that community concerns would be lost as collateral damage.

The Optimism of Will against the Pessimism of Intellect: The Gains of Nagoya

When the final round of negotiations began in Nagoya, indigenous peoples and traditional communities were clear that they had to secure five key positions in a potential ABS Protocol if it were to have any rights potential. These key positions were:

i. To eliminate the Article 8(j) term 'subject to national law' from the Protocol provisions dealing with rights of communities over their traditional knowledge and genetic resources before it became a legal 'term of art' and started being used in other COP resolutions.
ii. To secure the rights of communities over their genetic resources in the Protocol thereby creating a precedent for the dynamic interpretation of the CBD in the light of the UNDRIP.[36]
iii. To retain references to compliance with customary laws and community protocols of communities in the text of the Protocol thereby securing in treaty law, obligations of states to respect community systems of governance.
iv. To ensure reference to the UNDRIP in the preamble of the Protocol thereby locking in the legal opportunity to interpret the provisions of the Protocol from the perspective of the UNDRIP.

[36] United Nations General Assembly Resolution 61/295 adopted on 13 September 2007.

v. To prevent the forum shifting to the WIPO-IGC[37] of compliance provisions relating to traditional knowledge and affirm that the Protocol is the main instrument to enforce CBD related rights.[38]

These key positions had two dimensions: First, they were ends in themselves as significant 'rights victories' that secured the rights of communities over their traditional knowledge and genetic resources. Second, the hard-nosed pragmatists understood that the outcomes of Nagoya would not be perfect but that these positions should be viewed as levers for greater gains in the long run under the CBD and related WIPO, WTO, and UNFCCC processes.

The elimination of the term 'subject to national law' was a crucial hurdle to overcome. It had found itself back into the Co-Chairs' text in Montreal and some Parties were sticking to their guns about the provision being retained. Interestingly, countries like New Zealand and Canada had begun to have reservations about the term since it undermined the treaties that they already had with their indigenous peoples. These were not '*subject to national law*' but were akin to agreements between nations.

The African Group of states proposed a way out by replacing this term with a more temperate '*in accordance with national law*'. This would retain the facilitative role of the state in situations where Parties argued that communities within their jurisdiction needed state protection against exploitation. At the same time it would affirm the GTLE interpretation of Article 8(j) that the rights of communities under the CBD are not dependent on the discretion of states. This way forward was readily accepted by New Zealand and Canada, and Article 7 in the Nagoya Protocol finally read:

> In accordance with domestic law, each Party shall take measures, as appropriate, with the aim of ensuring that traditional knowledge associated with genetic resources that is held by indigenous and local communities is accessed with the prior and informed consent or

[37] *See* http://www.wipo.int/tk/en/igc/(accessed 13 September 2011).

[38] Based on conversations between the author and members of the IIFB.

> approval and involvement of these indigenous and local communities, and that mutually agreed terms have been established.[39]

While Article 7 was not perfect, it had clearly achieved what it set out to do. It had eliminated the term 'subject to national law', reinterpreted Article 8(j) in favour of community rights and created a new legal term of art that could henceforth be used in other parts of the Protocol and future COP decisions. This term—'in accordance with domestic law'—was clearly a lever that would lead to big gains in the future.

The next hurdle was the retention of references to 'customary laws and community protocols' in the text of the Protocol. France, at a rather late stage in the negotiations, had received instructions from its foreign ministry to withhold any agreement to references to 'customary laws, community protocols and indigenous and local community laws' in the draft Protocol. The French negotiators argued that this would affect the interests of France vis-à-vis their overseas territories and would create a new precedent of references to customary laws in international treaties between states.

It was clear that, as far as France was concerned, legal pluralism was definitely non-negotiable, and, through France's insistence, the rest of the EU had to back this position. France proposed 'community level procedures' as an alternative to 'customary laws and community protocols'. This phrase however was rejected by the African indigenous peoples' organizations (through the African Group) that argued that 'community level procedures' was a euphemism for state control and lacked the authenticity of genuine community processes.

The final wording in Article 12 (1) of the Nagoya Protocol now reads:

> In implementing their obligations under this Protocol, Parties shall in accordance with domestic law take into consideration indigenous and local communities' customary laws, community protocols and procedures, as applicable, with respect to traditional knowledge associated with genetic resources.[40]

[39] *See*, Nagoya Protocol on Access to Genetic Resources and the Fair and Equitable Benefits Arising from their Utilization (2010), http://www.cbd.int/abs/text/ (accessed 13 September 2011).

[40] Ibid.

How did communities manage to retain references to customary laws and community protocols despite the opposition?

The short history of this un-bracketed text is that an agreement was reached in the margins of the negotiations between France, the African Group, and the IIFB about the retention of the term 'customary laws and community protocols' in exchange for removal of the reference to 'indigenous and local community laws'. The African Group and the IIFB felt that the words 'customary laws' would in any case cover 'indigenous and local community laws'. France was also placated by the addition of 'in accordance with domestic law', the phrase that had replaced 'subject to national law', and was now beginning to reap dividends.

France, in return, had to agree to the use of the phrase 'Parties shall' at the beginning of the Article, thereby making it a binding obligation on Parties to take into consideration 'customary laws and community protocols' in implementing their obligations under the Protocol. Thanks to some very shrewd negotiating, the door in international law to legal pluralism, and self-determination of indigenous peoples and local communities, was now ajar.

The next crucial step was to secure the rights of communities over their genetic resources. This had always been a long shot in the negotiations since the CBD made no provision for such a right and one thing was clear in the September ING in Montreal: no Party would go out of its way to support this claim. On the penultimate day of the negotiations in Nagoya, there was still no support for this claim and the Co-Chairs constituted a small closed group (restricted to Parties) to discuss the still bracketed provisions relating to communities. A suggestion was made to drop this provision altogether. The African Group, however, on behalf of the IIFB suggested that a decision such as this should not be taken within a closed group but should be discussed within the larger group.

In the larger group Parties repeated that, while they were willing to recognize the rights of communities over genetic resources, it had to be strictly limited to national discretion, especially since the CBD did not recognize such a right. Communities, on the other hand stated that they had emerging rights to genetic resources through the UNDRIP, which despite being a UN General Assembly resolution, and therefore, not legally binding, had the moral authority that obliged countries to take it seriously. Communities further stated that, while they were willing to go along with references to their rights over genetic resources in national law, they also wanted a clear reference to their rights in international law. This argument was promptly rejected by the GRULAC.

Finally, a compromise text was developed and agreed to by all Parties and is now in the Nagoya Protocol. Article 6 (2) of the Protocol reads:

> In accordance with domestic law, each Party shall take measures, as appropriate, with the aim of ensuring that the prior informed consent or approval and involvement of indigenous and local communities is obtained for access to genetic resources where they have the established right to grant access to such resources.[41]

Two legal victories are worthy of note. First, the sentence begins with 'in accordance with domestic law' thereby eliminating the 'subject to law' term and making this a facilitative provision. The obligation on Parties is phrased as 'shall', which is mandatory. The sentence ends with 'where they have the established right to grant access to such resources'. The words 'established right' are unqualified thereby leaving it to interpretation as to whether these rights are established in national or international law. In negotiations speak this is known as a 'strategic ambiguity', that is, a shrewd silence, that leaves enough room for interpretation and jurisprudential growth.

If we approach the law as a site of struggle, Article 6 (2) of the Nagoya Protocol is a monumental achievement by communities. It is testimony to six years of hard work and careful lobbying, and it has extended the scope of Article 8(j) in ways that were inconceivable in 1993. It capitalized on the important victory in the GLTE report on traditional knowledge, that is, for indigenous peoples and local communities, there is an inseparable link between genetic resources and traditional knowledge. What is more, the preamble to the Nagoya Protocol explicitly recognizes this link in the paragraph:

> Noting the interrelationship between genetic resources and traditional knowledge, their inseparable nature for indigenous and local communities,

[41] *See*, Nagoya Protocol on Access to Genetic Resources and the Fair and Equitable Benefits Arising from their Utilization (2010), http://www.cbd.int/abs/text/ (accessed 13 September 2011).

> the importance of the traditional knowledge for the conservation of biological diversity and the sustainable use of its components, and for the sustainable livelihoods of these communities.[42]

The last two hurdles for communities were to ensure that compliance provisions relating to traditional knowledge were retained in the Protocol, and that the Protocol made reference to the UNDRIP in its preamble. For both these provisions communities had significant support from states. Regarding the compliance provisions relating to traditional knowledge, a deal was finally made with the EU that, in exchange for a paragraph in the COP 10 decision (that required the Parties to the Protocol to take note of the developments at the WIPO-IGC), the EU would agree to un-bracketing these provisions. The agreed text in the Nagoya Protocol under Article 16 reads:

1. Each Party shall take appropriate, effective and proportionate legislative, administrative or policy measures, as appropriate, to provide that traditional knowledge associated with genetic resources utilized within their jurisdiction has been accessed in accordance with prior informed consent or approval and involvement of indigenous and local communities and that mutually agreed terms have been established, as required by domestic access and benefit-sharing legislation or regulatory requirements of the other Party where such indigenous and local communities are located.
2. Each Party shall take appropriate, effective and proportionate measures to address situations of non-compliance with measures adopted in accordance with paragraph 1.
3. Parties shall, as far as possible and as appropriate cooperate in cases of alleged violation of domestic access and benefit-sharing legislation or regulatory requirements referred to in paragraph 1.[43]

[42] *See,* Nagoya Protocol on Access to Genetic Resources and the Fair and Equitable Benefits Arising from their Utilization (2010), http://www.cbd.int/abs/text/ (accessed 13 September 2011).

[43] Ibid.

Regarding the reference to the UNDRIP in the preamble of the Protocol, Canada ended up being the only Party that refused to accept. In order to goad Canada into un-bracketing this provision, the terms were made more acceptable by phrasing it as: 'Noting the United Nations Declaration on the Rights of Indigenous Peoples'.[44]

On the last day of the negotiations in Nagoya, Canada, after late night consultations with their capital, finally relented to un-bracket this text. This decision owes a great debt to media releases, press conferences, and lobbying undertaken by Canadian indigenous peoples' organizations in both Canada and Japan.[45] In many ways Canada's acceptance of this paragraph also contributed to the recent Canadian endorsement of the UNDRIP. While Canada had remained the last country that opposed even a reference to the UNDRIP in the Nagoya Protocol, a number of other countries were unwilling to have any strong affirmation of UNDRIP in the preamble to the Protocol. Indigenous peoples' organizations, however, repeatedly asserted that the UNDRIP is customary international law and the CBD would have to be interpreted in harmony with it. In this context it would be useful to note the views of James Anaya (the UN Special Rapporteur on the situation of human rights and fundamental freedoms of indigenous people) in his 15 July 2010 statement before the EMRIP where he made the case that UNDRIP should be recognized as customary international law by arguing thus:

> Of course it can be conceded that, as a resolution of the General Assembly, the Declaration (UNDRIP) is by its nature, not in an of itself legally binding .... But understanding about the normative significance and legal obligations related to the Declaration does not end there. First, whatever its legal significance, the Declaration has a significant normative weight grounded in its high degree of legitimacy. This legitimacy is a function of not only the fact that it has been formally endorsed by an overwhelming majority of UN Member States, but also the fact that it is the product of years of advocacy

[44] Ibid.

[45] 'Indigenous Representatives Denounce Canada's Obstructionist Position at COP 10', *Canada News Wire*, 2010. http://www.newswire.ca/en/story/636655/indigenous-representatives-denounce-canada-s-obstructionist-position-at-cop10 (accessed 23 March 2012).

> and struggle by indigenous peoples themselves. The Declaration is the result of a cross-cultural dialogue that took place over decades, in which indigenous peoples took a leading role. The norms of the Declaration substantially reflect indigenous peoples own aspirations, which after years of deliberation have come to be accepted by the international community. The Declaration's wording, which has been endorsed by Member States, explicitly manifests a commitment to the rights and principles the Declaration embodies. It is simply a matter of good faith that States adhere to that expression of commitment to the norms that indigenous peoples themselves have advanced. Furthermore, even though the Declaration itself is not legally binding in the same way that a treaty is, the Declaration reflects legal commitments that are related to the United Nations Charter, other treaty commitments and to customary international law. The Declaration builds upon the general human rights obligations of States under the Charter and is grounded in fundamental human rights principles such as non-discrimination, self-determination and cultural integrity that are incorporated into widely-ratified human rights treaties, as evident in the work of United Nations treaty bodies. In addition, core principles of the Declaration can be seen to connect to a consistent pattern of international and state practice, and hence to that extent they reflect customary international law ...[46]

Field Notes from the Frontline: The Emergence of Biocultural Jurisprudence

The previous sections endeavoured to take seriously Thompson's advice to avoid the 'profound condescension of posterity' by mapping the biocultural rights gains in the Nagoya Protocol resulting from six years of painstaking negotiations. The rights of communities we see in the Protocol today cannot be attributed to manna from heaven or the munificence of Parties. They are the result of hard fought battles by the IIFB over every comma and every word. With the strong support of sympathetic Parties, especially the African Group, Philippines, Peru, and Norway, communities gained significant ground vis-à-vis

[46] *See* http://unsr.jamesanaya.org/statements/statement-on-the-united-nations-declaration-on-the-rights-of-indigenous-peoples-to-the-emrip (accessed 13 September 2011).

their rights over traditional knowledge and genetic resources and the recognition of their customary laws.

The oft quoted homily in the ABS negotiations was 'perfection is the enemy of the good'. While there were times when it sounded trite, it rings true when analysing the Nagoya Protocol. The rights that were gained by communities in the Nagoya Protocol may not be perfect, but they are undeniably a giant gain from the tame provisions of Articles 8 (j) and 10 (c) of the CBD. Going back to the guiding questions posed at the outset—to truly understand the colossal achievement regarding community rights in the Nagoya Protocol, we must learn to see how far we have come since 1993. Slowly but surely indigenous peoples' groups have started transforming their non-binding rights in the UNDRIP into binding rights in treaty law relying on nothing more than the moral force of the Declaration.

Every gain in the Nagoya Protocol is not an end in itself but the flat end of a lever inserted into the interstices of other negotiations to pry open community rights under TRIPS, WIPO-IGC, FAO, and the UNFCCC. From the perspective of negotiations, this is the fine art of cross-leveraging rights, that is, to take gains from one Convention and insist that they be respected in another Convention dealing with similar subject matter. This emphasis by communities on a rights-based approach to all multilateral environmental negotiations is an effective nostrum against the tendency of the law to fragment life by splitting it up into different legal subjects, such as land, intellectual property, cultural issues, etc.

So, how do we begin to make sense of the emerging rights discourse? In the first place this growing phenomenon must be named. If thrown into the general grab bag of rights, both community lawyers and organizations will insufficiently understand the full potential of these new hard-fought rights. This possibility has led to their inadequate use in domestic activism, which has allowed states to ignore international commitments in the development and implementation of national law and policy.

To begin the naming process: in the last two decades, through the movement for indigenous peoples' rights, a discourse of third generation rights called 'group rights or collective rights' has developed. These are different from the first generation civil and political rights, and the second generation social and economic rights.

While group rights cover the gamut of rights required for the survival and flourishing of indigenous peoples and ethnic groups, a subset of third generation rights has emerged almost unnoticed as an offshoot of 'group rights'. This subset of rights is what is being termed as 'biocultural rights'.[47]

Biocultural rights are group rights, but they differ from the general category of third generation rights through their explicit link to conservation and sustainable use of biological diversity. Indigenous peoples and traditional communities who assert biocultural rights, base their claims on two foundations:

i. Conservation and sustainable use of biological diversity by communities is reliant on a way of life, and biocultural rights must protect this way of life.
ii. The way of life relevant for conservation and sustainable use of biological diversity is linked to secure land tenure, use rights, and rights to culture, knowledge and practices.

Biocultural rights are not claims to property by groups marginalized by markets. This link however is worked out through the assertion of a bundle of property rights. It is critical to understand the spirit of biocultural rights as not a pure property claim by a hitherto excluded group in the typical market sense of property being universally commensurable, commodifiable and alienable. On the contrary, biocultural assertions of property rights are claims in the form of use, stewardship, and fiduciary rights that emphasize use over exchange value. The 'peoplehood' of biocultural communities is integrally linked to the rights to stewardship of their lands and

[47] The term 'biocultural rights' is a classificatory term that we use here to distinguish this set of rights from the gamut of 'group rights'. As of yet, this term does not have common usage; regarding the three generations of human rights *see generally*, Karel Vasak, 'Human Rights: A Thirty-Year Struggle: the Sustained Efforts to give Force of Law to the Universal Declaration of Human Rights', *UNESCO Courier* 30(11), (Paris: United Nations Educational, Scientific, and Cultural Organization, November 1977), p. 29.

concomitant traditional knowledge through a complex system of customary use rights and fiduciary duties.

Biocultural jurisprudence then is the theory and practice of applying a biocultural rights framework to law and policy, when such law and policy affects a community whose peoplehood is integrally tied to their traditional stewardship role and fiduciary duties vis-à-vis their lands and concomitant knowledge. The infrapolitics of communities in the negotiations towards the Nagoya Protocol have firmly established biocultural rights in hard law. The story of these biocultural rights needs to be told and retold to ensure their realization on the ground. It is by repeated public declamation and proactive use that these biocultural rights will come alive. The Nagoya Protocol is a significant event, and it is only by celebrating its gains that we can fully honour the indigenous peoples and local communities who made it happen.

Biocultural rights, established through multilateral environmental negotiations, have begun to make their impact felt in property jurisprudence. In fact, biocultural jurisprudence seems to draw its strength from historicizing and deconstructing the legal discourse of private property to challenge its naturalness. Biocultural rights make the claim that it is not property that should determine personhood or peoplehood but the other way round. In the next chapter, we will turn to exploring the veracity of this radical claim.

CHAPTER SIX

Rethinking Property

A Biocultural Approach

The first person who, having fenced off a plot of ground, took it into his head to say 'this is mine' and found people simple enough to believe him, was the true founder of civil society. What crimes, wars, murders, what miseries and horrors would the human race have been spared by someone who, uprooting the stakes or filling in the ditch had shouted to his fellow-men: Beware of listening to this imposter; you are lost if you forget that the fruits belong to all and the earth to no one!

—*Jean-Jacques Rousseau:* 'Discourse on the Origin and Foundations of Inequality'[1]

The emergence of biocultural rights asks for a fundamental rethink of property jurisprudence itself. The understanding of property in law has never been constant, and discussions around the concept are among the most contested areas of jurisprudence. In fact, if we approach law as politics, then the discourse of property is perhaps the epicentre. The very notion of personhood, and hence the juridical subject in liberal democracies, is based on an assumption that a right to property is integral to what we understand as 'person'.[2]

The courts in liberal democracies, where property litigation is conducted, are also sites where our personhood is defined, contested,

[1] Jean-Jacques Rousseau (trans. by Roger D. Masters, ed. by Roger and Judith Masters), 'Discourse on the Origin and Foundations of Inequality', in *The First and Second Discourses of Rousseau* (New York: St. Martin's Press, 1964), p.141.

[2] Social contract theories of various shades that form the philosophical foundations of liberal democracies all understand personhood as incorporating a bundle of individual rights including the right to property.

and redefined. In their challenging of commodity or private property fetishism, and the estrangement it engenders, communities are relying on biocultural jurisprudence as a means to counter the two main fallacies regarding property in capitalist societies.

The first fallacy is one where property is understood as a thing rather than a right. The influential Canadian political scientist C.B. Macpherson in his analysis of property notes: 'In current common usage, property is *things*; in law and in the writers, property is not things, but *rights*, rights *in* or *to* things'.[3] The second fallacy is one where property is understood as predominantly private property. It is, therefore, treated as an individual exclusive right; a right to exclude others from use or benefit. Again Macpherson says that: 'Another difficulty is that property, in the works of most modern writers, is usually treated as identical with *private* property, an exclusive individual right, my right to exclude you from some use or benefit of something'.[4] The reason why these two dominant perceptions of property are fallacies is because both of them are a product of historical circumstances, specifically of the dominance of market economies, which like the *homo economicus* are passed off as ahistorical and natural.

WHAT IS PROPERTY?

Property in its most fundamental sense is a political relationship; it distinguishes itself from mere possession by establishing a right or a claim that is supported by law, custom, state, or society. At this elemental level, property is not a thing, but an enforceable claim. While the morality of any property claim is subject to contestation, it is undeniable that to assert a property right is to lay claim to a particular political relationship.

The transformation of property from a political relation to a thing is tied to the dominance of the market economy and the fetishism of commodities it engenders. The erasure of use value and

[3] C.B. Macpherson, 'The Meaning of Property', in C.B. Macpherson (ed.), *Property: Mainstream and Critical Positions* (Oxford: Basil Blackwell, 1978), p. 2.

[4] Ibid.

predominance of exchange value result in a phenomenon where commodities and not people become ends in themselves. As long as markets were embedded in social relations, notions of property were based on rights to access, use, and, under certain conditions, exchange. The moment markets began to eclipse all social relations, the emphasis palpably shifted from the rights to access and use, to the rights to exclude and alienate.

Macpherson notes:

> The change in common usage, to treating property as things themselves, came with the spread of the full capitalist market economy from the seventeenth century on, and the replacement of the old limited rights in land and other valuable things by virtually unlimited rights. As rights in land became more absolute, and parcels of land became more freely marketable commodities, it became natural to think of the land itself as property .... It appeared to be the things themselves, not just rights in them that were exchanged in the market. In fact the difference was not that things rather than rights in things were exchanged, but that previously unsalable rights in things were now saleable; or to put it differently, that limited and not always saleable rights *in* things were being replaced by virtually unlimited saleable rights *to* things.[5]

The blurring between right and thing in contemporary property discourse is a result of universal commoditization wrought by capitalism.[6] The transformation of property from a right to a thing, also transformed the notion of personhood[7] from the *homo socialis* to the *homo economicus.* If who we are, is an 'ensemble of social relations' or 'nodes in a web of social relations', then how we understand property determines the extent of our relationality and thereby our very notion of self. Property as a right affirms relationality since the

[5] Macpherson, 'The Meaning of Property', (1978), pp. 7–8.

[6] *See generally,* Michael J. Sandel, 'What Money Can't Buy: The Moral Limits of Markets', *The Tanner Lectures on Human Values* (Oxford University Press, 1998). www.tannerlectures.utah.edu/lectures/documents/sandel00.pdf (accessed 13 September 2011).

[7] *See,* Margaret Jane Radin, 'Property and Personhood', *Stanford Law Review* 34(5) (May 1982), pp. 957–1015 for an excellent analysis of the link between property and personhood.

human being is the ultimate end, whereas property as a thing results in estrangement since the commodity and not the human being becomes the legitimate end.

The second fallacy that Macpherson highlights is the conflation of property with private property, a conflation that goes back no further than the seventeenth century. While debates about property are as old as political theory itself, private property historically has always been contentious. According to Macpherson, this is not surprising since private property, which involved the right to exclude and alienate, was not just an economic but also a moral issue. Property, as a right rather than a thing, was viewed as a bundle of access and use claims. In this regard customary law jurist Thomas Bennett notes that:

> The great watershed in the formation of a fully-fledged concept of ownership was clearly trade. Before this occurred, property of economic significance attracted many highly specific rights, each of which could vest in a different person .... If the optimum condition of a free market was to be realized, these goods had to be loosened from the specific rights of particular interest holders. Ownership provided the answer. It was a concept applicable to any type of property and it was available to all traders .... The proprietary rights of the pre-trade era can be distinguished from ownership by the fact that the former usually implied a number of specific interests vesting in various different holders, whereas ownership implies a collection of interests vesting in a single holder.[8]

In fact, the predominant conception of property until the seventeenth century was that of common property, with private

[8] Thomas W. Bennett, *Customary Law in South Africa* (Landsdowne: Juta, 2004), p. 375; Bennett also notes that the notion of ownership as an indefeasible right is no longer appropriate to describe contemporary proprietary relations (or the requirements of modern society). Nevertheless this notion of absolute ownership lingers even in the contemporary Hohfeldian understanding of ownership as a bundle of rights and powers, which do not include any rights for others. *See also* Melville Herskovits, *Economic Anthropology* (New York: Knopf, 1952), p. 325 and Van der Walt. 'The Future of Common Law Land Ownership', in A.J. Van der Walt (ed.), *Land Reform and the Future of Landownership in South Africa* (Landsdowne: Juta, 1991), pp. 21 and 31–4.

property being a subset. Echoing Polanyi's argument of the recent vintage of the market economy, Macpherson argues:

> From the sixteenth and seventeenth centuries on, more and more of the land and resources in settled countries was becoming private property, and private property was becoming an individual right unlimited in amount, unconditional on the performance of social functions, and freely transferable, as it substantially remains to the present day ... the modern right, in comparison to the feudal right which preceded it, may be called an absolute right in two senses: it is a right to dispose of, or alienate as well as to use; and it is a right which is not conditional on the owner's performance of any social function.[9]

The displacement of common property and the consequent conflation of private property with property as a whole have had dire consequences for liberal political theory. If the *grundnorm* of liberal democracy is the right of all individuals to develop their potential, it becomes extremely difficult to reconcile this ethic with the growing concentration of ownership in the hands of a few. The notion of personhood in liberal democracies is linked to some form of property rights without which the person is unable to flourish or even remain a person. However, according to Macpherson, the erosion of common property in favour of private property with highly concentrated ownership adversely affected the liberal understanding of full and effective personhood.

Pre-empting a biocultural jurisprudence, Macpherson asserts:

> [P]roperty ... need not be confined, as liberal theory has confined it, to a right to exclude others from the use or benefit of something, but may equally be an individual right not to be excluded by others from the use or benefit of something. When property is so understood, the problem of liberal-democratic theory is no longer a problem of putting limits on the property rights, but of supplementing the individual right to exclude others by the individual right not to be excluded by others. The latter right may be held to be the one that is most required by the liberal-democratic ethic, and most implied in a liberal concept of the human essence. The right not to be excluded

[9] Macpherson (ed.), *Property: Mainstream and Critical Positions* (1978), p. 10.

by others may provisionally be stated as the individual right to equal access to the means of labour and/or the means of life.[10]

JOHN LOCKE AND JUSTIFICATIONS FOR PRIVATE PROPERTY

> *Though the Earth and all inferior Creatures be common to all Men, yet every Man has a Property in his own Person. This no Body has any Right to but himself. The Labour of his Body, and the Work of his Hands, we may say, are properly his. Whatsoever he removes out of the state that Nature hath provided, and left it in, he hath mixed his Labour with, and joined to it something that is his own, and thereby makes it his Property. It being by him removed from the common state Nature placed it in, it hath by this labour something annexed to it, that excludes the common right of other Men. For this Labour being the unquestionable Property of the Labourer, no Man but he can have a right to what that is once joined to, at least where there is enough, and as good left in common for others.*
>
> —*John Locke, Second Treatise of Government*[11]

An understanding of the views of the English philosopher John Locke, first published in 1689, could usefully inform the current discussion around the nature of property. A critical reading of Locke provides us with an insight into what happened in the seventeenth century to justify unlimited private property.

By the end of the seventeenth century Locke had for the first time developed a political theory that justified the right of individuals to limitless appropriation and accumulation of property.[12] As we shall see later, historically, private property in land was always a morally contentious issue that required justification. Macpherson comments:

[10] Ibid. p. 201.

[11] John Locke, 'Two Treatises of Government', in John Locke (ed. by Peter Laslett), *Locke's Two Treatises of Government: A Critical Edition with an Introduction and Apparatus* (New York: New American Library, 1965), excerpt from Macpherson (ed.), 'John Locke', *Property: Mainstream and Critical Positions* (1978), p. 18.

[12] *See generally*, C.B. Macpherson, *The Political Theory of Possessive Individualism: Hobbes to Locke* (Oxford: Oxford University Press, 1962), pp. 194–262.

> His (Locke's) case remained the standby of those who shaped the thinking of the ruling class in England, from the Whig Revolution for a century or more, and the eighteenth century. His justification of property was thus in effect written into, or at least was implied in, the constitutions of the first great modern capitalist nation-states.[13]

It is uncanny how close Locke's notion of personhood and its link to property is to Marx's understanding of the labour theory of value, and the estrangement that wage labour causes due to the worker's lack of control over the means of production. This is perhaps where the similarities between Marx and Locke also end, but this similarity nevertheless is worthy of note. As Locke observes in the excerpt at the beginning of this section: 'every Man has a Property in his own Person'.[14] This observation is the cornerstone of Locke's understanding of the link between property and personhood, and the building block of his theory on property.

If a person has a property in his own person, then Locke proceeds to say that, 'The Labour of his Body, and the Work of his Hands, we may say, are properly his'.[15] The basis of Locke's argument is that a person owns what his body labours over because he owns his body. His labour is an extension of his body or his personhood and therefore what his labour contributes to belong to him: 'Whatsoever he removes out of the state that Nature hath provided, and left it in, he hath mixed his Labour with, and joined to it something that is his own, and thereby makes it his Property'.[16]

Locke's justification for property by linking it to personhood is simple enough, and even Marx would not disagree with him. What is interesting though is Locke's need to justify appropriation. This need provides us with a window into the predominant moral principle of Locke's time; that God gave the earth in common to humankind, implying that what is common is natural, and private property is a moral exception that would need to be justified. Locke says:

[13] Macpherson, 'The Meaning of Property' (1978), p. 13.
[14] Macpherson, 'John Locke', *Property: Mainstream and Critical Positions* (1978).
[15] Ibid.
[16] Ibid, p. 17.

> Whether we consider natural *Reason*, which tells us that Men, being once born, have a right to their Preservation, and consequently to Meat and Drink, and such other things, as Nature affords for their subsistence: Or *Revelation* which gives us an account of those Grants God made of the World to *Adam* and to *Noah*, and his Sons, 'tis very clear, that God, as King *David* says, *Psal* CXV.xvj, *has given the Earth to the Children of Men*, given it to Mankind in common. But this being supposed, it seems to some a very great difficulty how any one should ever come to have a *Property* in anything.[17]

For Locke, the first step to a theory of private property is to justify the act of taking something out of the commons and enclosing it. Locke, as we have seen, does this by establishing an ownership over one's body and, by extension, an ownership over things that one's body expends labour over. Property then is an extension of one's bodily exertions and integrally tied to personhood. Up to this point Locke would not have faced much opposition, but he still had some way to go to be able to justify unlimited accumulation of private property. Locke acknowledges the moral limits to private property when he says:

> It will perhaps be objected to this, That if gathering the Acorns, or other Fruits of the Earth, *&c.* makes a right to them, then any one may *ingross* as much as he will. To which I Answer, Not so. The same Law of Nature, that does by this means give us Property, does also *bound* that *Property* too. *God has given us all things richly*, 1 Tim. Vi. 17. Is the Voice of Reason confirmed by Inspiration. But how far has he given to us? *To enjoy*. As much as anyone can make use of to any advantage of life before it spoils .... Whatever is beyond this, is more than his share and belongs to others. Nothing was made by God for Man to spoil or destroy.[18]

Here Locke acknowledges a clear moral dictum of his time, which is the 'spoilage limitation', a limitation that was also noted by Polanyi and Sahlins in economies preceding fully-fledged market economies. The limitation states that one can only appropriate for one's essential needs. Any accumulation beyond one's needs, to the extent that what

[17] Ibid.
[18] Ibid., p. 19.

is accumulated is not used or is spoiled amounts to breach of this moral code of sufficiency.

The spoilage limitation is buttressed by the other moral dictum which is the 'sufficiency or the distribution limitation'. This limitation states that one should not appropriate so much as to prejudice others from having access to the same resources. Locke notes this limitation too when he states:

> For this *Labour* being the unquestionable Property of the Labourer, no Man but he can have a right to what that is once joined to, *at least where there is enough, and as good left in common for others* (emphasis mine). [19]

At this stage, it is hard to see how Locke could have overcome three very powerful moral limits that common property sets on private property: i) the earth and everything on it is common property and we can only appropriate that to which we have joined our labour; ii) we can only appropriate enough to meet our needs but not beyond what we can use; and iii) the amount we appropriate should still leave enough for others to fulfil their personhood. Locke however transcends the spoilage and sufficiency limitation by arguing that:

> That the same Rule of Propriety, (viz.) that every man should have as much as he could make use of, would hold still in the World, without straitning any body, since there is Land enough in the World to suffice double the Inhabitants had not the Invention of Money, and the tacit Agreement of Men to put a value on it, introduced (by Consent) larger Possessions, and a Right to them....[20]

Locke goes on to add:

> That in the beginning, before the desire of having more than Men needed, had altered the intrinsick value of things, which depends only on their usefulness to the Life of Man; of (Men) had agreed, that a little piece of yellow Metal, which would keep without wasting or decay should be worth a great piece of Flesh, or a whole heap of Corn; though Men had a Right to appropriate, by their Labour, each one to himself, as much of the things of Nature, as he could use; Yet this

[19] Macpherson (ed.), 'John Locke' in *Property: Mainstream and Critical Positions* (1978), p. 18.

[20] Ibid., p. 21.

> could not be much, nor to the Prejudice of others, where the same plenty was still left, to those who would use the same Industry. To which let me add, that he who appropriates land to himself by his labour, does not lessen but increase the common stock of mankind. For the provisions serving to the support of humane life, produced by one acre of inclosed and cultivated land, are … ten times more, than those, which are yielded by an acre of land, of an equal richnesse, lying wast in the common.[21]

In the above two excerpts Locke, with a single stroke, makes two assertions that represent the ideology of seventeenth century mercantilism shot back through history and presented as the natural evolution of the *homo economicus*. The first assertion is that the invention of money, and the tacit consent to it in terms of a social contract, overrides the spoilage limitation. Money or gold does not spoil and therefore as long as one is earning money or converting to exchange value what is appropriated from common property, one is not breaching any moral code. The real sin for Locke's version of mercantilism is when money or capital is hoarded. As long as money is put to work, or is kept in circulation, to generate more money, unlimited appropriation is justified.[22]

Locke's second assertion in the seventeenth century resonates nearly 280 years later with the views of Garett Hardin in his essay on the 'Tragedy of the Commons'.[23] Long before Hardin, Locke had begun dismantling the sufficiency limitation to private property by stating that private property incentivizes production, which benefits society as a whole, and common property leads to waste. Locke's point that one acre of enclosed land leading to an output that exceeds ten acres of land in the commons strategically shifts the discourse of social well-being from sufficiency to profit: society as a whole benefits not when each takes from the commons only what s/he needs but when profit seeking is incentivized by lifting the limits on private property.

It is useful to observe the gradual development and normalization of the figure of the *homo economicus* over the last three hundred years.

[21] Ibid., pp. 21–2.

[22] Macpherson, *The Political Theory of Possessive Individualism: Hobbes to Locke* (1962).

[23] Hardin, 'The Tragedy of the Commons' (1968).

Locke had to work a lot harder to justify unlimited private property at a time when the moral climate leaned in favour of common property. Locke even had to develop the fictional theory of social contract, which argued that society as a whole had tacitly agreed to lift limits to accumulation by its adoption of money. Mercantilist economy had to be portrayed as the natural outcome of social evolution rather than as the interest of a capitalist class.

Locke's assumption about the naturalness of wage labour in his theory of property is also intriguing. According to Locke's first principle, if one can rightfully appropriate what one mixes with labour, it becomes difficult to justify the capitalist accumulating the product of a worker's labour in exchange for wages. According to Locke's theory the labourer could well have a right over the means of production itself since labour is joined to the system of production. Locke deftly overcomes this obstacle by implying in his theory that, if one owns one's labour through the ownership of one's body, then one also has the right to alienate or dispose of one's labour in exchange for wages.

By this implication, Locke provides a justification for capitalism wherein wage labourers freely consent to the estrangement or alienation of their labour and its products in an exercise of their rights over their bodies. This was a justification that Marx would spend his life dismantling. Locke notes:

> Thus the Grass my Horse has bit; the Turfs my Servant has cut; and the Ore I have digg'd in any place where I have a right to them in common with others, become my *Property*, without the assignation or consent of any body. The *labour* that was mine, removing them out of that common state they were in, hath *fixed* my *Property* in them.[24]

It is obvious here that Locke, by developing a theory of private property in seventeenth century England, transposed the class relations prevalent in his time back to the history of humankind itself, where wage labour in the form of ownership over the 'Turfs my Servant has cut' is assumed as completely 'natural'.

Working through Macpherson's interrogation of contemporary property jurisprudence and its historical justifications, beginning

[24] Macpherson (ed.), 'John Locke' in *Property: Mainstream and Critical Positions* (1978), p. 18.

with Locke, has better equipped us to analyse critically the issues that biocultural jurisprudence would need to confront, and potential dangers along the way. It is to undertake such a critical analysis that we must now turn.

THE 'BIOCULTURE' IN BIOCULTURAL RIGHTS

The political justification for biocultural rights by communities is, for the most part, rooted within the liberal rights discourse and relies on advocacy within national and supranational law and policy forums. When farmers' groups, pastoralists, and indigenous peoples' activists demand biocultural rights, they are also demanding the right to common property or, in Macpherson's terms, the right not to be excluded through private property or state appropriations of their lands, waters, and cultures. For example, farmers' rights challenge seed monopolies of agribusinesses by asserting their common property rights to save and exchange their seeds; pastoralists declare their right to their historical grazing commons; and indigenous peoples affirm the right to collectively manage and govern their forests.

As was previously noted, the successes of the movement for biocultural rights are undeniable with the Nagoya Protocol on ABS being a case in point. Unless there is great clarity, however, in what constitutes the ethic of stewardship, biocultural rights within market economies could end up being co-opted into a discourse of private property rights. This co-option could then individualize the collective, wherein claimant groups begin to interpret their newly acquired biocultural rights as akin to rights of corporate entities to exclude others from collective property and alienate it.

This real possibility has been well documented by anthropologists Jean and John Comaroff in their book *Ethnicity Inc.* where they explore the incorporation of identity and commodification of culture by analysing the San Hoodia case (previously discussed here) and Royal Bafokeng Nation's platinum mining interests.[25] Such a co-option could possibly stymie the real potential of the movement

[25] *See generally*, John Comaroff and Jean Comaroff, *Ethnicity Inc.* (Chicago: University of Chicago Press, 2009).

for biocultural rights, which is a movement that challenges both the conflation of property with private property and the justification of limitless accumulation through reducing property from a right to pure capital (thing).

The right to common property, where property is a right that guarantees well-being, has slowly transformed into the right to unlimited private property, where property is understood as capital. It is submitted that the reinterpretation of property then should not be reduced to access to capital but should be enlarged to include access to well-being which is underpinned by a right to common property. This does not mean that common property is an unregulated 'free for all', but rather is regulated by the ethic of stewardship that emphasizes responsibility to collective well-being and restricts unlimited private appropriation or enclosure.

In the context of the Nagoya Protocol on ABS, one could well argue that the recognition of the rights of communities to their traditional knowledge is essentially recognition of private property rights to enclose such knowledge and exclude non-community members from using it. While this is clearly a possibility, the ethos of biocultural rights within the Nagoya Protocol makes the link between the right to a way of life that embodies stewardship and the conservation of ecosystems. This ethos stems less from the need to establish private property rights for the purposes of exchange value and more from a need to affirm common property rights in order to establish a right to use value, one that is integrally linked to the way of life of indigenous people and traditional communities, and hence to their well-being.

As noted previously, the campaign for biocultural rights is not a campaign against commodification or markets *per se*. On the contrary, it is a campaign for the re-embedding of the market within social relations or reasserting the predominance of use over exchange value. It is a campaign against the complete eclipse of all social relations by market relations through an assertion of the duty of stewardship over the unbridled absolutism of private property discourses.

The fact that communities will rely on their biocultural rights to enter into commercial benefit sharing agreements with potential users of their resources and knowledge is not necessarily a bad thing. Commodification by communities of natural products and the knowledge relating to it have a long history, one that both Polanyi and Sahlins acknowledge when they theorize on the role of markets in pre-capitalist societies.[26] The real value of biocultural rights, however, lies in the re-centering of the community's stewardship values and its challenge to the preponderance of market values.

Biocultural rights therefore establish both the right of communities to set the terms of access by outsiders to their cultures, territories, and resources while at the same time, affirming the community's ethic of stewardship over what is considered common property belonging to the whole community. Biocultural rights in effect challenge the current conflation of property with private property thereby expanding the concept of property to reclaim the rightful place of common property and the rights of those who are its stewards.

PUTTING PERSONHOOD IN PROPERTY

> *Most people possess certain objects they feel are almost part of themselves. These objects are closely bound up with personhood because they are part of the way we constitute ourselves as continuing personal entities in the world. They may be different as people are different, but some common examples might be a wedding ring, a portrait, an heirloom, or a house .... The opposite of holding an object that has become a part of oneself is holding an object that is perfectly replaceable with other goods of equal market value. One holds such an object for purely instrumental reasons. The archetype of such a good is, of course, money, which is almost always held to but other things .... Other examples are a wedding ring in the hands of the jeweler, the automobile in the hands of the dealer, the land in the hands of the developer ... I shall call these theoretical opposites-property that is bound up with a person and property that is held purely instrumentally- personal property and fungible property respectively.*
>
> — *Margaret Jane Radin- Property and Personhood*[27]

While Marx highlighted the loss of personhood through alienation caused by exchange value, Locke argued the opposite by stating that personhood is affirmed through the freedom to alienate. However, both Marx and Locke seemed to acknowledge that personhood was

[26] *See generally*, Chapter Two.

[27] Radin, 'Property and Personhood' (1982), pp. 959–60.

not purely an internal subjectivity, with the external world being somehow separate. Their notion of personhood extended beyond the self as an enclosed subject to a subjectivity that included objects of one's labour. For Marx, wage labour led to estrangement, since one's labour and its object were intimately tied to one's self. Locke also agreed that one's labour was a part of oneself, but, precisely because of this, one had the right to alienate one's labour for a wage or appropriate that which one's labour was joined with. Neither Marx nor Locke, however, developed a nuanced understanding of what aspects of the world constituted integral aspects of personhood and what could be could be understood as fungible.

The above excerpt by Margaret Jane Radin, arguably one of the most significant contemporary property jurists, offers us an insight into the critical importance of examining the nature of personhood and developing an understanding of property on this basis. For Marx, the erasure of use value through the hegemony of exchange value results in a fetishism of commodities, which causes an estrangement from our real personhood.

Personhood for Marx, as we noted previously, is an ensemble of social relations, and the transforming of all social relations into market relations makes our lives one dimensional thereby alienating us from the fullness of our lived experience. Polanyi, however, said that the market or commodification per se is not a bad thing, since a number of societies through history had engaged in market exchanges. The danger was when markets were no longer embedded in society. Instead society had to justify itself in market terms.

It is precisely Polanyi's argument that Radin works through to its logical conclusion by asking the following question, one that is restated in different ways to highlight the different angles from which one could approach it:

i. What are the moral limits of commodification? Or
ii. What should our understanding of personhood or 'human flourishing' be in order to enable us to distinguish between personal property that should not be commodified and fungible property that can be? Or
iii. What are the different kinds of rights that should be available to people, to offer them different kinds of protection depending on whether property is personal or fungible?

By asking these questions, Radin was going to the heart of the matter: 'human flourishing'. Such a flourishing for Radin depended on our understanding of personhood and thereby an understanding of the distinction between personal and fungible property. From this basis, we could develop a theory of what should be 'market alienable', that is, freely bought and sold in the market to which an economic rationality can be applied and what should be 'market inalienable', that is, should not be viewed as purely fungible because they are so integral to personhood that a purely economic rationality cannot be applied. Radin makes this point with great clarity when she notes:

> In conceiving of all rights as property rights that can (at least theoretically) be alienated in markets, economic analysis has (at least in principle) invited markets to fill the social universe. It has invited us to view all (market) inalienabilities as problematic ... Indeed I try to show that the characteristic rhetoric of economic analysis is morally wrong when it is put forward as the sole discourse of human life .... I think we should evaluate inalienabilities in connection with our best current understanding of human flourishing.[28]

The point that Radin makes includes our earlier discussion of common versus private property. This is because the key issue at hand is not the legal distinction between common and private property but rather the different ways in which personhood or flourishing is tied to access and use of certain 'things', be they land, culture, or resources. The question therefore is 'what kind of rights do we require in order to safeguard integral aspects of personhood, including rights to common property or stewardship duties over community territories' or even rights to certain kinds of property which are partly fungible and partly personal. The incisiveness of Radin's argument lies in the manner it brings any discourse on property back to personhood.

Radin's value also lies in the manner in which she breaks out of the straitjacket of commodity fetishism that Marx warned about. She refuses to fetishize property by treating it as a thing in itself. Property for Radin must have a reason, and the only legitimate reason it could have is its contribution to human flourishing or well-being. By

[28] Margaret Jane Radin, 'Market-Inalienability', *Harvard Law Review* 100(8) (June 1987), p. 1851.

putting human flourishing and personhood at the centre of property discourse, Radin provides us with an ethical compass with which to negotiate property jurisprudence.

In essence, Radin's compass works by asking two questions, the answering of which provides us with an ethical solution to a property conundrum. They are: Is a 'thing' (be it land, resources, culture, etc.) absolutely integral to the flourishing of one's personhood? If so, would the loss of such a thing adversely affect one's personhood or curtail one's flourishing?

Radin concludes that:

> Where we can ascertain that a given property right is personal, there is a prima facie case that that right should be protected to some extent against invasion by government and against cancellation by conflicting fungible property claims of other people. This case is strongest where without the claimed protection of *property as personal* (emphasis mine), the claimants' opportunities to become fully developed persons in the context of our society would be destroyed or significantly lessened ... Where we can ascertain that a property right is fungible, there is a prima facie case that that right should yield to some extent in the face of conflicting recognized personhood interests, not embodied in property. This case is strongest where without the claimed *personhood interest* (emphasis mine), the claimants opportunity to become fully developed persons in the context of our society would be destroyed or significantly lessened.[29]

Note that Radin makes two critical points here. First, where property claims are personal the claims should in general override fungible property claims. For example, an individual's property claim to her home should override a real estate developer's claim to the same piece of property. Second, even where the claimant may not have a legal property claim, but merely a strong personhood interest, such an interest should still override a fungible property claim. For example a claim to a sacred site on state land that is to be leased to a golf resort.

Radin of course understands the difficulty of identifying objective criteria for human flourishing for the things that are essential for

[29] Radin, 'Property and Personhood' (1982), pp. 1014–15.

personhood. In an age of commodity fetishism, so much of people's sense of self is tied up with the acquiring or possessing of things. Well-being has been replaced by 'well-having' and questions regarding what is essential for the good life or what Aristotle termed, as *eudaimonia* are lost in the maelstrom of commodities. In such circumstances, it seems a formidable, if not impossible, task to delineate criteria for when personal property or personhood interests must be allowed to trump fungible property claims. Radin in her seminal 1982 Stanford Law Review article 'Property and Personhood' clearly outlines this problem when she says that:

> It intuitively appears that there is such a thing as property for personhood because people become bound up with 'things'. But this intuitive view does not compel the conclusion that property for personhood deserves moral recognition or legal protection, because arguably there is bad as well as good in being bound up with external objects. If there is a traditional understanding that a well-developed person must invest herself to some extent in external objects, there is no less a traditional understanding that one should not invest oneself *in the wrong way or to too great an extent* in external objects. Property is damnation as well as salvation, object-fetishism as well as moral groundwork.[30]

Radin nevertheless concludes that, as with most things in life, there are no absolutes but rather a spectrum where, at the one end we have things that are absolutely fungible and, at the other, things that are essentially personal. We then have things that fall somewhere along this continuum, some lying more to the fungible end and others to the personal end. Judges then have to engage in the task of identifying what is personal and what is fungible on a case-by-case basis. In any event, judges make this distinction unconsciously, be it in deciding the amount of damages to be paid for pain and suffering in tort law or in determining whether the state can expropriate a residential neighbourhood for some public works.

Five years later, in 1987, Radin published her much acclaimed article 'Market-Inalienability' in the *Harvard Law Review*. This article was a decisive response to advocates of universal commodification

[30] Ibid., p. 961.

led by Richard Posner of the Law and Economics school of jurisprudence.[31] Here Radin had further developed her argument regarding criteria for determining property for personhood by attempting to distinguish between those goods and services that are market alienable or can be commodified and those that ought to be market inalienable or should not be commodified.

Radin's attempts brought her back to the same question that she had posed in 1982 albeit from a different angle. If the question posed in 'Property and Personhood' was 'how do we distinguish between personal property or personhood interest and fungible property?' then the question that Radin posed in 'Market-Inalienability' was 'how do we distinguish between those things that can be commodified and those that shouldn't?' The answer to both these questions lay in the most ancient of all human quests: to understand what constitutes 'well-being' or, in Radin's terms, 'human flourishing'.

There is ultimately only one question here, which can be asked in various different ways. The fact remains that, in whichever the fashion we pose this question the answer will ultimately come down to a shared understanding of human flourishing. One cannot answer the question 'what is property?' without answering the question of 'what is personhood?'; and one cannot answer the latter question without answering 'what is well-being?' A shared understanding of well-being informs our perception of personhood and the rights that must be availed to affirm such personhood. A common conception of personhood would then clarify what constitutes personhood interests or personal property and what constitutes fungible or market alienable property.

When Marx accused the commodity form of being the very cell of capitalism, he was essentially criticizing capitalism's caricature of personhood through universal commodification. Estrangement or alienation for Marx was a separation from our essence or personhood caused by the commodification of what is most intimate or integral to who we are. For Marx, the human essence can be seen in our social

[31] Radin, 'Market-Inalienability' (1987), pp. 1849–1937. For Posner's arguments on Law and Economics, *see generally*, Richard Posner et al., 'The Economics of the Baby Shortage', *Journal of Legal Studies* 7 (1978), pp. 323–48.

being: we are both *homo faber* and *homo socialis*, we are our works and an ensemble of social relations. Radin, despite her differences with Marx, does not diverge too far from his humanism in her conclusions about what constitutes human flourishing. On the contrary Radin nuances Marx's humanism by identifying three interrelated aspects or criteria for personhood: freedom, identity, and contextuality.[32]

Rather than resting her understanding of personhood on any one particular trait, Radin argues that it involves a balance of all these three traits. At the same time she is pragmatic enough to note that we live in a non-ideal world with unequal power relations that sometimes result in personal property being traded as fungible property or being incompletely commodified. Commercial sex work is a typical example, where the lines are blurred between the body as personal property and the body as fungible property. Another example is a community deciding to lease its ancestral lands to a logging company. These are cases of a moral 'double bind'[33] where it would be patronizing to tell the unemployed woman with children to feed or a desperately poor community that needs an income that the body or ancestral lands are personal property that should not be commodified. In fact, to force these people to do otherwise curtails their freedom to make choices, choices that are sometimes 'desperate exchanges'.[34] For Radin, however, these situations should not be presented as examples of the possibility of universal commodification but rather as situations of incomplete commodification, where the woman's body or the community's ancestral lands are still personal property that in certain non-ideal situations are commodified.

The above examples could represent the freedom or autonomous aspect of personhood, which highlights will or the ability to make one's own choices. Freedom is nevertheless not the only aspect of personhood. For Radin, personhood includes 'identity' and 'contextuality'. The identity aspect involves the integrity or continuity of the self, which is necessary for individuation. Our personhood is based on an enduring self. This self of course goes through various transformations in an individual's lifetime, but it nevertheless is the

[32] Ibid., p. 1904.
[33] Ibid., pp. 1915–16.
[34] Ibid., pp. 1917–18.

manifestation of a memory that knits together the various events that this self experiences.

Personhood in the context of identity is analogous to a node or a knot in a web of relations wherein it is clear that the knot is nothing if not the various strands of relations. It is also clear, however, that these relations can only become real if they are embodied through the knot or, so to speak, through the person. The identity aspect of personhood then contextualizes the freedom aspect. Identity constitutes the self that exercises the freedom to choose what is important to it, a self that is able to distinguish between what is personal and what is fungible.

Marx's notion of estrangement in capitalist societies is in essence one where the self or identity is slowly being cut off from the ensemble of social relations within which it is embedded. The *homo economicus* is an estranged being because it recognizes and affirms only one kind of relation, which is the market relation, thereby denying all other social relations that constitute the self. It is this idea of the self as an ensemble of social relations that Radin develops in attributing contextuality as the third aspect of personhood. Radin elaborates:

> The contextuality aspect of personhood focuses on the necessity of self-constitution in relation to the environment of things and other people. In order to be differentiated human persons, unique individuals, we must have relationships with the social and natural world .... I focus primarily on a certain view of contextuality and its consequences: the view that connections between the person and her environment are integral to personhood.[35]

Then again Radin adds:

> The relationship between personhood and context requires a positive commitment to act so as to create and maintain particular contexts of environment and community .... Universal commodification undermines personal identity by conceiving of personal attributes, relationships, and philosophical and moral commitments as monetizable and alienable from self. A better view of personhood should understand many kinds of particulars — one's politics, work, religion, family, love, sexuality, friendships, altruism, experiences,

[35] Radin, 'Market Inalienability' (1987), p. 1904.

wisdom, moral commitments, character and personal attributes- as integral to the self.[36]

Radin makes three critical contributions to property jurisprudence that greatly aid us in distinguishing different kinds of property and how they must be treated. The significance of the first contribution is the link between property and personhood thereby breaking free from the fetishism that is caused by discussing property as a thing in itself, disassociated from its link to human flourishing. Within this framework of 'property for personhood', Radin's second contribution is her understanding of personhood from the perspective of human flourishing. Personhood is not merely an exercise of freedom and identity but also contextuality. The self, therefore, is not simply free but also relational, and this relationality is integral to human flourishing and positive liberty. Radin's third major contribution is to tie personal property or personhood interests to contextuality, arguing that the non-precedence of personal property or personhood interests over fungible property in capitalist societies is detrimental to contextuality and thereby to human flourishing and personhood itself.[37]

[36] Ibid., pp. 1905–6.

[37] There is growing research on well-being in the context of the CBD and ABS. Some researchers have applied the 'capabilities framework' developed by Martha Nussbaum and Amartya Sen. The capabilities framework helps to describe the well-being of a social group (community) whose members have made decisions within the 'freedoms given to them' and available 'capabilities' (including natural endowments, skills, norms, values, and markets). It does not presuppose well-being based solely on 'rational economic choice', but anchors well-being in both moral and economic choices. Other researchers such as Mathew Clarke have attempted to measure the well-being of nations by correlating it to the achievement of Maslow's 'hierarchical framework of human needs', which include 'basic needs', 'safety', 'belonging', 'self-esteem', and 'Self-actualization'. One of the most interesting tools to measure well-being is developed by M.S. Suneetha and Balakrishna Pisupati where Clarke's application of the Maslow framework is used in tandem with the Sen and Nussbaum 'capabilities framework'. The result is a framework of needs and related indicators to measure well-being where: basic needs: is captured by indicators related to food, health, and shelter; safety needs: is captured by indicators related to settled lives and security from risks, including

PROPERTY FOR PEOPLEHOOD

Radin made a meticulous case for personhood as the very raison d'être of property, arguing that the litmus test for any property jurisprudence is whether it positively contributes to human flourishing and thereby to personhood. Radin's arguments have had a far-reaching impact on the emerging jurisprudence for the rights of indigenous peoples to their territories, sacred sites, and cultures. In 2009 the *Yale Law Journal* published a pivotal article entitled 'In Defense of Property'.[38] The article was co-authored by three professors of law, Angela Riley, Kristen Carpenter, and Sonia Katyal. These authors, twenty-seven years after Radin's seminal arguments on the relationship between property and personhood, sought to adapt her ideas to argue for the rights of American Indians to their cultural property.

A year before in 2008, Kristen Carpenter in her article titled 'Real Property and Peoplehood'[39] had reasoned that if, according to Radin, the protection of certain kinds of property was relevant for personhood, then equally the protection of some kinds of property interests was critical for 'peoplehood'. Carpenter explained:

> Much in the way that Radin's discussion of 'personhood' invokes what is most essential to the individual human condition, "peoplehood" refers to the qualities that define a group and inspire individuals to

---

economic and natural risks; belonging needs: is captured by indicators related to social groups and equity in transactions, including gender equity and non-discrimination and; self-esteem and self-actualization needs: is captured by indicators related to autonomy, confidence, and education. *See generally*, Martha C. Nussbaum and Amartya Sen (eds), *The Quality of Life* (Oxford: Clarendon Press, 1996); Matthew Clarke, 'Assessing Well-being using Hierarchical Needs', in Mark McGillivray and Matthew Clarke (eds), *Understanding Human Well-being* (Tokyo: United Nations University Press, 2006); *cited in* M.S. Suneetha and Balakrishna Pisupati, *Learning from the Practitioners: Benefit Sharing Perspectives from Enterprising Communities* (Nairobi: UNEP/UNU-IAS, 2009), pp. 31–2.

[38] Angela Riley, Kirsten Carpenter, and Sonia Katyal, 'In Defense of Property', *Yale Law Journal* 118 (2009), pp. 1022–1125.

[39] Kristen Carpenter, 'Real Property and Peoplehood', *Stanford Environmental Law Journal*, Vol. 27 (2008) p. 313.

participate in the collective. In common parlance, peoplehood is the state of being a people or the sense of belonging to a people.[40]

Carpenter, in her article, argued that American Indians as a people have rights to the use and management of sacred sites despite the fact that these sites were on public lands owned by the government. The rights of American Indians to their sacred sites were similar to Radin's notion of rights to personal property or personhood interests, which in most cases would trump fungible property rights. Carpenter argued that American Indians had rights to peoplehood interests in their sacred sites since their very existence as a people depended on access, use, and management of these sites. Therefore, these peoplehood interests must override any state directive that determines the use of the public lands in ways that would profane sacred sites.

Carpenter's thesis made a strong case for the legal recognition of peoplehood interests in property despite the lack of formal ownership. The basis of her argument was that the flourishing, or sometimes the very survival of certain groups or peoples, depended on access and control of these properties. In 2009, Riley, Carpenter, and Katyal further developed this argument into a fully-fledged theory for the right to 'cultural property' in order to secure peoplehood. They proposed that:

> Peoplehood, we argue, dictates that certain lands, resources, and expressions are entitled to legal protection as cultural property because they are integral to the group identity and cultural survival of indigenous peoples ... some cultural resources are so sacred and intimately connected to a people's collective identity and experience that they deserve special consideration as a form of cultural property .... Classic ownership theory tends to overlook the possibility of non-owners exercising custodial duties over tangible and intangible goods in the absence of title or possession. Yet indigenous peoples have historically exercised such custodial duties .... Indigenous cultural property claims ... thus reflect a fiduciary approach to cultural property and takes into account indigenous peoples' collective obligations toward land and resources .... To the extent that indigenous peoples' cultural property claims are premised on custodial duties toward specific properties, we

[40] Ibid., p. 348.

> argue that such claims are more appropriately characterized through the paradigm of stewardship rather than ownership ... cultural property law ... seeks to distribute entitlements along a spectrum so as to accommodate both the ownership and stewardship interests that attach to owners and non-owners. We contend that indigenous cultural property claims can be both explained and justified by this more expansive understanding of property, which we articulate through peoplehood and stewardship.[41]

Tracing the genealogy of a critical understanding of property beginning with Marx, through Macpherson and Radin and leading to Riley et al., one can see a common theme emerging despite the different angles through which each of these theorists approached property. The theme is one that deconstructs the fetishism of property as a sacrosanct legal concept from which people derive certain rights. It argues that property has human origins, and that it is not human beings and communities who need to fit within the framework of property, but the discourse of property that must align itself with our collective understanding of flourishing of personhood and peoplehood.

Among the valuable contributions Riley et al. make to a critical understanding of property jurisprudence is the notion of cultural property and its significance for peoplehood. Cultural property is analogous to Radin's notion of personhood interests and personal property, except that the former applies to peoplehood interests or 'peoples' property'. Notions of cultural property also resonate with Macpherson's notions of common property with a bundle of access and use rights. The denial of cultural property rights result in a phenomenon very similar to what Marx refers to as alienation or estrangement. Except that the kind of estrangement Riley et al. refer to is the alienation of a people from what they understand to be the essence of their peoplehood.

The groundbreaking proposition made by Riley et al. is that stewardship or custodianship by communities of certain lands and waters should entitle them to cultural property rights integral to peoplehood. Such cultural property rights should be available irrespective of whether the community owns the lands or waters. In

[41] Riley et al., 'In Defense of Property' (2009), pp. 1028–9.

situations where the land is owned by the state or privately owned, fungible interests should make space for peoplehood interests rather than excluding the latter simply because it is private property entailing an absolute right to exclude and alienate. Using an approach that argues that historical fiduciary obligations of a community towards certain lands, waters, and sacred sites entitle them to cultural property rights, Riley et al. persuasively argue that:

> Fluid conceptions of property underlie indigenous peoples' group claims to those items most closely and intimately tied to peoplehood and group identity: indigenous cultural property. Once indigenous peoples' cultural property claims are examined within the framework of stewardship, as opposed to ownership alone, a more nuanced conception of property emerges that captures the unique ways in which indigenous groups may exercise cultural property entitlements as non-owners. Consider, for example, the complexities that arise when dealing with certain objects that may not be owned at all, those that are inalienable by definition, or those for which possession is subject to shifting custodial arrangements rather than absolute rights of title. In many such cases, the custody of such items may in fact be situated in the fiduciary obligations of a collective 'people,' rather than rooted in the claims of individual ownership.[42]

The pertinence of the arguments of Riley et al. to biocultural rights is significant. The notion of cultural property rights based on stewardship and their relevance for peoplehood makes an effective case for biocultural rights. The difference between rights to cultural property and biocultural rights however is threefold. First, biocultural rights are not restricted to a people in terms of indigenous peoples, but also extend to other traditional communities. Second, biocultural rights are those rights that are essential for a community to look after the ecosystems they inhabit. Third, biocultural rights derive their legitimacy not so much from the fact that property is vital for peoplehood but rather from the stewardship role that certain communities play vis-à-vis their lands and waters. In fact the stewardship of ecosystems is the raison d'être of biocultural rights.

[42] Ibid., pp. 1088–9.

Biocultural rights trace their origins not through property jurisprudence but through the crucial paradigm shift in environmental law over the last two decades, and the call for the legal protection of the roles played by communities in conserving ecosystems. The growing strength of these rights in environmental law and policy however, have had a huge impact on property jurisprudence gradually forcing a paradigm shift from the private property imperatives, which have had an adverse impact on ecosystems, to a stewardship ethic, which has conserved these ecosystems.

Biocultural rights begin from the perspective that human flourishing cannot be disassociated from the flourishing of ecosystems. Human flourishing is also based on nurturing the contextuality aspect of personhood, (which Radin identifies) or the relational aspect of the self (which Marx identifies). From the perspective of biocultural rights, however, human flourishing will always be warped if such a contexuality or relationality does not give due regard to our relationship with Nature.

The foundational ethic for biocultural rights is not peoplehood per se but rather the stewardship ethic that some communities have with their lands and waters. Third generation rights foreground peoplehood or group rights and are rooted in a communitarian ethic that identifies human flourishing as being dependent on strong and vibrant communities. While the first and second generation rights address civil and political, and socio–economic rights, respectively, which are critical for human flourishing, third generation rights assert that our individual well-being is tied to the flourishing of communities to which we belong: personhood attains its full meaning not only through the fulfilling of our individual potential but also through belonging to communities.

Biocultural rights add a vital element to this discourse of group rights by making the case that the flourishing of some communities, and hence their individual members, is dependent on securing the stewardship relation these communities have with their ecosystems. Biocultural rights, therefore, add a stewardship dimension to group rights by foregrounding the ethic rather than the group as a justification for a right. This means that the demand for biocultural rights does not take as its point of departure the inherent right of a group or community to flourish, but rather from the ethic of stewardship: it is the ethic of stewardship and not the group per se that justifies the right.

Among the most significant of Radin's contributions to property jurisprudence is her forcing any discourse of property to justify itself from the standpoint of human well-being. While Radin is commonly acknowledged as making the all-important link between property and personhood, her efforts at developing an ethical grammar of personhood needs greater attention. Radin's advocacy of an evolutionary pluralism that constantly aspired towards a better view of personhood is both the beginning and the end of her intellectual labours. She embarked on a critique of private property jurisprudence since the personhood it relied upon was that of the '*homo economicus*', which denied the fullness of human potential, and the richness of life. Radin concluded her critique by advocating a 'better view of personhood' and thereby a different understanding of property that would sustain this 'better person'.

Biocultural rights in many ways engage in the same exercise in the context of communities. They begin by requiring property jurisprudence to justify itself from the standpoint of peoplehood or community. Biocultural rights do not stop there, however. They aspire towards a 'better view of community or peoplehood' by arguing that communities that have stewarded territories have rights to use and manage these lands and waters simply by virtue of having cared for them. It is the ethic of care for Nature that is the cornerstone of biocultural rights: Communities that have historically cared for their ecosystems should have the rights to use and manage their lands and waters irrespective of whether or not they have a formal title to it. The increasing number of international and domestic environmental law and policies that have begun to recognize biocultural rights of communities is a testimony to their moral force in the face of an impending ecological crisis.

The operative question at this stage is whether this 'better view of community or peoplehood' has had any notable impact on how judges have begun to decide cases involving indigenous peoples and traditional communities and their lands. We shall turn, in the next chapter, to survey a possible emergence of a biocultural tendency in the jurisprudence of regional courts and tribunals.

CHAPTER SEVEN

A Jurisprudence of Stewardship

Creating Biocultural Precedents

In the language of my people . . . there is a word for land: Eloheh. This same word also means history, culture and religion. We cannot separate our place on earth from our lives on the earth nor from our vision nor our meaning as people. We are taught from childhood that the animals and even the trees and plants that we share a place with, are our brothers and sisters. So when we speak of land, we are not speaking of property, territory, or even a piece of ground upon which our houses sit and our crops are grown. We are speaking of something truly sacred.

—*Peter Mathiessen quoting Jimmie Durham, a Cherokee litigant in a sacred sites case*[1]

On 31 August 2001, the Inter-American Court of Human Rights handed down a landmark judgment in the case of *Mayagna (Sumo) Awas Tingni Community* v. *Nicaragua*.[2] It was the first ever legally binding decision by an international tribunal to secure the collective and resource rights of indigenous peoples when a state failed to do so. The *Awas Tingni* case is therefore, a useful starting point to begin tracing the emergence of biocultural rights in the jurisprudence of the regional tribunals.[3]

[1] Peter Mathiessen, *Indian Country* (New York: Penguin, 1984), p. 119.

[2] *Mayagna (Sumo) Awas Tingni Community* v. *Nicaragua*, Inter-Am. C.H.R., No. 79, Ser. C (2001), http://www.corteidh.or.cr/docs/casos/articulos/seriec_79_ing.pdf (accessed 13 September 2011) (hereinafter *Awas Tingni*).

[3] 'The Inter-American Court of Human Rights, an affiliate of the Organization of American States, has jurisdiction to adjudicate claims

THE AWAS TINGNI CASE

The Awas Tingni is a community among the many Mayagna indigenous communities in Nicaragua living in the dense jungles of the Atlantic Coast region. The Mayagna is one of the three groups native to the region and has lived in the area since the fourteenth century at least and speaks Mayagna as a common language. The Awas Tingni number around 150 families or 650 individuals and they hold their lands communally and subsist on hunting, fishing, and agriculture. Each family has several plantations of about a hectare and a half each where they practice a traditional form of *swidden* or 'slash and burn' agriculture that is common amongst the indigenous peoples of the Americas.[4] The *swidden* system of farming under certain conditions is considered ecologically sustainable and mimics the growth of the natural forest pattern.[5]

---

alleging violations of the American Convention on Human Rights and to issue decisions binding upon states that are parties to the Convention and that have formally acceded to the Court's jurisdiction, as has Nicaragua. Cases may be brought to the Court either by the states that are subject to the Court's jurisdiction or, as is typically done, by the Inter-American Commission on Human Rights, the principal human rights investigative and monitoring body of the Inter-American system. The Inter-American Commission initiated the proceedings before the Court in the Awas Tingni case in June 1998 with its filing of a complaint against Nicaragua, after having investigated the case and found in favor of the Community. The Community itself—through its *Síndico*, or principal leader, and with the assistance of legal counsel—had submitted a petition in October 1995 seeking the Commission's intervention to abate the threats to its land and resource tenure'. *See* James S. Anaya and Claudio Grossman, 'The Case of Awas Tingni v. Nicaragua: A New Step in the International Law of Indigenous Peoples', *Arizona Journal of International and Comparative Law* 19(1) (2002), pp. 2–3.

[4] Jonathan P. Vuotto, 'Awas Tingni v. Nicaragua: International Precedent for Indigenous Land Rights?', *Boston University International Law Journal*, Vol. 22 (2004), p. 226.

[5] 'In most densely-settled areas of the world, swidden agriculture long ago gave way to other systems. As one might deduce, swidden agriculture is only sustainable so long as there are 50 hectares or more of forest land per family, so that there can be at least 50 years of forest regrowth between

The Awas Tingni grow beans, rice, plantains, corn, and bananas and cultivate a piece of land until its nutrients are nearly exhausted. They then burn the vegetation on the land and leave it fallow for a period of nearly 15 years until the soil can replenish itself and regain its nutrients. Awas Tingni villages are constructed on the peripheries of the plantations and during the period where the land is left fallow, they dismantle their villages and move them to another fertile area of their territory, where they begin again to cultivate this area.[6]

The Awas Tingni also hunt deer and wild fowl for subsistence and an important aspect of their hunting tradition is the hunt for the pecari (a kind of a wild boar, which is held in high spiritual esteem). Families go on pecari hunts that could last for days or weeks, and the significance of the hunt goes beyond meat and skin to include rites of passage and social bonding. In many ways the spiritual place occupied by the pecari in the lives of the Awas Tingni affirms the link between the community and their territory. In fact, the Awas Tingni lands affirm a link between the community and their ancestors buried there and the spirits that dwell in the mountains. These spirits can affect the success of a hunt, can heal the sick, protect the community, if appeased, or jeopardize the community, if displeased. Awas Tingni

---

cropping cycles on any given parcel. Once population rises above that level, fallow periods become shorter, allowing less forest regrowth, until eventually the ten years or less allowed between cropping cycles produces only a grassy savanna instead of a full-fledged forest. At that point the forest has effectively been lost, and it makes sense to change the cropping system to one more suited to a grassy savanna. This process took place in Europe just before Classical Antiquity, leaving the dry scrublands of the Mediterranean where oak forests had once flourished. But in other parts of the world, namely those that remain covered in dense forest, the population has never risen above the density that can be sustainably supported by swidden agriculture. In such places as the mountains of Southeast Asia and the inner Amazon forest, over half a billion of the world's people continue to earn their livelihood satisfactorily and sustainably through swidden agriculture'. Greg Vaughan. 2010. 'Swidden Agriculture: Sustainable Slash and Burn?', *Good Eater Collaborative,* http://www.goodeater.org/2010/07/02/swidden-agriculture-sustainable-slash-and-burn/ (accessed 13 September 2011).

[6] Vuotto, 'Awas Tingni v. Nicaragua' (2004), p. 226.

ancestors are buried with their possessions, and families pass on information of burial sites generation to generation.[7]

In 1993, the Nicaraguan Ministry of Environment and Natural Resources (MARENA) gave a logging concession to a Dominican company Maderas y Derivados de Nicaragua, S.A. (MADENSA). The concession covered around 43,000 hectares of forest that fell within the Awas Tingni traditional lands. As a result of pressure from the World Wildlife Fund (WWF) a trilateral agreement was signed in 1994 between the Awas Tingni, MARENA, and MADENSA. The Awas Tingni was assisted in its negotiations by the College of Law of the University of Iowa (the IOWA project), which was supported by the WWF. The agreement provided for sustainable timber harvesting in Awas Tingni territory along with the sharing of economic benefits arising from the logging with the Awas Tingni. The most important aspect of the agreement was that it committed MARENA to a process of formal identification and titling of the Awas Tingni lands, and secured an undertaking from the government that it would not undertake any action that would adversely affect the community's land claim.[8]

Before the ink had dried on the agreement, however, the government had already entered into negotiations with a Korean logging company Sol del Caribe, S.A. (SOLCARSA) seeking a logging concession on 63,000 hectares of land adjacent to the MADENSA concession. A significant portion of this land fell within the Awas Tingni territory and no efforts had been made by MARENA to begin to identify and title the community's lands as agreed. When the Awas Tingni learnt of this development in 1995, MARENA had already provided SOLCARSA with an exploration licence and a preliminary approval.[9]

On receiving no response by MARENA to its protests, and when agents of SOLCARSA began to undertake timber inventories on the lands, the Awas Tingni concluded that MARENA was determined to grant the logging concession to SOLCARSA on the basis that the

[7] Ibid., p. 227.

[8] Anaya and Grossman, 'The Case of Awas Tingni v. Nicaragua' (2002), p. 3.

[9] Ibid., p. 3.

lands were state-owned. The community filed for emergency relief in the Nicaraguan courts relying on provisions of Nicaraguan law that provided for the rights of indigenous communities to their communally owned traditional lands. When the necessary relief was not forthcoming, the community petitioned the Inter-American Commission on Human Rights claiming violations of the right to property (Article 21), cultural integrity (Article 12), and other relevant rights in the American Convention on Human Rights to which Nicaragua is a party.[10]

Remarkably, in 1997 as a result of a separate action by two members of the Regional Council of the North Atlantic Autonomous Region claiming that the approval of the Regional Council as required by law was not sought, the Supreme Court of Nicaragua declared the SOLCARSA concession unconstitutional. MARENA sought to cure this defect by securing a post hoc approval by a majority of the Regional Council. Another legal action by the dissenting members of the Regional Council ensued and the Supreme Court declared the concession null and void stating that a defect in due process cannot be cured by a retrospective approval by the Regional Council.

At this stage the Awas Tingni were convinced that the Nicaraguan government was not willing to honour its agreement with the community to identify and title their lands. Therefore, despite the revocation of the SOLCARSA concession due to the decision by the Supreme Court, the Inter-American Commission on Human Rights submitted the Awas Tingni petition to the Inter-American Court of Human Rights with the hope of getting a remedy that would bind the Nicaraguan government to officially demarcate and title lands of indigenous communities.

In a groundbreaking decision that found in favour of the Awas Tingni, the Inter-American Court affirmed the community's right to property despite an absence of official recognition of the title to its traditional lands by the Nicaraguan government. The Court in a decision that stated that the government had violated Article 21 of the American Convention on Human Rights noted:

[10] Adopted at the Inter-American Specialized Conference on Human Rights, San José, Costa Rica, 22 November 1969.

> Given the characteristics of the instant case, some specifications are required on the concept of property in indigenous communities. Among indigenous peoples there is a communitarian tradition regarding a communal form of collective property of the land, in the sense that ownership of the land is not centered on an individual but rather on the group and its community. Indigenous groups, by the fact of their very existence, have the right to live freely in their own territory; the close ties of indigenous peoples with the land must be recognized and understood as the fundamental basis of their cultures, their spiritual life, their integrity, and their economic survival. For indigenous communities, relations to the land are not merely a matter of possession and production but a material and spiritual element, which they must fully enjoy, even to preserve their cultural legacy and transmit it to future generations.[11]

The above paragraph in the judgment shows signs of the emerging biocultural jurisprudence through interpretation of the American Convention on Human Rights. The Court could have stopped at stating that the Awas Tingni had a right to their communal lands, but it continued to establish a link between land and peoplehood. The Court's emphasis on the ties between the community's culture, spirituality, and territory highlights the principle of stewardship.

This relationship between culture and property that the Court affirms is not a value-neutral relationship. As Radin noted, we can have personal and cultural attachments to all kinds of property, but attachment in itself should not warrant legal protection. The fetish for luxury goods in capitalist societies, for example, can be understood as a relationship between some forms of contemporary culture and property; but such an attachment can hardly be seen as something that needs to be protected in law, where one's right to expensive cars should be upheld. The nature of attachment that the Court sought to uphold in the Awas Tingni case was one of stewardship of land.

It is unlikely that the Court would have upheld the Awas Tingni right to property if the intent of the community was to profit financially from the land by providing logging concessions to SOLCARSA or MADENSA. What the Court upheld was a particular kind of relationship to the land, and this is a relationship

[11] *Awas Tingni*, paragraph 149.

of stewardship. From the Court's perspective attachment to land was an attachment to property for peoplehood rather than to fungible property. Hence the Court emphasized the cultural and spiritual connections to the land. The subtext of the Court's decision in this case is that a communal land title is established not merely through historical occupation but through historical occupation coupled with a positive attachment of care manifested through the bioculture of the community.

The momentum towards biocultural rights set off by the Inter-American Court in the Awas Tingni judgment continued inexorably in its later decisions, where it privileged a biocultural attachment to the land over the nature of the community and the length of historical occupation of territory.

MOIWANA VILLAGE V. *SURINAME*: AFFIRMING BIOCULTURAL RELATIONS

> *Nevertheless, this Court has held that, in the case of indigenous communities who have occupied their ancestral lands in accordance with customary practices — yet who lack real title to the property — mere possession of the land should suffice to obtain official recognition of their communal ownership. That conclusion was reached upon considering the unique and enduring ties that bind indigenous communities to their ancestral territory. The relationship of an indigenous community with its land must be recognized and understood as the fundamental basis of its culture, spiritual life, integrity, and economic survival. For such peoples, their communal nexus with the ancestral territory is not merely a matter of possession and production, but rather consists in material and spiritual elements that must be fully integrated and enjoyed by the community, so that it may preserve its cultural legacy and pass it on to future generations.*
>
> — *Case of Moiwana Village* v. *Suriname*[12]

The reasoning of the Inter-American Court in the Awas Tingni decision was extended to create new criteria for determining a right to common property, the criteria of stewardship or a biocultural relationship. In the 2005 judgment of the Court in the *Case of*

[12] *Moiwana Village* v. *Suriname* Inter-Am. Ct. H.R. (ser. C) No. 124 (15 June 2005), paragraph 131.

Moiwana Village v. *Suriname,*[13] one could already see the shift in property jurisprudence from a focus on possession and production to a greater emphasis on cultural and spiritual connections in order to establish communal land title. The main thrust of the Moiwana Village case was less about land and more about the state sponsored massacre of members of the N'djuka Maroon community and the continued victimization of this community by the government of Suriname through denying them effective protection and redress. Nevertheless, the Court also pronounced on the property rights of the N'djuka to their communal lands extending these rights to non-indigenous communities who were able to establish a biocultural bond with their territories.

While in the Awas Tingni decision, the establishment of land title stressed the fact that the Awas Tingni were an indigenous people who were entitled to rights to their ancestral territories, the Court in the Moiwana Village case emphasized as the deciding factor, the stewardship relation of the community with their land. The Court held that:

> The Moiwana community members are not indigenous to the region; according to the proven facts, Moiwana Village was settled by N'djuka clans late in the 19th Century ... Nevertheless, from that time until the 1986 attack, the community members lived in the area in strict adherence to N'djuka custom. Expert witness Thomas Polimé described the nature of their relationship to the lands in and around Moiwana Village:
>
> [The] N'djuka, like other indigenous and tribal peoples, have a profound and all- encompassing relationship to their ancestral lands. They are inextricably tied to these lands and the sacred sites that are found there and their forced displacement has severed these fundamental ties. Many of the survivors and next of kin locate their point of origin in and around Moiwana Village. Their inability to maintain their relationships with their ancestral lands and its sacred sites has deprived them of a fundamental aspect of their identity and sense of wellbeing. *Without regular commune with these lands and sites, they are unable to practice and enjoy their cultural and religious traditions, further detracting from their personal and collective security and sense of wellbeing* (emphasis mine).

[13] Ibid.

> In this way, the Moiwana community members, a N'djuka tribal people, possess an 'all-encompassing relationship' to their traditional lands, *and their concept of ownership regarding that territory is not centered on the individual, but rather on the community as a whole* (emphasis mine). Thus, this Court's holding with regard to indigenous communities and their communal rights to property under Article 21 of the Convention must also apply to the tribal Moiwana community members: their traditional occupancy of Moiwana Village and its surrounding lands ... should suffice to obtain state recognition of their ownership.[14]

The N'djuka are not an indigenous people in the strict sense of term. But, for the Court, it was not merely being indigenous that entitled a community to the right to its traditional lands. Rather it was through having a 'profound and all-encompassing relationship' with their territories. Such a relationship is a one where a community's very identity or peoplehood is tied to the land. It is critical to note that the Court is affirming the rights of the Moiwana to their ancestral lands on two grounds. The first is the community's historical occupation of the said lands, but the second ground (to which the court devotes considerable attention) is the community's 'profound and all-encompassing relationship' with the land.

Here the Court appears to use the same reasoning as Radin's notion of contextuality for human flourishing and Riley et al.'s argument of 'cultural property rights'. Both Radin and Riley et al. point out that there are deep relations that people have with certain kinds of property that take it outside the realm of what is fungible, and place it squarely within the realm of personal. Within the latter realm, the relationship between a territory and a people is one of stewardship, where the flourishing of the people is tied to the well-being of the property. It is submitted, that the people *care* for this land not because they are conscious environmentalists but rather because their very selfhood is tied to the land: they feel that the land belongs to them and they belong to the land. The ethic of care for the land then is a natural by-product of this deep relationship, just as one would care for one's family.

[14] *Moiwana Village* v. *Suriname* Inter-Am. Ct. H.R. (ser. C) No. 124 (15 June 2005), paragraphs132–3.

The maturing of the jurisprudence on biocultural rights appeared in the 2007 decision of the Inter-American Court in the case of *Saramaka People* v. *Suriname.*[15] The Saramaka are one among the six Maroon tribes that live in the tropical rainforests of Suriname.[16] The Surinamese Maroons numbering around 1,20,000 are the largest Maroon population of the Americas. They were originally African slaves who in the seventeenth century, escaped from the Dutch settlers who brought them to Suriname to work their sugar, timber, and coffee plantations. The Maroons escaped into the dense Surinamese forests and established self-governing, linguistically and culturally distinct communities between the late seventeenth and mid-nineteenth centuries. For over 100 years they fought a war of liberation against their slave masters and in 1762 won their freedom and signed a treaty with the Dutch crown. Until the mid-twentieth century the Saramaka like the other Maroon tribes lived autonomously within Suriname until the growing encroachments on their lands in the name of development led to a war between the Maroons and the Surinamese military government. The end of the civil war in the mid-1990s led to a national government that turned its back on the Saramaka and the other Maroons and began to give large timber and mining concessions to foreign companies in Saramaka territory without any consultation.[17]

The Saramaka, who number about 55,000 and whose territory covers 9,000 square kilometres of rainforest, had in 1963 lost 50 per cent of their lands to a massive hydroelectric dam built to provide electricity to the Alcoa bauxite factory. The dam submerged some 43 Saramaka villages and nearly 6,000 Saramaka were displaced. Some were sent to resettlement camps where they still live. Others set up new villages on the Upper Suriname River.

[15] *Saramaka People* v. *Suriname* Inter-Am. Ct. H.R. (ser. C) No. 172 (28 November 2007) (hereinafter *Saramaka People*).

[16] Lisl Brunner, 'The Rise of Peoples' Rights in the Americas: The *Saramaka People* Decision of the Inter-American Court of Human Rights', *Chinese Journal of International Law* 7(3) (2008), pp. 699–711.

[17] *See* http://en.wikipedia.org/wiki/Saramaka (accessed 13 September 2011).

In the late 1990s, the Surinamese government permitted logging companies to begin timber harvesting on Saramaka territory, against Saramaka wishes.[18] The expert witness in the Sarmaka case—a noted anthropologist Richard Price who has written extensively on the Maroon populations of the Americas—describes the situation:

> In 1996, Saramaka women on their way to their gardens began to find their paths blocked by Chinese labourers. They heard heavy earth-moving machinery in the distance. When village headmen went to have a look, they were told that the land now belonged to the Chinese and that if they interfered with logging operations, they would be arrested and imprisoned. Soon, soldiers from the Suriname army were standing guard at the logging sites, refusing entry to Saramakas. The Saramakas began to organize against this invasion of their lands, but the depredations continued. Large swaths of the territory their ancestors had fought for, and which had been granted to Saramakas by the Dutch in the treaty of 1762, were now occupied by Chinese loggers, who had by the mid-1990s received official concessions from the Suriname government to much of Saramaka territory.[19]

As the logging continued unabated over the years, leaders of the Saramaka community began to mobilize their people across nearly 70 villages. They travelled from village to village organizing communities against the logging. They were assisted by NGOs, who aided them with GPS mapping of their territories, and human rights lawyers.[20] In 2000 they filed a petition before the Inter-American Commission on Human Rights. The Commission in 2002 and in 2004 asked Suriname to cease all logging concessions and mining exploration on Saramaka lands until a full and thorough investigation of the Saramaka complaint. However, when the Government of

[18] *See* http://www.goldmanprize.org/2009/southcentralamerica (accessed 13 September 2011).

[19] Richard Price. 'Contested Territory: The Victory of the Saramaka People vs. Suriname'. Paper prepared for *Simpósio Internacional: Territórios Sensíveis: Diferença, Agência e Transgressão,* Museu Nacional, Rio de Janeiro, 15 June 2009, available at www.richandsally.net.

[20] Mainly Fergus MacKay of the FPP and Hugo Jabini, a Saramaka law student at the local university; Ibid.

Suriname failed to comply with the remedial measures required by the Commission in its 2006 report, the Commission referred the case to the Inter-American Court for Human Rights.[21]

The Court in the Saramaka case elaborated on the biocultural relationship between indigenous and tribal peoples and their territories that the Moiwana Village case had referred to. In responding to the arguments of the Surinamese government that the Saramaka (who were brought as slaves in the seventeenth century) were not indigenous people with rights to their ancestral lands, the Court stated:

> Their (Saramaka's) culture is also similar to that of tribal peoples insofar as the members of the Saramaka people maintain a strong spiritual relationship with the ancestral territory they have traditionally used and occupied. Land is more than merely a source of subsistence for them; it is also a necessary source for the continuation of the life and cultural identity of the Saramaka people. The lands and resources of the Saramaka people are part of their social, ancestral, and spiritual essence. In this territory, the Saramaka people hunt, fish, and farm, and they gather water, plants for medicinal purposes, oils, minerals, and wood. Their sacred sites are scattered throughout the territory, while at the same time the territory itself has a sacred value to them. In particular, the identity of the members of the Saramaka people with the land is inextricably linked to their historical fight for freedom from slavery, called the sacred 'first time'.[22]

In the Court's statements, the emergence of biocultural jurisprudence with an emphasis on the values of stewardship is clear. The Court in the Saramaka case elaborated on the nature of the relationship between the community and the land that qualifies it for a right to property under Article 21 of the Inter-American Convention. While the Awas Tingni, Moiwana Village, and the Saramaka judgments are ordinarily read as establishing the rights of indigenous and tribal peoples to their ancestral territories, what is often missed is the principle that these judgments affirm. This is the principle of a

[21] Price, 'Contested Territory: The Victory of the Saramaka People vs. Suriname'. Paper prepared for *Simpósio Internacional: Territórios Sensíveis: Diferença, Agência e Transgressão*, Museu Nacional, Rio de Janeiro, 15 June 2009, available at www.richandsally.net, pp. 3–4.

[22] *Saramaka People*, paragraph 83.

relationship of stewardship. The deep structure of the jurisprudence of the Court in these cases is not that a community being indigenous or tribal necessarily vests it with a right to communal property, but rather that it is the stewarding relationship of the community to its lands and waters that determines the authenticity of the claim. In many ways, the subtext of these decisions reads that an indigenous or tribal identity is established through proving a strong biocultural link to the land.

The fact that the Court makes references to a 'strong spiritual relationship with their ancestral territory' or land as a part of 'social, ancestral or spiritual essence' of a community or the 'territory having sacred value' gives us an insight into the nature and the quality of the relationship a community must have with its land to for it to assert its indigenous or tribal identity and the concomitant right to property. Such a biocultural relationship with their territories is possible only when land is not seen as a fungible property, whose importance lies in its exchange value, but rather when it is seen as personal property, whose worth lies in it being at the core of peoplehood. The Court made this clear when it extended the right to community property under Article 21 of the Convention to the tribal communities on the condition of establishing a special relationship with their territories. The Court stated that:

> [T]he Court considers that the members of the Saramaka people make up a tribal community whose social, cultural and economic characteristics are different from other sections of the national community, particularly because of their special relationship with their ancestral territories, and because they regulate themselves, at least partially, by their own norms, customs, and/or traditions.
>
> Hence, this Tribunal declares that the members of the Saramaka people are to be considered a tribal community, and that the Court's jurisprudence regarding indigenous peoples' right to property is also applicable to tribal peoples because both share distinct social, cultural, and economic characteristics, including a special relationship with their ancestral territories, that require special measures under international human rights law in order to guarantee their physical and cultural survival.
>
> The Court's decisions to this effect have all been based upon the special relationship that members of indigenous and tribal peoples have with their territory, and on the need to protect their right to

> that territory in order to safeguard the physical and cultural survival of such peoples.[23]

The Court in the Saramaka case does not stop at recognizing the rights of indigenous and tribal peoples to their territories. It also secures the stewarding relationship between the community and its land by establishing the community's rights over natural resources on and within the land. Developing a biocultural approach to indigenous and tribal territories, the Court sought to uphold the principle of stewardship by stating that a communal right to land includes a right to all resources on and within the land necessary for the physical and cultural survival of the community.

Such an approach could be narrowly understood as arguing that an indigenous or tribal community has rights only over the resources it actually uses and not over sub-surface minerals, for example, since these are irrelevant for the cultural and physical survival of the community. The Court in the Saramaka case, however, emphasized the converse by indicating that the Saramaka would have the right to exclude any activities on their lands that adversely affected the resources that the community relies upon. For example, mining for gold could negatively affect fish populations in rivers where the communities fish for subsistence. This means that the community in question could restrict gold mining on their territories even though they did not need gold for their cultural or physical survival.

In effect the Court was making the point that indigenous and tribal communities could restrict any activities that ran counter to their stewarding relationship with their territories. Setting the stage for such an approach, the Court stated:

> In accordance with this Court's jurisprudence as stated in the *Yakye Axa* and *Sawhoyamaxa* cases, members of tribal and indigenous communities have the right to own the natural resources they have traditionally used within their territory for the same reasons that they have a right to own the land they have traditionally used and occupied for centuries. Without them, the *very physical and cultural survival of such peoples is at stake. Hence the need to protect the lands and resources they have traditionally used to prevent their extinction*

[23] *Saramaka People*, paragraphs 84–6 and 90.

> *as a people* (emphasis mine). That is, the aim and purpose of the special measures required on behalf of the members of indigenous and tribal communities is to guarantee that they may continue living their traditional way of life, and that their distinct cultural identity, social structure, economic system, customs, beliefs and traditions are respected, guaranteed and protected by states ...., due to the inextricable connection members of indigenous and tribal peoples have with their territory, the protection of their right to property over such territory, in accordance with Article 21 of the Convention, is necessary to guarantee their very survival. Accordingly, the right to use and enjoy their territory would be meaningless in the context of indigenous and tribal communities if said right were not connected to the natural resources that lie on and within the land. *That is, the demand for collective land ownership by members of indigenous and tribal peoples derives from the need to ensure the security and permanence of their control and use of the natural resources, which in turn maintains their very way of life* (emphasis mine). This connectedness between the territory and the natural resources necessary for their physical and cultural survival is precisely what needs to be protected under Article 21 of the Convention in order to guarantee the members of indigenous and tribal communities' right to the use and enjoyment of their property. From this analysis, it follows that the natural resources found on and within indigenous and tribal people's territories that are protected under Article 21 are those natural resources traditionally used and necessary for the very survival, development and continuation of such people's way of life.[24]

The implications of the judgment in this case are far-reaching. The Court makes the critical link between the communal right to land and the right to ensure the security and permanence of the community's control over its natural resources. The justification that the Court provides is that such control is integral to a 'way of life', which denotes a biocultural relationship with land. The Court in the Saramaka case built on the foundations laid in the Awas Tingni case, and firmly established that the right to communal property extends to tribal peoples and such a right includes the right to use and maintain the resources on their territories in accordance with the biocultural values of the community.

[24] *Saramaka People*, paragraphs 121–2.

ENDOROIS WELFARE COUNCIL V. *KENYA*: GLOBALIZING BIOCULTURAL RIGHTS

The Inter-American Court of Human Rights established the judicial protection of the relations of stewardship between indigenous and tribal peoples and their territories. This heralded the birth of biocultural rights in the case law of the American Convention on Human Rights and recently begun to inform the jurisprudence of the African Commission on Human and Peoples' Rights.[25]

In its recent 2010 judgment in the case of *Endorois Welfare Council* v. *Kenya,*[26], the African Commission on Human and Peoples' Rights relied upon the decisions of the Inter-American Court to support its interpretation of the African Charter on Human and Peoples' Rights[27], and firmly rooted the biocultural rights of indigenous and tribal peoples in the African context.

[25] The African Commission on Human and Peoples' Rights was established under Article 30 of the African Charter to 'promote human and peoples' rights and to ensure their protection in Africa'. It is composed of 11 human rights experts of high moral standing who are chosen from lists of nominations submitted by states. These experts act in their individual capacity and under Article 45.2 of the African Charter 'Ensure the protection of human and peoples' rights under conditions laid down under the African Charter'. This protective mandate of the Commission includes receiving complaints from individuals, groups, or NGOs of serious or massive violations of human rights by states. These complaints are admissible if the complainant can establish that all domestic remedies have been exhausted or that these remedies do not or will not provide an effective redress. While the decisions of the Commission are not legally binding, they are considered as authoritative interpretations of the African Charter. The decisions of the Commission are sent to the Assembly of Heads of State and Government of the AU who will decide on the course of action that would need to be taken. The Commission can also refer its decision in the form of a complaint to the African Court on Human and Peoples' Rights The decision of the African Court is binding upon all state parties who have ratified the Court Protocol.

[26] Communication 276/2003, Decision of the African Commission on Human and Peoples' Rights (hereinafter *Endorois Welfare Council*).

[27] The African Charter on Human and Peoples' Rights is an African regional human rights instrument. It was adopted by the OAU, now the African Union (AU). The Assembly of Heads of State and Government

The Endorois are a community of around 60,000 people who have lived sustainably for centuries as pastoralists around the Lake Bogoria in the Rift Valley area of Kenya. The Government of Kenya dispossessed them of their territories through the creation of the Lake Hannington game reserve in 1973, and a subsequent re-gazetting of the Lake Bogoria Game Reserve in 1978. Since that date the Endorois were effectively denied access to their lands, which adversely affected their way of life, cultural, and spiritual traditions all of which were inextricably connected to their land.

All the neighbouring communities had for hundreds of years accepted the Endorois as the effective 'owners' of their lands. Prior to Kenyan independence in 1963, although the British Crown claimed title over the Endorois lands, the community was allowed peaceful and undisturbed possession and use of its territories. When Kenya gained independence the Endorois land passed on to the respective local county councils, which under Section 115 of the Kenyan Constitution, held the land in trust on behalf of the Endorois community.

The Endorois grazed their cattle along the fertile green pastures surrounding Lake Bogoria and have historically relied upon the medicinal salt licks in the area to ensure their animals' health. Lake Bogoria is central to the Endorois cultural and spiritual traditions, including their historical prayer sites, places for circumcision and other ceremonies. The people believe that the spirits of all Endorois live on Lake Bogoria and that the Monchongoi forest is birthplace of their for bearers.

Shortly after the creation of the Lake Bogoria Game Reserve, the Kenyan Wildlife Service (KWS) informed a few elders of the Endorois community that 400 families would be provided with compensation of fertile pieces of land and the community as a whole would receive 25 per cent of the tourist revenue of the Game Reserve and 85 per cent of the employment generated therein. The KWS also promised to construct for the Endorois cattle dips and fresh

---

of the OAU adopted a resolution in July 1979 to form a committee of experts to draft an African Charter on Human and Peoples' Rights. The OAU adopted the Charter on 7 June 1981 and it entered into force on 21 October 1986.

water dams. None of these promises were kept and as a result of repeated petitioning by the Endorois, the government finally agreed to provide 3150 Kenya Shillings per family that had been dispossessed. It was only in 1986 however, eight years after the Endorois were excluded from their lands, that some money was given to 170 of the 400 families. The Endorois were also taken a back when they were informed that the 3150 Kenya Shillings was full compensation for their loss of land. They had understood that this money was for helping with relocation rather than for compensation for their exclusion from their ancestral lands.

The Endorois petitioned President Daniel Arap Moi to intervene to protect their rights, and, despite the President's directives to the local county councils in 1994 to respect the 1973 agreement on compensation and to pay the community 25 per cent of the annual tourist revenues, nothing was done. Due to the non-implementation of the presidential directives, the Endorois began legal action against the Baringo and Koibatek County Councils. The High Court in its judgment in 2002[28] dismissed the Endorois application and stated in its decision that the community had lost any legal claim as a result of the designation of their land as a game reserve. The Court also held that the money given to the 170 Endorois families in 1986 fulfilled all duties owed by the government to the community for the loss of their land.[29]

The High Court refused to recognize the Endorois as a community and their right to communal property as a result of historical occupation and cultural bonds to their lands. After the decision, the Endorois became aware that part of their land was being demarcated and sold off by the government to third parties, including concessions to a private company for mining rubies. The mining exacerbated the risk of polluting the waterways used by the Endorois for their personal consumption and for their cattle. Though as a result of their legal action the Endorois were permitted limited grazing rights and access to Lake Bogoria for cultural purposes, the fact that their

[28] Referenced in *Endorois Welfare Council.*

[29] Refer to Ibid., at paragraphs 1–25 for detailed facts of the case.

land was not titled meant that access to their territories was subject entirely to the discretion of the Game Reserve officials.

The Endorois community was breaking down due to the displacement from their ancestral lands and they were being forced to live on the peripheries of the Game Reserve. They no longer had access to their grasslands, salt licks, the Lake Bogoria, and medicinal plants, and instead had to survive in semi-arid areas. The human rights lawyer representing them was arrested in 1996, was accused of 'belonging to an unlawful society' and received death threats.

In 2003, 30 years after they had been dispossessed, denied compensation, and access to justice, the Endorois decided to approach the African Commission on Human and Peoples' Rights for relief. They were supported by the Centre for Minority Rights Development (CEMIRIDE). After three years of no response by the government of Kenya despite repeated requests and postponements of hearings by the African Commission, the Commission decided to admit the Endorois complaint and consider the case on its merits. The Endorois claimed the violation of Articles of the African Charter on Human and Peoples' Rights dealing with the right to property, the right to free disposition of natural resources, the right to religion, the right to cultural life, and the right to development.[30]

At the outset, the African Commission sought to clarify the status of indigenous populations in Africa in the context of Articles 20 to 24 in the African Charter that refers to 'peoples'. It cited the African Commission's work through its Working Group of Experts on Indigenous Populations/Communities, and referred to the four criteria for identifying indigenous peoples: occupation and use of a specific territory; voluntary perpetuation of peoples; self-identification as a distinct collectivity, as well as recognition by other groups; and experience of subjugation, marginalization, dispossession, exclusion, or discrimination.[31] What is interesting from the perspective of an emerging discourse of stewardship is the

[30] *See generally*, for the facts of the case, *Endorois Welfare Council*, at paragraphs 1–21.

[31] Report of the African Commission's Working Group of Experts on Indigenous Populations/ Communities (adopted at the Twenty-eighth Session, 2003).

African Commission's emphasis on another characteristic of African indigenous groups highlighted by its Working Group of Experts on Indigenous Populations/Communities:

> A key characteristic for most of them is that the survival of their particular way of life depends on access and rights to their traditional land and the natural resources thereon.[32]

The explicit linking of a way of life to traditional lands and resources therein reveals an added dimension to the concept of indigenous and tribal communities that has gained currency over the last two decades. This dimension emphasizes the strong bond these communities have to their ancestral lands, a bond that defines the very nature of their peoplehood. The African Commission stresses this point by adding:

> The African Commission is thus aware that there is an emerging consensus on some objective features that a collective of individuals should manifest to be considered as peoples, viz: a common historical tradition, racial or ethnic identity, cultural homogeneity, linguistic unity, religious and ideological affinities, territorial connection, and a common economic life or other bonds, identities and affinities they collectively enjoy—especially rights enumerated under Articles 19 to 24 of the African Charter—or suffer collectively from the deprivation of such rights. *What is clear is that all attempts to define the concept of indigenous peoples recognize the linkages between peoples, their land, and culture* (emphasis mine) and that such a group expresses its desire to be identified as a people or have the consciousness that they are a people.[33]

The Commission concluded that the Endorois culture, religion, and traditional way of life were integrally tied to their ancestral lands, Lake Bogoria and its surrounds including the Monchongoi forest. In its conclusion, the Commission made clear that, amongst the criteria for identifying indigenous and tribal groups, the relationship between the community and its territory is a defining factor:

> The African Commission is also aware that though some indigenous populations might be first inhabitants, validation of rights is not

32 *Endorois Welfare Council*, paragraph 150.
33 Ibid., at paragraph 151.

> automatically afforded to such preinvasion and precolonial claims. In terms of ILO Convention 169, even though many African countries have not signed and ratified the said Convention, and like the UN Working Groups' conceptualisation of the term, the African Commission notes that *there is a common thread that runs through all the various criteria that attempts to describe indigenous peoples — that indigenous peoples have an unambiguous relationship to a distinct territory and that all attempts to define the concept recognise the linkages between people, their land, and culture* (emphasis mine).[34]

The decisions of the Inter-American Court and the African Commission have resulted in a paradigm shift in property jurisprudence where new criteria for establishing common property rights of communities have emerged. These criteria resonate with the arguments of Riley et al. to establish a new principle: that the sense of peoplchood may arise through a mutually reinforcing relationship between land and culture/religion. The property claims of the Awas Tingni, the Saramaka, and the Endorois are never presented purely as a right to property but as a right to the cultural, and therefore, physical, survival of a people. The bond between the community and its territory is not just a bond established through historical occupation of land but a biocultural bond whose content is defined by culture, religion, and spirituality of the community. This bond includes the duty of stewardship and thereby contains the very essence of what 'flourishing' means to the community.

This paradigm shift in property jurisprudence is exemplified in the Endorois case where the community not only accused the Kenyan government of violating their right to property but also coupled this violation with a denial of the right to freely practise their religion and culture. The Endorois explicitly linked this denial to their dislocation from Lake Bogoria and their sacred sites in the vicinity. They argued that many of their rituals and ceremonies including circumcisions, initiations, and marriages could only take place on certain sacred sites around the Lake. Among the adverse impacts of the dispossession of their lands was their inability to conduct their annual ceremony to appease their ancestors, who had drowned at the time of the Lake's formation.

[34] *Endorois Welfare Council*, paragraph 154.

The African Commission clearly used culture as a bridge between property and peoplehood by noting that the denial of property in the case of the Endorois is tantamount to the denial of the right to freely practise religion and culture, and therefore threatens the very survival of a people. The African Commission underscored this by stating:

> This Commission also notes the views of the Human Rights Committee with regard to the exercise of the cultural rights protected under Article 27 of the UN Declaration on the Rights of Persons Belonging to National or Ethnic, Religious and Linguistic Minorities. The Committee observes that 'culture manifests itself in many forms, including a particular way of life associated with the use of *land resources*, especially in the case of indigenous peoples. That right may include such traditional activities as fishing or hunting and the right to live in reserves protected by law. The enjoyment of those rights may require positive legal measures of protection and measures to ensure the effective participation of members of minority communities in decisions which affect them.' The African Commission notes that a common theme that usually runs through the debate about culture and its violation is the association with one's ancestral land. It notes that its own Working Group on Indigenous Populations/ Communities has observed that dispossession of land and its resources is 'a major human rights problem for indigenous peoples.' It further notes that a Report from the Working Group has also emphasised that dispossession 'threatens the economic, social and *cultural survival* of indigenous pastoralist and huntergatherer communities.'[35]

Perhaps the most groundbreaking aspect of the decision was an assertion, in the context of property for peoplehood, that traditional possession is sufficient to establish a right and this right overrides any other competing property claim. Any infringement of the right of property for peoplehood would have to establish a most compelling and urgent public interest. Regarding the establishment of a communal property right through historical possession, the African Commission went so far as to say that in situations of forced displacement of indigenous peoples from their land, even the lack of possession of these lands does not extinguish the original right. The Commission elaborated its position by stating:

[35] *Endorois Welfare Council*, at paragraphs 243–4.

> In the view of the African Commission, the following conclusions could be drawn: (1) traditional possession of land by indigenous people has the equivalent effect as that of a stategranted full property title; (2) traditional possession entitles indigenous people to demand official recognition and registration of property title; (3) the members of indigenous peoples who have unwillingly left their traditional lands, or lost possession thereof, maintain property rights thereto, even though they lack legal title, unless the lands have been lawfully transferred to third parties in good faith; and (4) the members of indigenous peoples who have unwillingly lost possession of their lands, when those lands have been lawfully transferred to innocent third parties, are entitled to restitution thereof or to obtain other lands of equal extension and quality. Consequently, possession is not a requisite condition for the existence of indigenous land restitution rights.[36]

Regarding the encroachment on indigenous lands for public interest, the African Commission strictly circumscribes this limitation on indigenous property rights by pointing out that:

> The 'public interest' test is met with a much higher threshold in the case of encroachment of indigenous land rather than individual private property. In this sense, the test is much more stringent when applied to ancestral land rights of indigenous peoples. In 2005, this point was stressed by the Special Rapporteur of the United Nations SubCommission for the Promotion and Protection of Human Rights who published the following statement: *Limitations, if any, on the right to indigenous peoples to their natural resources must flow only from the most urgent and compelling interest of the state. Few, if any, limitations on indigenous resource rights are appropriate, because the indigenous ownership of the resources is associated with the most important and fundamental human rights, including the right to life, food, the right to self-determination, to shelter, and the right to exist as a people.*[37]

Finally the Commission decided against the government of Kenya, rejecting arguments of public interest to justify encroachment on the Endorois territory. The Commission found the state arguments that the land was being demarcated as a conservation area in public interest

[36] Ibid., at paragraph 209.
[37] Ibid., at paragraph 212.

as particularly disingenuous. Highlighting the stewardship role of the Endorois vis-à-vis their territories, the Commission unequivocally supported the Endorois' biocultural rights to their traditional lands and waters. The Commission noted:

> The reasons of the Government in the instant Communication are questionable for several reasons including: (a) the contested land is the site of a conservation area, and the Endorois—*as the ancestral guardians of that land—are best equipped to maintain its delicate ecosystems* (emphasis mine); (b) the Endorois are prepared to continue the conservation work begun by the Government; (c) no other community have settled on the land in question, and even if that is the case, the Respondent state is obliged to rectify that situation, (d) the land has not been spoliated and is thus inhabitable; (e) continued dispossession and alienation from their ancestral land continues to threaten the cultural survival of the Endorois' way of life, a consequence which clearly tips the proportionality argument on the side of indigenous peoples under international law.[38]

BIOCULTURAL RIGHTS AND LEGAL RECOGNITION OF STEWARDSHIP CLAIMS

It could well be argued that all the decisions of the regional tribunals and commissions are merely recognizing group rights to indigenous or tribal land title on the basis of historical occupation and not biocultural or stewardship rights. However, such an argument does not answer for the extensive treatment by the judges in these cases of the cultural, spiritual and, in effect, 'all-encompassing relationship' between a people and their territories. In fact the decisions of the courts turned on the important pivot of the relationship between property and peoplehood. This relationship is one where property is, in Radin's terms, personal not fungible and critical for human flourishing. The fact that the lands in question were materially, culturally, and spiritually integral to peoplehood, implied a relationship with a land that embodied an ethic of care. Such an ethic of care though culturally and spiritually expressed has its material basis in the cold

[38] Ibid., at paragraph 235.

fact that a destruction of the land would imperil the entire existence of a people, every aspect of whose lives depended on the land. The main issue in the decisions of the regional tribunals was less about the land belonging to the people and more about the people belonging to the land, without which they would cease to exist as a people.

In each of these cases the communities asserted their claims to the land not just by proving occupation but also by establishing strong cultural and spiritual ties to the land through showing a strong ethic of stewardship. If the communities were able to prove only historical occupation, but were unable to establish stewardship, the decisions of the courts may not have gone in their favour. For example, if there was widespread evidence of the aforementioned communities selling or leasing parts of their lands for strip mining and themselves engaged in ecologically destructive practices, then clearly they would not have been able to establish an 'all-encompassing relationship' with the land. The land would be treated as a fungible asset and at best the courts would have asked the governments to compensate the community. The fact that the courts required the governments to recognize community rights, not just to any lands, but specifically to ancestral lands evidences the emergence of biocultural rights in the jurisprudence of regional tribunals and commissions. At this juncture, it is important to include a caveat that the submissions here should not be interpreted as an assertion that indigenous peoples and traditional communities are invariably stewards of the land. On the contrary, the effort here is merely to marshal evidence to establish a discursive shift in law and policy towards the recognition of biocultural rights of communities where they are able to establish practices of stewardship.

The growing traction of biocultural rights in the afore-mentioned decisions marks the establishment of a stewardship discourse in property jurisprudence. If a discourse on stewardship brings with it a set of values that are markedly different from those of conventional property jurisprudence, then such a discourse necessarily requires the acceptance of a legal pluralism. The break that biocultural rights make from the dominant state-centred approach to land as fungible and alienable requires an engagement with a different worldview.

Stewardship of lands and waters is not an abstract concept but is embodied in a way of life that can only flourish if its cultural and material autonomy can be protected. The ethic of stewardship is rooted within a moral universe that will be crowded out if forced to fit within the dominant legal and material systems of the *homo economicus*. It is precisely for this reason that the jurisprudence of the Inter-American Court and the African Commission have begun to strongly affirm the rights of indigenous and tribal communities to cultural autonomy and to control and manage their territories.

In many ways the deep structure of the right of control over territories and cultural autonomy is the right to self-determination, albeit in a form that does not seek separate statehood but rather insists on respect for customary laws and local institutions of governance. This judicial affirmation of stewardship by regional tribunals builds on firm foundations laid down in Anglo–American jurisprudence. It is these foundations that we shall explore in the next chapter.

CHAPTER EIGHT

Biocultural Rights in Anglo-American Jurisprudence

There is a tendency, operating at times unconsciously, to render that (native) title conceptually in terms, which are appropriate only to systems, which have grown up under English law. But this tendency has to be held in check closely. As a rule, in the various systems of native jurisprudence throughout the Empire, there is no such full division between property and possession as English lawyers are familiar with. A very usual form of native title is that of a usufructuary right, which is a mere qualification of or burden on the radical or final title of the Sovereign where that exists. In such cases the title of the Sovereign is a pure legal estate, to which beneficial rights may or may not be attached. But this estate is qualified by a right of beneficial user which may not assume definite forms analogous to estates, or may, where it has assumed these, have derived them from the intrusion of the mere analogy of English jurisprudence .... The title, such as it is, may not be that of the individual, as in this country it nearly always is in some form, but may be that of a community. Such a community may have the possessory title to the common enjoyment of a usufruct, with customs under which its individual members are admitted to enjoyment, and even to a right of transmitting the individual enjoyment as members by assignment inter vivos or by succession. To ascertain how far this latter development of right has progressed involves the study of the history of the particular community and its usages in each case. Abstract principles fashioned a priori *are of but little assistance, and are as often as not misleading.*

— *The judgment of their Lordships delivered by Viscount Haldane in* Amodu Tijani v. The Secretary, Southern Nigeria, *Privy Council, 11th July 1921*[1]

[1] (1921) 2 A.C. 399.

The last two decades have resulted in landmark decisions on 'aboriginal title'[2] in Anglo-American jurisprudence. These decisions of the highest courts have conclusively established for domestic law the rights of indigenous and tribal communities to their traditional lands. While our focus in this chapter is on Anglo-American jurisprudence, it is pertinent to note that the doctrine of aboriginal title is *sui generis* rather than typical of common law notions of property.[3] It is recognized in legal systems other than Anglo-American[4] and is arguably a right recognized in

[2] 'Aboriginal title (or native title as it is so called) is a right to land, one vesting in a community that occupied the land at the time of colonization. Once such a title is established, the claimants may vindicate their land or, if it had been expropriated without adequate reimbursement, claim compensation'. [Thomas W. Bennett et al., 'Aboriginal Title in South Africa Revisited', *South African Journal of Human Rights* 15 (1999), p. 449.]

[3] On 18 October 2007, the Supreme Court of Belize in *Cal* v. *Attorney General* (Claims Nos. 171 and 172, 2007) ruled that the national government must recognize indigenous Mayans' customary tenure to land and refrain from any act that might prejudice their use or enjoyment of their ancestral domain. The Court also held that the Mayan tenure pre-dates European colonization and survives today. The decision noted 'A mere change in sovereignty does not extinguish native title to land.... Extinguishment of rights to or interests in land is not to be lightly inferred'. Referring to *Delgamuukw* v. *British Columbia* (see below), the High Court observed that 'Indigenous title is now correctly regarded as *sui generis*'. In other words, the very fact of 'Original Peoples' having inhabited a land over time confers land title rights to them. It cited the Belizean Constitution and several international legal precedents that affirmed the existence of indigenous peoples' collective rights to their land and other natural resources. While stating that the UNDRIP is considered to be non-binding, the Court averred that principles of general international law contained in the declaration should be respected. Moreover, it noted that the UNDRIP was adopted by an 'overwhelming number' of states thus reflecting 'the growing consensus and the general principles of international law on indigenous peoples and their lands and resources. *See* Owen J. Lynch, *Mandating Recognition: International Law and Native/Aboriginal Title* (Washington DC: Rights and Resources Initiative, 2011), p. 15.

[4] The 1988 Brazilian Constitution for the first time recognized the existence of collective rights of Brazilian Indians and acknowledged the

international law.[5] Hence the current chapter should be viewed as less about Anglo-American jurisprudence per se and more about the judicial recognition of a pre-existing aboriginal title that lies outside the common law system.[6] Where South African case law has been analysed, it does not in any way deny its Roman-Dutch elements but rather seeks to explore its common law and *sui generis* influences.

Aboriginal title differs from common law property rights because it is a communal right vesting in an aboriginal people and originated in a pre-colonial system of indigenous law. It therefore,

---

legitimacy of community-based indigenous autonomy and social structures. The Brazilian Constitution states that 'Land traditionally occupied by Brazilian Indians are those that they have occupied and permanently possessed and they shall have the exclusive usufruct of the riches of the soil, the rivers and the lakes existing therein'. In 2009 Brazil's Supreme Court handed down a decision giving indigenous Amazonians legal control over 1.7 million hectares of the Raposa Serra do Sol Indigenous Reserve. *See* ibid., p. 16.

[5] The UNDRIP in Article 26 states that 'Indigenous peoples have the right to the lands, territories and resources which they have traditionally owned'. In Article 10, the Declaration goes further by providing that 'Indigenous peoples shall not be forcibly removed from their lands or territories. No relocation shall take place without the free, prior and informed consent of the indigenous peoples concerned and after agreement on just and fair compensation and, where possible, with the option of return'. International Labour Organization (ILO) Convention Nos. 107 and 169 on the Rights of Indigenous and Tribal Peoples in Developing Countries came into force in 1957 and 1989, respectively. Prior to the UNDRIP, the ILO Conventions were seen as the most explicit statements in international law on aboriginal title. While ILO Convention No. 107 has been ratified by 27 countries, Convention No. 169 has been ratified by 20 countries.

[6] Bennett et al., 'Aboriginal Title in South Africa Revisited' (1999), p. 462; Bennett et al. also note in this article that the courts in Canada and Australia have declared that aboriginal title is not a part of English common law but is in fact an equitable principle of constitutional common law and that its doctrine is applicable even in colonies, such as Quebec, which retained French law as the basic law of the land.

lies at the intersection of indigenous laws and the received systems of colonial law.[7]

Many of the decisions dealing with aboriginal title rest on the clear foundations laid by the Privy Council in 1921 in its decision in *Amodu Tijani* v. *The Secretary, Southern Nigeria*.[8] Nevertheless it is important to note that the American Supreme Court in *Johnson* v. *M'Intosh* nearly a hundred years before *Amodu Tijani* had already begun to recognize the rights of the conquered American Indian tribes to property. Chief Justice Marshall in his judgement stated that:

> The rights of the conquered to property should remain unimpaired .... the new subjects should be governed as equitably as the old, and .... confidence in their security should gradually banish the painful sense of being separated from their ancient connections.[9]

Amodu Tijani Case

Before discussing the reasoning of the Privy Council in *Amodu Tijani* it is important to provide some context to the common law history that underlies these significant advances in Anglo-American case law. Courts in countries that were former colonies of the British Crown (or what are often referred to as common law jurisdictions) have on occasion had to clarify the status of the rights of indigenous, native or aboriginal communities to their traditional lands after annexation by the British Empire. The reason behind such clarification was

[7] In fact some commentators have gone as far as to say that aboriginal title is already recognized under aboriginal law and has nothing to do with common law. However, the recognition by common law of aboriginal title is what is termed as 'native title'. While the lack of recognition by common law of aboriginal title extinguishes native title, aboriginal title continues to exist due to its recognition by aboriginal law. See Noel Pearson, 'The Concept of Native Title at Common Law', *Australian Humanities Law Review* (March 1997), http://www.australianhumanitiesreview.org/archive/Issue-March-1997/pearson.html (accessed 13 September 2011).

[8] (1921) 2 A.C. 399. (hereinafter *Amodu Tijani*).

[9] 21 US (8 Wheaton) 541 at 589 (1823). *See also US* v. *Percheman* 32 US (7 Peters) 51 at 86–7 (1831).

the need to establish whether these rights survived the handover of power by the Crown to the respective national governments when the colonies gained independence. Simply put, if the jurisprudence of these former colonies traced its lineage to common law, then the operative question was whether common law recognized the customary land rights and the relevant customary laws of the native populations when these colonies were under the rule of the British Empire. If common law did recognize such rights, then one could argue that they would have survived the transfer of power to the new governments, who in turn would also have to recognize such rights since their jurisprudence was based on common law.[10]

In the above excerpt from *Amodu Tijani*, Viscount Haldane reasoned that 'native title' is a burden on the 'radical title' of the Crown. The presumption of the Crown's 'radical title' over all lands in its colonies implied that the Crown, like any government, asserted its sovereignty over the area within its jurisdiction. Such title means that the land in question is within the administrative jurisdiction of the Crown. However, the fact that land is under the jurisdiction of the Crown or any government for that matter does not mean that the pre-existing rights of individuals or communities over such land can be denied. Rather, such rights (in this case 'native title') become a burden on the 'radical title', which means that the Crown or the government would have to recognize these rights and in cases where such rights are to be extinguished, due process of the law would need to be followed and compensation provided. In a nutshell, in common law, the rights of communities and individuals over land are protected against any wholesale expropriation by governments despite the fact that all such land is under state jurisdiction.[11]

[10] Lord Hailey, *An African Survey: A Study of Problems Arising in Africa South of the Sahara*, Revised to 1956 (Oxford: Oxford University Press, 1968). No reserves were created in West Africa, because in this region only a small amount of land had been appropriated by settlers or declared Crown property. Indigenous landholdings were, by and large, undisturbed by colonization.

[11] 'Radical title, which is an assertion of the right of the Crown over all land in its jurisdiction, should be distinguished from eminent domain, the power to take land. Radical title enables the Crown to become paramount

While this state of affairs is generally accepted in common law countries, the pertinence of *Amodu Tijani* is its clarification of the relationship between common law and customary law. The property rights of British citizens under common law being a burden on the Crown is one thing, since both the rights of the citizens and the radical title of the Crown are derived from within the same legal system. However, the recognition in common law of land rights of individuals and communities that are derived from indigenous systems of customary law is another thing altogether, and it is here that the importance of the Privy Council's judgment in *Amodu Tijani* lies.

As Viscount Haldane noted in his oft quoted dictum:

> There is a tendency, operating at times unconsciously, to render that (native) title conceptually in terms, which are appropriate only to systems which have grown up under English law. But this tendency has to be held in check closely.[12]

---

lord in respect of a tenure created by Crown grant. Once the Crown grants particular land to a subject, by definition, the Crown no longer has radical title to that land; that is, the sovereign loses its radical title to the land for the duration of the grant. Thus, radical title is only relevant in respect of land, which is not subject to a Crown grant, that is, unalienated land. It is in the context of alienated land, therefore, that the concept of eminent domain is relevant. Although the Crown does not have a radical title to land, which has been granted to a subject (the land is no longer Crown land), it has a power of eminent domain in relation to the land. Thus the concept of eminent domain compliments the concept of radical title. Until the Crown has exercised its sovereign power to grant an interest in unalienated land, bringing it within the doctrine of tenure, the Crown cannot exercise its powers of eminent domain to effect acquisition of property. Because unalienated land comes within the definition of Crown land, that is land in respect of which the Crown has a radical title, the Crown can simply exercise its sovereign power to appropriate to itself ownership of the land. By formally entitling itself to the land, the land loses its character as Crown land and becomes Crown property'. *See* Ulla Secher, 'Implications of the Crown's Radical Title for Statutory Regimes Regulating the Alienation of Land: "Crown Land" v "Property of the Crown" Post- *Mabo*', *Monash University Law Review* 34 (1) (2008), p. 50.

[12] *Amodu Tijani*, p. 403. Viscount Haldane's views were in marked contrast to the Privy Council decision in In *Re Southern Rhodesia* (1919) AC

What needs to be held in check is the tendency in common law to recognize customary law only where it fits within the pre-existing categories of common law. The potential injustice caused to traditional occupants or users of land due to the lack of recognition of customary law title to land extends even to this day.[13] In many ways this situation is as much political as it is legal, since the non-recognition of communal title paves the way for the dominant understanding of land as a marketable commodity that is fungible, alienable, and tradable (with no biocultural links to peoplehood).

Amodu Tijani was a case that came before the Privy Council on appeal from the Supreme Court of Nigeria in 1921. Amodu Tijani, the appellant, was one of the native chiefs, the land under whose control was acquired by the government of the colony for public purposes under the Public Lands Ordinance. The Public Lands Ordinance entitled Amodu Tijani to compensation for the state's acquisition of his lands. What was in dispute, however, was the basis on which the compensation that was due was to be calculated. The government of the colony decided to compensate Tijani only to the extent of the revenues and tributes that he would receive from the communities occupying the land. Tijani on the other hand argued that the land was held in communal title and the transfer of ownership of the land to the government necessitated compensation for the full value of the land. The case went on appeal all the way to the Supreme Court of Nigeria, which upheld the government's decision on the basis that native chiefs in Lagos do not have absolute ownership of the lands but were merely entitled to receive tributes and rents from occupiers to these lands. Tijani appealed the decision of the Supreme Court before the Privy Council pressing the point that the land was held in communal title and the community had usufructuary rights over the land.

---

211 (PC) which held that customary tenure was too primitive to warrant recognition as a recognizable land right in common law.

[13] Examples of this includes the recent appeal by the Hai//om people of Etosha in Namibia to the Minister of Environment and Tourism Netumbo Nandi-Ndaitwah to recognize their customary law title to their traditional lands in the Etosha National Park. Letter from the Etosha Hai||om Association dated 21 April 2011. On file with author.

After analysing the facts of the case, their Lordships overruled the decision of the Supreme Court of Nigeria noting that:

> Their Lordships think that the learned Chief Justice (of the Supreme Court) in the judgment thus summarised, which virtually excludes the legal reality of the community usufruct, has failed to recognize the real character of the title to land occupied by a native community. That title, as they have pointed out, is prima facie based, not on such individual ownership as English law has made familiar, *but on a communal usufructuary occupation, which may be so complete as to reduce any radical right in the Sovereign to one which only extends to comparatively limited rights of administrative interference* (emphasis mine). In their opinion there is no evidence that this kind of usufructuary title of the community was disturbed in law, either when the Benin Kings conquered Lagos or when the cession to the British Crown took place in 1861. The general words used in the treaty of cession are not in themselves to be construed as extinguishing subject rights. The original native right was a communal right, and it must be presumed to have continued to exist unless the contrary is established by the context or circumstances. There is, in their Lordships' opinion, no evidence which points to its having been at any time seriously disturbed or even questioned. Under these conditions they are unable to take the view adopted by the Chief Justice and the full Court.[14]

What makes *Amodu Tijani* a foundational decision in common law jurisprudence is the resolution by the Privy Council (the highest appellate body in the British Empire) of two key issues regarding native title:

(i) There is always a presumption in common law that the Crown recognizes the customary rights of native populations when it asserts its radical title and that these rights become a burden on the radical title of the Crown; and

[14] *Amodu Tijani*, pp., 409–410. This conception followed *St. Catherine's Milling & Lumber Co.* v. *The Queen* (1889) 14 App Cas 46 (PC), where the Privy Council also held that radical title remained vested in the Crown, and that the First Nations had a personal usufructuary right dependent upon the goodwill of the Sovereign.

(ii) An attempt should be made to understand native title that is, customary law relating to land use, on its own terms and not on the basis of categories in English law.

The Privy Council in *Amodu Tijani* in effect accepted that common law can recognize and coexist with an indigenous system of customary law.[15] More importantly the Privy Council opened the jurisprudential doors to recognition of other ways of understanding property, and by implication peoplehood, that could substantially differ from the approaches of English law.[16]

Establishing Native Title in the Nineties: *Mabo* v. *Queensland (No. 2)*

> *Whatever the justification advanced in earlier days for refusing the rights and interests in land of the indigenous inhabitants of settled colonies, an unjust and discriminatory doctrine of that kind can no longer be accepted. The expectations of the international community accord in this respect with the contemporary values of the Australian people. The opening up of international remedies to individuals pursuant to Australia's accession to the Optional Protocol to the International Covenant on Civil and Political Rights ... brings to bear on the common law the powerful influence of the Covenant and the international standards it imports.*

[15] *See also, Sobhuza II* v. *Miller* (1926) AC 518 (PC) at 525 where the Privy Council held that 'the title of the native community generally takes the form of a usufructuary right, a mere qualification of a burden on the radical or final title of whoever is sovereign. Obviously such a usufructuary right, however difficult to get rid of by ordinary methods of conveyancing, may be extinguished by the action of a paramount power which assumes possession or the entire control of the land'.

[16] The recognition of aboriginal title in the United States and New Zealand through treaties pre-dates *Amodu Tijani*. The expansion of the United States after independence from Britain was achieved by treaties between the federal government and American Indians. These treaties usually provided that the latter, as sovereign nations, were entitled to retain their lands and a degree of internal autonomy. *See Worcester* v. *Georgia* 31 US (6 Peters) 515, 559–60 (1832). In New Zealand the recognition of aboriginal title was based, in the first instance, on the Treaty of Waitangi of 1840.

> *The common law does not necessarily conform with international law, but international law is a legitimate and important influence on the development of common law especially when international law declares the existence of universal human rights. A common law doctrine founded on unjust discrimination in the enjoyment of civil and political rights demands reconsideration. It is contrary both to international standards and to the fundamental values of our common law to entrench a discriminatory rule which, because of the supposed position on the scale of social organization of the indigenous inhabitants of a settled colony, denies them a right to occupy their traditional lands.*
>
> *Justice Brennan in Mabo v. Queensland (No. 2)*[17]

The *Mabo case (No. 2)* involved a declaration sought by the Meriam people, a seafaring and gardening community of the eastern Torres Strait Islands, for their entitlement as traditional owners and occupiers over three Torres Strait Islands, collectively known as the Murray Islands. The Meriam people argued that they had lived on these islands in accordance with their customary laws for a number of generations even prior to annexation by the British Crown. They asserted that their native title was not extinguished after the annexation and establishment of a British Colony of New South Wales in 1788, and that the title continued to exist to the present.

In 1982 members of the Meriam community, Eddie Koiki Mabo, Sam Passi, David Passi, Celuia Mapo Salee, and James Rice claimed legal ownership of their lands on the Murray Islands. While the Supreme Court of Queensland was considering the case, the state Parliament enacted the *Torres Strait Islands Coastal Islands Act*, which formally extinguished, without compensation, all rights that Torres Strait Islanders had to their land after its annexation by the British Crown in 1879. This Act was challenged in the High Court of Australia, which decided in *Mabo No. 1* that the Act was invalid as it conflicted with the *Commonwealth Racial Discrimination Act of 1975*.[18]

However, *Mabo No. 1* did not resolve the question of legal ownership of the Meriam people over their lands. On 3 June 1992, the High

[17] (1992) HCA 23, (1992) 175 CLR 1 (hereinafter *Mabo No. 2*). *See* paragraph 42.

[18] *See* Documenting Democracy, *Mabo* (No. 2), http://foundingdocs.gov.au/item-did-33.html (accessed 13 September 2011).

Court of Australia handed down a landmark decision (*Mabo No.2*) that affirmed the native title and therefore, the customary land rights of the Meriam people. Eddie Mabo and Celuia Mapo Salee had died in the ten years it took from the initiation of the land title claim to the decision of the High Court of Australia. Nevertheless the process they began transformed Anglo-American jurisprudence relating to land rights of indigenous peoples in ways that they probably never conceived.

Mabo No.2 traced a line of precedents in common law beginning with *Amodu Tijani* that upheld 'native title' and therefore, customary systems of land holding. In doing so the case overruled Australian decisions in common law that did not recognize traditional land rights.[19] The fact that Justice Brennan in the above excerpt went as far as saying that international law was a legitimate and important influence on common law and common law could not violate human rights is an indication of the delicate balance he sought to maintain, a balance between holding fast to the centuries of common law tradition and keeping step with the growing human rights discourse in international law.

Justice Brennan, speaking on behalf of himself, Chief Justice Mason, and Justice McHugh, was confronted with a political dilemma. On the one hand, he could not embrace the advances in international law to the extent that they would undercut the very foundations of the Australian legal system, that is, disrupt the existing land rights of Australian citizens despite the fact that some of this land was acquired as a result of great injustices against the aboriginal populations. On the other hand, he could not uphold aspects of common law that were clearly contrary to generally accepted human rights standards. The way out of this dilemma was for Justice Brennan to propound the 'skeleton principle':

> In discharging its duty to declare the common law of Australia, this Court is not free to adopt rules that accord with contemporary notions of justice and human rights if their adoption would fracture the *skeleton of principle* (emphasis mine) which gives the body of our

[19] See, *Cooper* v. *Stuart* (1889) 14 App Cas 286 and *Milirrpum* v. *Nabalco Pty Ltd.* (1971) 17 FLR 141.

> law its shape and internal consistency. Australian law is not only the historical successor of, but is an organic development from, the law of England. Although our law is the prisoner of its history, it is not now bound by decisions of courts in the hierarchy of an Empire then concerned with the development of its colonies.[20]

The challenge for Justice Brennan, however, was to clarify what was meant by this skeletal principle of Australian law that could override international human rights law. He sidestepped this difficulty by stating that:

> The peace and order of Australian society is built on the legal system. It can be modified to bring it into conformity with contemporary notions of justice and human rights, but it cannot be destroyed. It is not possible a priori to distinguish between cases that express a skeletal principle and those, which do not, but no case can command unquestioning adherence if the rule it expresses seriously offends the values of justice and human rights (especially equality before the law) which are aspirations of the contemporary Australian legal system. If a postulated rule of common law expressed in earlier cases seriously offends those contemporary values, the question arises whether the rule should be maintained and applied. Whenever such a question arises, it is necessary to assess whether the particular rule is an essential doctrine of our legal system and whether, if the rule were to be overturned, the disturbance to be apprehended would be disproportionate to the benefit flowing from the overturning.[21]

At this stage it would help to clarify the common law principle that was being argued by the government of Queensland, which was at odds with the rule propounded by *Amodu Tijani*. In fact the government of Queensland was making the case that, while *Amodu Tijani* held that common law should recognize native title, this recognition was subject to two caveats: the international law rule of *terra nullius* (uninhabited land) and the Privy Council ruling in the 1919 case of *In re Southern Rhodesia*[22] which had held that certain forms of aboriginal social organization in relation to land were so

[20] *Mabo No. 2*, paragraph 29, judgment of Brennan J.
[21] Ibid., at paragraph 29, judgment of Brennan J.
[22] (1919) AC 211.

'backward' that it was as good as considering the land unoccupied.[23] Lord Sumner in *In re Southern Rhodesia* expressed this view by stating:

> The estimation of the rights of aboriginal tribes is always inherently difficult. Some tribes are so low in the scale of social organization that their usages and conceptions of rights and duties are not to be reconciled with the institutions or the legal ideas of civilized society. Such a gulf cannot be bridged, it would be idle to impute to such people some shadow of the rights known to our law and then to transmute it into the substance of transferable rights of property as we know them.[24]

The logical conclusion of such a view propounded by the Privy Council was that the moment the colonial government classified certain tribes in the colonies as 'so low in the scale of social organization' that their way of life cannot be reconciled with 'civilized society', then the Crown no longer had to recognize their customary laws relating to land. These lands could be deemed ownerless. The declaration that a land was ownerless implied that the 'radical title' of the Crown would expand to include beneficial ownership of the land. This would imply that the land was not only within the jurisdiction of the Crown but also that the Crown in effect became the owner of the land.

At this stage the High Court of Australia had a choice of critically analysing the doctrine of *terra nullius* or engaging in the unsavoury task of examining the customs and traditions of the Meriam people to determine whether they can be reconciled with Lord Sumner's views

[23] Justice Brennan articulated his reasoning by stating that: 'The theory that the indigenous inhabitants of a "settled" colony had no proprietary interest in the land thus depended on a discriminatory denigration of indigenous inhabitants, their social organization and customs. As the basis of the theory is false in fact and unacceptable in our society, there is a choice of legal principle to be made in the present case. This Court can either apply the existing authorities and proceed to inquire whether the Meriam people are higher "in the scale of social organization" than the Australian Aborigines whose claims were "utterly disregarded" by the existing authorities or the Court can overrule the existing authorities, discarding the distinction between inhabited colonies that were terra nullius and those which were not'. *Mabo No 2* at paragraph 39, judgment of Brennan J.

[24] Ibid., at paragraph 38, judgment of Brennan J.

of 'civilized society'. Justice Brennan and his fellow judges chose the former course of action and thereby overruled *In re Southern Rhodesia* and all the decisions thereafter that had relied on that case to deny native title. Importantly they disagreed with *Milirrpum* v. *Nabalco Pty. Ltd.*,[25] the only reported decision of an Australian court directly dealing with the merits of an Aboriginal claim to particular traditional tribal or communal lands. In interrogating the doctrine of *terra nullius*, the High Court of Australia had at its disposal the advisory opinion of the International Court of Justice (ICJ) on the status of the Western Sahara, where the ICJ unequivocally clarified what *terra*

[25] (1970) 17 FLR 141. Deane and Gaudron JJ stated that in *Milirrpum*:

> ... a group of Aborigines representing native tribes sued a mining company and the Commonwealth in the Supreme Court of the Northern Territory claiming relief in relation to the possession and enjoyment of areas of land which had initially been part of the Colony of New South Wales. The learned trial judge (Blackburn J.) rejected the plaintiffs' claim of common law communal native title. The primary reason for that rejection was that his Honour found that the plaintiffs had not established, on the balance of probabilities, that their predecessors had had the same links as themselves to the relevant areas of land at the time of the establishment of New South Wales. It is not necessary, for present purposes, to examine the correctness or the relevance of that particular finding in the context of the evidence in *Milirrpum*. The importance of the case for present purposes lies in Blackburn J.'s conclusion that, quite apart from that finding, there were general reasons of principle which precluded the plaintiffs' success. One was that a doctrine of common law native title had no place in a settled Colony except under express statutory provisions. Another was that, under any such doctrine, the narrow and somewhat rigid approach referred to in In re Southern Rhodesia would be appropriate and that the plaintiffs had failed to establish any pre-existing interest in relation to the land which satisfied the requirement that it be of the category of "rights of property". It should be apparent from what has been written above that we disagree with each of the above conclusions of general principle reached by Blackburn J. in *Milirrpum*. As has been seen, the doctrine of presumptive common law native title, which has long been recognized by the common law, is applicable to a settled British Colony.

(Ibid., at paragraphs 41 and 42, judgment of Deane and Gaudron JJ) *nullius* meant in law. The majority judgment in the *Advisory Opinion on Western Sahara*[26] noted that:

> The expression *'terra nullius'* was a legal term of art employed in connection with "occupation" as one of the accepted legal methods of acquiring sovereignty over territory. 'Occupation' being legally an original means of peaceably acquiring sovereignty over territory otherwise than by cession or succession, it was a cardinal condition of a valid 'occupation' that the territory should be *terra nullius*- a territory belonging to no-one — at the time of the act alleged to constitute the 'occupation' .... Whatever differences of opinion there may have been among jurists, the state practice of the relevant period indicates that territories inhabited by tribes or peoples having a social and political organization were not regarded as *terra nullius*.[27]

The Vice-President of the ICJ, Justice Ammoun, in a separate opinion supported the views of Mr. Bayona-Ba-Meya, Senior President of the Supreme Court of Zaire, and Mr. Mohammed Bedjaoui, Algerian Ambassador in Paris, representatives respectively of the Republic of Zaire and the Democratic and Popular Republic of Algeria regarding the concept of *terra nullius*. Justice Ammoun's views on *terra nullius* in his separate judgment deserve to be presented in full considering its explicit recognition of a biocultural relationship with the land. The majority in *Mabo No.2* concurred in their judgment with the views of Justice Ammoun where he noted:

> Mr. Bayona-Ba-Meya goes on to dismiss the materialistic concept of *terra nullius*, which led to this dismemberment of Africa following the Berlin Conference of 1885. Mr. Bayona-Ba-Meya substitutes for this a spiritual notion: the ancestral tie between the land, or "mother nature", and the man who was born therefrom, remains attached thereto, and must one day return thither to be united with his ancestors. This link is the basis of the ownership of the soil, or better, of sovereignty. This amounts to a denial of the very concept of *terra nullius* in the sense of a land which is capable of being appropriated by someone who is not born therefrom. It is a condemnation of the modern concept, as defined by Pasquale Fiore, which regards as *terra nullius* territories inhabited by populations whose civilization, in the sense of the public

[26] *Western Sahara, Advisory Opinion* I.C.J. Reports (1975), p. 12.
[27] Ibid., p. 39.

> law of Europe, is backward, and whose political organization is not conceived according to Western norms. One might go still further in analysing the statement of the representative of Zaire so as to say that he would exclude from the concept of *terra nullius* any inhabited territory. His view thus agrees with that of Vattel, who defined *terra nullius* as a land empty of inhabitants. This is the reply which may be given to the participants in the Berlin Conference of 1885, who, during the fierce blaze of nineteenth-century colonialism, the success of which they sought to ensure by eliminating competition, regarded sub-Saharan Africa as an immense *terra nullius* available for the first occupier, whereas that continent had been inhabited since prehistoric times, and flourishing kingdoms had there been established—Ghana, Mali, Bornu—whose civilization survived until the colonial period, and only succumbed to the wounds inflicted by colonization and the slave trade .... It was in the southern part of this continent and in Kenya that the ethnologists discovered the remains of the first hominoids.[28]

Justice Brennan and his fellow judges in *Mabo No. 2* relied on the advisory opinion of the ICJ in *Western Sahara* to overrule the views of Lord Sumner in *Inre Southern Rhodesia* and clarified that native title in common law is not extinguished simply because the administrators of the colonies did not think that the social organization of the natives met the standards of 'civilized society'. In situations of such a nature, one would do well to cleave to the dictum of Viscount Haldane in *Amodu Tijani* that native title should not be conceived of only in terms of English law but on its own terms.

Once the High Court of Australia had done away with the notion of *terra nullius* in the Australian context, it cleared the way for the recognition of native title in common law. Justice Brennan noted that the assertion of radical title by the Crown does not imply that the Crown acquires beneficial ownership of the land in question. He makes this point explicitly by the notion that 'it is only the fallacy of equating sovereignty and beneficial ownership of land that gives rise to the notion that native title is extinguished by the acquisition of sovereignty'.[29]

[28] Separate opinion of Ammoun J. Ibid., pp. 85–6.

[29] *Mabo No. 2*, paragraph 52, judgment of Brennan J.

Going further to clarify the different ways in which land is held by indigenous peoples and the need for legal recognition of the same, Justice Brennan notes:

> The fact that individual members of the community .... enjoy only usufructuary rights that are not proprietary in nature is no impediment to the recognition of a proprietary community title. Indeed, it is not possible to admit traditional usufructuary rights without admitting a traditional proprietary community title. There may be difficulties of proof of boundaries or of membership of the community or of representatives of the community which was in exclusive possession, but those difficulties afford no reason for denying the existence of a proprietary community title capable of recognition by common law.[30]

While the majority of the High Court of Australia were in agreement thus far, they still left open the question of whether and how native title could be extinguished by the state, and, if native title was extinguished, whether the communities who lost their lands were entitled to compensation. It was on this issue that the majority was spilt. Justices Brennan, Mason, and McHugh held that native title is a form of permissive occupancy at the will of the Crown, and Justices Toohey, Deane, and Gaudron held that, in the absence of clear and unambiguous statutory provisions to the contrary, extinguishment of native title by the Crown by inconsistent grant is wrongful and gives rise to a claim for compensatory damages.[31]

Justice Brennan on behalf of himself and Justices Mason and McHugh explained native title as a term that 'conveniently describes the rights and interests of indigenous inhabitants in land, whether communal, group or individual possessed *under the traditional laws acknowledged by and the traditional customs observed by the indigenous inhabitants*'[32] and that the dispossession of the indigenous peoples of Australia was not a result of the application of the principles of common law or the fact that native title did not survive the acquisition of sovereignty by the Crown but by the recurrent exercise of paramount power.[33] The real question then was whether

[30] *Mabo No. 2,* at paragraph 53, judgment of Brennan J.

[31] Ibid., at paragraph 2.

[32] Ibid., at paragraph 61, judgment of Brennan J.

[33] Ibid., at paragraph 63, judgment of Brennan J.

the exercise of paramount or executive power could validly extinguish native title, and on this issue the majority in *Mabo No.2* split.

Justice Brennan noted that native title is different from an interest in land granted by the Crown. He thereby distinguished between the rights of indigenous peoples to their lands in Australia and other Australians whose land was granted by the Crown or who purchased their lands according to statute. Outlining a rationale that posed a grave risk to native title, Justice Brennan noted:

> (A)n interest validly granted by the Crown or a right or interest dependent on an interest validly granted by the Crown cannot be extinguished by the Crown without statutory authority. As the Crown is not competent to derogate from a grant once made, a statute which confers a power on the Crown will be presumed (so far as consistent with the purpose for which the power is conferred) to stop short of authorizing any impairment of an interest in land granted by the Crown or dependent on a Crown grant. But, as native title is not granted by the Crown, there is no comparable presumption affecting the conferring of any executive power on the Crown the exercise of which is apt to extinguish native title.[34]

The implications of this view are grave for the security of native title. In effect, the executive, with no statutory authority, can decide to extinguish native title without necessarily getting the consent of the communities holding the native title.[35] What is worse is that an action by the executive that is inconsistent with native title could be tantamount to extinguishing that title. For example, a decision by the Crown to reallocate some of the land under native title for a public purpose could extinguish native title if it conflicted with such a purpose, irrespective of whether the Crown intended to extinguish it or not. This means public purpose as deemed by the Crown would always trump native title thus making native title particularly vulnerable. Justice Brennan notes that: 'A Crown grant which vests in the grantee an interest in land which is inconsistent

[34] Ibid., at paragraph 74, judgment of Brennan J.

[35] The judges here refused to make the concession of eminent domain for native title wherein full compensation would have to be paid when the executive expropriated private property for public good. See Secher, 'Implications of the Crown's Radical Title for Statutory Regimes Regulating the Alienation of Land' (2008).

with the continued right to enjoy a native title in respect of the same land necessarily extinguishes the native title'.[36]

Justices Brennan, Mason, and McHugh emphasized the vulnerability of native title by concluding that while such title remains unaffected by the Crown's acquisition of radical title, such an acquisition nevertheless exposes native title to extinguishment by a valid exercise of sovereign power inconsistent with the continued enjoyment of native title. Their brother judges, Justices Toohey, Deane, and Gaudron, however, strongly disagreed with this conclusion, arguing that it would exacerbate the vulnerability of native title to the extent that would render it hollow.

Justices Deane and Gaudron in their joint judgment added significant limitations to the executive's power to extinguish native title. They reasoned that even though native title, like other forms of property, can be extinguished by the state, it can only be done through legislation where it is stated in clear and unambiguous terms that there is an intent to expropriate native lands. The judges asserted in no uncertain terms that acts of the executive inconsistent with native title or general waste lands (or Crown lands) legislation cannot be construed, in the absence of clear words to this effect, as extinguishing or diminishing native title. The judges went so far as to say:

> If lands in relation to which such (native) title exists are clearly included within the ambit of such legislation, the legislative provisions conferring executive powers will, in the absence of clear and unambiguous words, be construed so as not to increase the capacity of the Crown to extinguish or diminish native title. That is to say, the power of the Crown wrongfully to extinguish the native title by inconsistent grant will remain but any liability of the Crown to pay compensatory damages for such wrongful extinguishment will be unaffected. The executive acts of the Crown under Crown or waste lands legislation will likewise be presumed not to have been intended to derogate from native title.[37]

[36] *Mabo No. 2,* at paragraph 81, judgment of Brennan J.

[37] Ibid., at paragraph 61, judgment of Deane and Gaudron JJ; *see also, The Commonwealth* v. *Hazeldell Ltd.* [1918] HCA 75; (1918) 25 CLR 552, at 563; *Central Control Board (Liquor Traffic)* v. *Cannon Brewery Company Ltd.* (1919) AC 744, at 752; *Clissold* v. *Perry* [1904] HCA 12; (1904) 1 CLR 363, at 373–4 (affirmed (1907) AC 73): a case dealing with possessory title.

Justice Toohey in a separate judgment went a step further to question the limits of the Crown's power to extinguish native title. Should the power be exercised only with the consent of the title holders or can it be exercised unilaterally? Is there a right to compensation by the titleholders whose rights have been extinguished or diminished? For Justice Toohey in order to establish native title, or what he refers to, as 'traditional title', the existence of an aboriginal society occupying the lands in question at the time of annexation has to be proved. However, the fact that this society has transformed does not extinguish native title. He says that:

> Traditional title arises from the fact of occupation, not the occupation of a particular kind of society or way of life. So long as occupation by a traditional society is established now and at the time of annexation, traditional rights exist. An indigenous society cannot, as it were, surrender its rights by modifying its way of life.[38]

The judges in *Mabo No. 2* however, did not dwell on the extent to which the lifestyle of an aboriginal community should change for it to lose its native title. Decisions thereafter, as we shall see, have further elaborated on the content of aboriginal or native title. But for now, the most significant aspect of Justice Toohey's judgment was his tracing of a clear line of authority in common law that restricted the power of the state or the Crown from unilaterally extinguishing native title. While agreeing that there is precedent supporting the power of the Crown to extinguish native title through legislating in clear and simple language, Justice Toohey stressed that there is no reason to treat native title as more vulnerable than other kinds of rights in land and stated that:

> [T]o say that, with the acquisition of sovereignty, the Crown has the power to extinguish traditional title does not necessarily mean that such a power is any different from that with respect to other interests in land. The Crown has the power, subject to constitutional, statutory or common law restrictions, to terminate any subject's title to property by compulsorily acquiring it.[39]

[38] Ibid., at paragraph 51, judgment of Toohey J.
[39] Ibid., at paragraph 55, judgment of Toohey J.

Justice Toohey noted that the tendency to think that native title is more vulnerable to extinguishment by the Crown than other kinds of title arises from the view that it is a 'personal or usufructuary right' as opposed to a 'proprietary right'. Here the judge underscored the principle of *Amodu Tijani*, where Viscount Haldane cautioned against understanding traditional title from the perspective of English law rather than by reference to the indigenous system. Justice Toohey concluded that the fact that native title could be personal or usufructuary should not make it any more vulnerable to extinguishment than other kinds of proprietary rights.

At this stage Justice Toohey was confronted with the same dilemma that confronted Justice Brennan: To limit the power of the Crown to extinguish native title would necessarily be to render a number of previous actions of the Crown acquiring aboriginal lands illegal thereby destabilizing the rights of the current occupants. At the same time not to subject the Crown's power to due process would be to continue to expose aboriginal peoples to the same kind of injustices of the past, in effect making their rights purely academic. Justice Brennan chose the more conservative route to resolve this dilemma. He stated that, as long as the extinguishment was for a public purpose, it was valid. Justice Toohey, on the other hand, chose the more progressive route, which he embarked upon only after firmly closing behind him any opening that could expose previous actions of the Crown to legal challenge. He did so by observing that:

> Where there has been an alienation of land by the Crown inimical to the continuance of traditional title, any remedy against the Crown may have been lost by the operation of limitation statutes. And nothing in this judgment should be taken to suggest that the titles of those to whom land has been alienated by the Crown may now be disturbed.[40]

Having thus secured the 'skeletal principle' of Australian law, Justice Toohey developed a line of reasoning initiated by the American courts on the 'fiduciary duty' of the Crown with respect to native title.[41] In responding to the plaintiffs' claim that the Crown was under

[40] *Mabo No. 2*, at paragraph 61, judgment of Toohey J.

[41] One of the earliest cases in this line of reasoning was *Cherokee Nation* v. *Georgia* 5 Peters 1 (1831) where Chief Justice Marshall held that the Indian

a fiduciary duty to recognize and protect the rights of the Meriam people to the Murray islands, Justice Toohey began with analysing the existence of fiduciary obligations of the Crown. The Government of Queensland argued that because they had the power to extinguish native title, they had no fiduciary obligations towards the holders of such title. However, Justice Toohey's response to this argument was counter-intuitive to the extent that he noted that the Crown's fiduciary obligations towards native titleholders arose precisely because the Crown had the power to extinguish or diminish native title.[42] Justice Toohey further noted that the fact that native title in common law jurisprudence is inalienable except to the Crown further affirmed the Crown's fiduciary duty to indigenous peoples. He elaborated:

---

tribes were akin to constitutional 'wards' under the 'guardianship' of the United States federal government. In *Seminole Nation* v. *US* 316 US 286 (1942) at 296–7, the US Supreme Court decided that the state's assumption of a trust implied a binding obligation. The trust, in other words, was to be interpreted in a strict or 'lower sense'. *Pyramid Lake Paiute Tribe* v. *Morton* 354 F Supp 252 (1972) at 256–7 established the principle that the government's responsibility as a trustee overrode whatever administrative powers it might enjoy. Soon afterwards, *Navajo Tribe* v. *US* 624 F2d 981 (1980) held that, when administering Indian property, the government was under a special duty of care and that, whenever the government had control of tribal moneys or property, it was subject to an actionable fiduciary duty, even though the statute or other foundation document specifying government powers had not mentioned a trust fund. The latter point was endorsed in *US* v. *Mitchell II* 463 US 206 (1983) where the Supreme Court held that a fiduciary obligation necessarily arose whenever the elements of a common-law trust were present—'a trustee (the United States), a beneficiary (the Indian allottees), and a trust corpus (Indian timber, lands, and funds)'—even though nothing was expressly said in the foundation document about a trust or fiduciary relationship. *See* Thomas W. Bennett et al., 'The State as Trustee of Land', *South African Journal of Human Rights* 16 (2000), pp. 601–22.

[42] *See also*, *Seminole Nation* v. *United States* 316 U.S. 286, 296–7 (1942) where the Court maintained that the government by entering into a treaty with the Indians has taken upon itself the 'moral obligations of the highest responsibility and trust,' and that its conduct will be scrutinized by 'the most exacting fiduciary standards'.

> [I]f the Crown in the right of Queensland has the power to alienate land the subject of the Meriam people's traditional rights and interests and the result of that alienation is the loss of traditional title, and if the Meriam people's power to deal with their title is restricted in so far as it is inalienable, except to the Crown, then this power and corresponding vulnerability give rise to a fiduciary obligation on the part of the Crown. *The power to destroy or impair people's interests in this way is extraordinary and is sufficient to attract regulation by Equity to ensure that the position is not abused. The fiduciary relationship arises, therefore, out of the power of the Crown to extinguish traditional title by alienating the land or otherwise; it does not depend on an exercise of that power* (emphasis mine).[43]

Justice Toohey went on to explain that the nature of this fiduciary obligation of the Crown was similar to that of a constructive trustee, since the legal interest in the traditional rights is in the Crown whereas the beneficial interest in the rights is in the indigenous owners. The content of this fiduciary obligation prima facie was a duty to act in the interest of the beneficiaries.

The cutting edge of Justice Toohey's judgment however, lies in his reasoning that a fiduciary obligation puts a special burden on the Crown not to act in a way that unduly impairs the interests of the indigenous peoples. Interestingly these views undercut the position of Justice Brennan, by implying that the Crown cannot discharge its duty by merely claiming that the extinguishing or diminishing of native title is for a public purpose. On the contrary, the Crown's primary duty in the case of native title is towards the indigenous holders of this title which overrides any larger public purpose intent of the Crown.

This means that consultation with and the consent of the native title holders is imperative to fulfil the Crown's fiduciary duty before it takes any decision to impair native title. By reasoning thus, Justice Toohey conclusively restricted the Crown's power to extinguish native title thereby providing native title the security it had been historically denied.

The majority in *Mabo No.2* agreed that native title in common law survived the assertion of sovereignty by the Crown, thereby

[43] *Mabo No. 2*, at paragraph 85, judgment of Toohey J.

entitling indigenous people to beneficial ownership of their traditional lands. The precedent value of *Mabo No.2* for indigenous peoples' rights in common law jurisprudence is significant since it recognized customary land rights in the common law. In many ways *Mabo No.2* opened the door to protecting other forms of property in Anglo-American jurisprudence, forms of property that went beyond absolute ownership of fungible assets to personal, usufructuary, and communal biocultural relations to traditional lands. However the critical question that split the majority still remained: what are the limits to state power in the context of land rights of indigenous peoples and traditional communities? Is this power unmitigated as Justices Brennan, McHugh, and Mason held or is it strictly restricted, as Justices Toohey, Gaudron, and Deane believed?

BEYOND MABO: CLARIFYING ABORIGINAL TITLE IN *DELGAMUUKW* V. *BRITISH COLUMBIA*[44]

> *A total of 61 witnesses gave evidence at trial, many using translators from their native Gitksan or Wet'suwet'en language; 'word spellers' to assist the official reporters were required for many witnesses; a further 15 witnesses gave their evidence on commission; 53 territorial affidavits were filed; 30 deponents were cross-examined out of court; there are 23,503 pages of transcript evidence at trial; 5898 pages of transcript of argument; 3,039 pages of commission evidence and 2,553 pages of cross-examination on affidavits (all evidence and oral arguments are conveniently preserved in hard copy and on diskettes); about 9,200 exhibits were filed at trial comprising, I estimate, well over 50,000 pages; the plaintiffs' draft outline of argument comprises 3,250 pages, the province's 1,975 pages, and Canada's over 1,000 pages; there are 5,977 pages of transcript of argument in hard copy and on diskettes. All parties filed some excerpts from the exhibits they referred to in argument. The province alone submitted 28 huge binders of such documents. At least 15 binders of reply argument were left with me during that stage of the trial.*
>
> — *Chief Justice McEachern's description of the trial at the British Columbia Supreme Court*[45]

[44] *Delgamuukw* v. *British Columbia* (1997) 3 S.C.R. 1010. [hereinafter *Delgamuukw* (1997)].

[45] (1991) 3 W.W.R. 97 at 116–17.

The trial of *Delgamuukw* v. *British Columbia* at the British Columbia Supreme Court heard 318 days of testimony and resulted in a 400-page judgment by the trial judge with another 100 pages of schedules.[46] The proceedings began in 1984 with a claim from the hereditary chiefs of the Gitksan and Wet'suwet'en First Nations, who, both individually and on behalf of their 'Houses', claimed 'ownership' of territory and 'jurisdiction' over separate portions of 58,000 square kilometres in British Columbia. The claim for jurisdiction meant that, where there was a conflict between tribal and provincial law, the tribal law would prevail.

For the purpose of the claim, the area was divided into 133 individual territories, claimed by 71 Houses. This represented all of the Wet'suwet'en people, and all but 12 of the Gitksan Houses. The province of British Columbia counter-claimed for a declaration that the Gitksan and Wet'suwet'en had no right to or interest in the territory or alternatively, that their cause of action ought to be for compensation from the Government of Canada.

In 1991 the British Columbia Supreme Court held that aboriginal title was limited to aboriginal rights and did not extend beyond occupation or use of land to hunt, fish, collect wood, berries, and other foods for sustenance in a traditional manner. This meant that, while Canadian law recognized the rights of aboriginal people to carry on some of their traditional practices, it did not recognize customary law relating to land title.

The Supreme Court also held that the rights of the Gitksan and Wet'suwet'en were extinguished through pre-Confederation enactments providing unencumbered titles to settlers, and that the land of the Gitksan and Wet'suwet'en became vested in the Imperial Crown upon its assertion of sovereignty over the mainland colony of British Columbia in the early or mid-nineteenth Century. Finally the Court ruled that since its entry into Confederation in 1871, the Province of British Columbia had the right to dispose of Crown lands unburdened by aboriginal title, and the right to govern the province within the terms of Section 92 of the Constitution Act, 1867.[47] This meant that the aboriginal title claimed by the tribes no

[46] *Delgamuukw* (1997), at 1028.

[47] Mary C. Hurley, *Aboriginal Title: The Supreme Court of Canada Decision in Delgamuukw v. British Columbia*, Law and Government

longer existed and the Gitksan and Wet'suwet'en would not qualify to claim their rights under Section 35(1) of the Constitution Act of 1982 that sought to recognize existing rights of aboriginal peoples in Canada.

The Gitksan and Wet'suwet'en appealed the decision of the Supreme Court to the British Columbia Court of Appeal, which heard 374 days of evidence and arguments. In 1993 the Court of Appeal overturned the decision of the Supreme Court stating that the rights of the Gitksan and Wet'suwet'en's had not been extinguished and were protected by common law, and, since 1982 by Section 35 (1) of the Constitution Act. The scope and content of these rights was not addressed by the Court of Appeal, which referred these issues back to the trial judge. Nevertheless the Court of Appeal asked the parties to resolve their differences through consultation and negotiation.

In March 1994 the parties were granted leave to appeal and cross-appeal the decision of the Court of Appeal to the Supreme Court of Canada. In the meantime the parties requested an adjournment of proceedings to try to work out a negotiated settlement. By February 1996, the negotiations between the Gitksan and British Columbia's Ministry of Aboriginal Affairs were deadlocked. The parties then decided to continue with the proceedings before the Supreme Court of Canada.[48]

The Supreme Court of Canada did not enter into the merits of the case to decide whether or not the Gitksan and Wet'suwet'en had aboriginal title to the lands that they claimed. Instead it ordered a new trial on the basis that the trial judge had not given due weight to the oral histories of the tribes. In addition the Court gave a groundbreaking decision clarifying the content of aboriginal title in Canada, the power of the state to extinguish or diminish aboriginal title, and the evidentiary value of oral histories in establishing aboriginal title.

Chief Justice Lamer, who handed down the judgment on behalf of his fellow justices, began by examining the status of oral histories as evidence in establishing aboriginal title. The contention of the

---

Division, Parliamentary Information and Research Service (January 1998, revised February 2000).

[48] Ibid.

Gitksan and Wet'suwet'en was that the trial judge did not give due weight to the *adaawk* of the Gitksan and the *kungax* of the Wet'suwet'en. The *adaawk* and the *kungax* are:

> (S)acred official litany, or history, or recital of the most important laws, history, traditions and traditional territory of a House. The content of these special oral histories includes a physical representation in totem poles, crests and blankets. Their importance is underlined by the fact that they are repeated and performed and authenticated at important feasts.[49]

At the trial the *adaawk* was relied upon as an aspect of and proof of land tenure law of the Gitksan and evidence of their historical use and occupation of the lands to which they claimed title. The *kungax* was relied upon by the Wet'suwet'en as the main proof of the significance of the lands to the culture of the tribe. The trial judge had refused to give any independent weight to these histories to establish aboriginal title of the Gitksan and Wet'suwet'en. Instead, he held that oral traditions at best can be used to confirm the facts established by other forms of evidence. The judge noted that it was not easy to distinguish between the mythological and real aspects of oral history; oral history tended to confound facts and beliefs and projected a romantic view of the history of the tribes. Most importantly, the trial judge felt that the *adaawk* and *kungax* lacked the necessary detail regarding the specific lands that were being claimed.[50]

The Supreme Court of Canada overruled the trial judge's reasoning and ordered a new trial, thereby breaking new ground on recognition of non-codified and oral customary laws and traditions relating to community land rights. This Court noted that, if the oral traditions of the Gitksan and Wet'suwet'en had been given due weight, the conclusions of the trial judge on fact may have been different. It stressed that, if the trial judge's understanding of oral evidence were upheld, then the oral histories of aboriginal peoples would be 'consistently and systematically undervalued by the Canadian legal system'.[51] Chief Justice Lamer quoted with approval the 1996 *Report*

[49] *Delgamuukw* (1997), paragraph 93, judgment of Lamer, C.J.
[50] Ibid., at paragraph 97, judgment of Lamer, C.J.
[51] Ibid., at paragraph 98, judgment of Lamer, C.J.

of the Royal Commission on Aboriginal Peoples as a useful approach to understanding oral history:

> The Aboriginal tradition in the recording of history is neither linear nor steeped in the same notions of social progress and evolution [as in the non-Aboriginal tradition]. Nor is it usually human-centred in the same way as the western scientific tradition, for it does not assume that human beings are anything more than one—and not necessarily the most important—element of the natural order of the universe. Moreover, the Aboriginal historical tradition is an oral one, involving legends, stories and accounts handed down through the generations in oral form. It is less focused on establishing objective truth and assumes that the teller of the story is so much a part of the event being described that it would be arrogant to presume to classify or categorize the event exactly or for all time. In the Aboriginal tradition the purpose of repeating oral accounts from the past is broader than the role of written history in western societies. It may be to educate the listener, to communicate aspects of culture, to socialize people into a cultural tradition, or to validate the claims of a particular family to authority and prestige .... Oral accounts of the past include a good deal of subjective experience. They are not simply a detached recounting of factual events but, rather, are 'facts enmeshed in the stories of a lifetime'. They are also likely to be rooted in particular locations, making reference to particular families and communities. This contributes to a sense that there are many histories, each characterized in part by how a people see themselves, how they define their identity in relation to their environment, and how they express their uniqueness as a people.[52]

Giving of independent weight to the oral traditions of aboriginal customary laws was a jurisprudential landmark. It paved the way for courts to appreciate aboriginal worldviews wherein traditional lands are not identified with title deeds or even occupation, but through relationships that include stories, songs, myths, and legends. Having ordered a retrial with an instruction to the trial court to give the oral traditions of the Gitksan and Wet'suwet'en independent and not

[52] *Report of the Royal Commission on Aboriginal Peoples*, Vol. 1: Looking Forward, Looking Back (1996), p. 33, quoted by Lamer C.J., Ibid., at paragraph 85.

merely confirmatory weight in establishing aboriginal title, Chief Justice Lamer turned his attention to the content of the title.

In the first place, he needed to make a clear distinction between aboriginal title and aboriginal rights. The trial court had held that aboriginal title is essentially a bundle of aboriginal rights and did not extend beyond occupation or use of land to hunt, fish, collect wood, berries, and other foods for sustenance in a traditional manner. Chief Justice Lamer noted that:

> Aboriginal title is a right in land and, as such, is more than the right to engage in specific activities which may be themselves aboriginal rights. Rather, it confers the right to use land for a variety of activities, not all of which need be aspects of practices, customs and traditions which are integral to the distinctive cultures of aboriginal societies. Those activities do not constitute the right *per se*; rather, they are parasitic on the underlying title. *However, that range of uses is subject to the limitation that they must not be irreconcilable with the nature of the attachment to the land which forms the basis of the particular group's aboriginal title* (emphasis mine).[53]

With this understanding of aboriginal title, Chief Justice Lamer did two things. First, he extended aboriginal title beyond the right to merely carry on traditional activities on aboriginal lands. Secondly, he limited the title to the fact that such activities should not be in direct conflict with the biocultural relations with the land that forms the basis of the title. While noting that aboriginal title is *sui generis* and that its elements include its inalienability, occupation by the tribes prior to annexation, and communal control, Justice Lamer stressed its inherent limits: that '*lands held pursuant to aboriginal title cannot be used in a manner that is irreconcilable with the nature of attachment to the land which forms the basis of the group's claim to the aboriginal title*'.[54]

The Supreme Court of Canada, by establishing this limit, clearly located aboriginal title in a category that was different from other kinds of land title. The Court seemed to emphasize that aboriginal title was based on a special relationship with the land, which could

[53] *Delgamuukw* (1997), at paragraph 111, judgment of Lamer, C.J.
[54] Ibid., at paragraph 124, judgment of Lamer, C.J.

well be interpreted as a biocultural relationship and that any activities undertaken by the tribe which would threaten such a relationship would weaken the title. It is submitted that by approaching aboriginal title in this fashion, it appears that the Court stressed the tribe's duty of stewardship. While such an approach has been viewed by some commentators as a patronizing limit on aboriginal self-government,[55] it would help to dwell rather on the rationale provided by Chief Justice Lamer for taking such an approach.

The Chief Justice explained:

> Accordingly, in my view, lands subject to aboriginal title cannot be put to such uses as may be irreconcilable with the nature of the occupation of that land and the relationship that the particular group has had with the land which together have given rise to aboriginal title in the first place ... one of the critical elements in the determination of whether a particular aboriginal group has aboriginal title to certain lands is the matter of the occupancy of those lands. Occupancy is determined by reference to the activities that have taken place on the land and the uses to which the land has been put by the particular group. If lands are so occupied, there will exist a special bond between the group and the land in question such that the land will be part of the definition of the group's distinctive culture. It seems to me that these elements of aboriginal title create an inherent limitation on the uses to which the land, over which such title exists, may be put. For example, if occupation is established with reference to the use of the land as a hunting ground, then the group that successfully claims aboriginal title to that land may not use it in such a fashion as to destroy its value for such a use (e.g., by strip mining it). Similarly, if a group claims a special bond with the land because of its ceremonial or cultural significance, it may not use the land in such a way as to destroy that relationship (e.g., by developing it in such a way that the bond is destroyed, perhaps by turning it into a parking lot).[56]

By reasoning thus, it could be argued that the Supreme Court of Canada based aboriginal title not purely on the fact that the tribes

[55] Kent McNeil, *Defining Aboriginal Title in the 90's: Has the Supreme Court Finally Got it Right?*, 12th Annual Robarts Lecture, York University, Toronto, Ontario (25 March 1998).

[56] *Delgamuukw* (1997), paragraph 128, judgment of Lamer, C.J.

occupied the lands at the time of annexation by the Crown, but also on a special biocultural relationship with the land. In a sense, this line of reasoning is linked to Chief Justice Lamer's views on the admissibility of and weight that needs to be given to oral histories in establishing aboriginal title. Oral histories in many ways establish occupation through emphasizing specific cultural and spiritual ties to the land which are ritualized through stories, songs, and myths. These cultural and spiritual ties assert that the aboriginal community in question does not just refer to any land (or land as a fungible asset), but to specific traditional land that defines them as a people. Such an approach to land, according to the Supreme Court, necessarily makes aboriginal title inalienable.

Elaborating on this view Chief Justice Lamer notes:

> It is for this reason also that lands held by virtue of aboriginal title may not be alienated. Alienation would bring to an end the entitlement of the aboriginal people to occupy the land and would terminate their relationship with it .... *What the inalienability of lands held pursuant to aboriginal title suggests is that those lands are more than just a fungible commodity. The relationship between an aboriginal community and the lands over which it has aboriginal title has an important non-economic component. The land has an inherent and unique value in itself, which is enjoyed by the community with aboriginal title to it* (emphasis mine). The community cannot put the land to uses which would destroy that value.[57]

Having said this Justice Lamer, expanded further on the nature of aboriginal title, thereby distinguishing it from aboriginal rights. He emphasized that a variety of aboriginal rights can be contained within aboriginal title, but that the main difference between them is the proof needed to establish them. In order to assert title the tribe must prove occupancy of the lands at the time the Crown asserted sovereignty. So, the fact that a group is able to make out a claim for aboriginal rights would not necessarily imply an aboriginal title. Chief Justice Lamer elucidated this as:

> Constitutionally recognized aboriginal rights fall along a spectrum with respect to their degree of connection with the land. At the one end

[57] Ibid., at paragraph 129, judgment of Lamer, C.J.

are those aboriginal rights which are practices, customs and traditions integral to the distinctive aboriginal culture of the group claiming the right but where the use and occupation of the land where the activity is taking place is not sufficient to support a claim of title to the land. In the middle are activities which, out of necessity, take place on land and indeed, might be intimately related to a particular piece of land. Although an aboriginal group may not be able to demonstrate title to the land, it may nevertheless have a site-specific right to engage in a particular activity. At the other end of the spectrum is aboriginal title itself which confers more than the right to engage in site-specific activities which are aspects of the practices, customs and traditions of distinctive aboriginal cultures.[58]

The next significant question addressed by the Court was the power of the federal and provincial governments to diminish or extinguish aboriginal rights and title. Here Chief Justice Lamer and his brother judges did agree that, in common law, aboriginal rights or title are not absolute and can be infringed. The Canadian Supreme Court however, differed from the views of Justice Brennan in *Mabo No. 2* by requiring a much heavier burden on the government when it sought to do so. The Court in Canada laid down two conditions: an infringement must further a compelling and substantial legislative objective; it must be consistent with the fiduciary duties of the Crown to the aboriginal peoples.[59]

At this stage the Canadian Supreme Court seemed to give the Crown a fairly generous power to infringe aboriginal title and rights by stating that a general public purpose like the development of agriculture, forestry, mining, and hydroelectric power, the general economic development of the interior of British Columbia, protection of the environment or endangered species, and the building of infrastructure and the settlement of foreign populations to support those aims, can be sufficient reason for infringement. At the same time, however, the Court limited this power by stressing the Crown's fiduciary duty to act in the interests of the aboriginal peoples.

Chief Justice Lamer listed three aspects of this duty:

[58] Ibid., p. 8.

[59] Ibid., pp. 1021.

> First, the right to exclusive use and occupation of land is relevant to the degree of scrutiny of the infringing measure or action. Second, the right to choose to what uses land can be put, subject to the ultimate limit that those uses cannot destroy the ability of the land to sustain future generations of aboriginal peoples, suggests that the fiduciary relationship between the Crown and aboriginal peoples may be satisfied by the involvement of aboriginal peoples in decisions taken with respect to their lands. There is always a duty of consultation and, in most cases, the duty will be significantly deeper than mere consultation. And third, lands held pursuant to aboriginal title have an inescapable economic component which suggests that compensation is relevant to the question of justification as well. Fair compensation will ordinarily be required when aboriginal title is infringed.[60]

Compared with decision of the High Court of Australia in *Mabo No. 2*, the Supreme Court of Canada in *Delgamuukw* restricted the power of the Crown to infringe or extinguish aboriginal rights and title to a much greater extent. In *Delgamuukw* the Court held that depending on the strength of the right or the title, it could be argued that consultation with and sometimes consent of the aboriginal tribes in question would be required prior to any state action. Nevertheless, in cases where there is an infringement by the Crown of aboriginal title, compensation would have to be provided to the aboriginal tribes concerned.

Indigenous Title in Africa: Alexkor Limited v. The Richtersveld Community[61]

> *While in the past indigenous law was seen through the common law lens, it must now be seen as an integral part of our law. Like all law it depends for its ultimate force and validity on the Constitution. Its validity must now be determined by reference not to common law, but to the Constitution .... It is clear, therefore that the Constitution acknowledges the originality and distinctiveness of indigenous law as an independent source of norms within the legal system. At the same time the*

[60] *Delgamuukw* (1997) p. 1021.

[61] (CCT19/03) [2003] ZACC 18; 2003 (12) BLR 1301 (CC) (hereinafter *Richtersveld*).

Constitution, while giving force to indigenous law, makes it clear that such law is subject to the Constitution and has to be interpreted in the light of its values. Furthermore, like the common law, indigenous law is subject to any legislation, consistent with the Constitution that specifically deals with it. In the result, indigenous law feeds into, nourishes, fuses with and becomes part of the amalgam of South African law.

— Judgment of the Constitutional Court of South Africa in Alexkor v. The Richtersveld Community[62]

The decisions of the High Court of Australia in *Mabo No.2* and the Supreme Court of Canada in *Delgamuukw* were not alone in recognizing native or aboriginal title. The Constitutional Court in South Africa in 2003 handed down a significant judgement recognizing the indigenous title of the Richtersveld community to their traditional lands. In doing so the Court clarified the status of indigenous land rights in South Africa vis-à-vis both common law and the South African Constitution.

The Richtersveld is an area of land in the Northern Cape Province of South Africa that had for centuries been inhabited by the Richtersveld community. In the 1920s, when diamonds were discovered, the state dispossessed the community of its lands. In 1994 after the end of apartheid and the first democratic elections, the new South African government passed the Restitution of Land Rights Act of 1994[63] which entitled communities dispossessed of their lands after 19 June 1913 resulting from past racially discriminatory laws to claim restitution of such lands. The Richtersveld community then lodged a claim for their traditional lands with the Land Claims Court. In 2001 the Land Court dismissed the claim. The community appealed the decision to the Supreme Court of Appeal, which set aside the order and granted relief to the community. Both Alexkor (which is a South African state-owned mining company with interests in the Richtersveld) and the South African government then appealed the decision of the Supreme Court of Appeal to the Constitutional Court of South Africa. The latter decided in favour of the Richtersveld community holding that it had a right to ownership

[62] Ibid., at paragraph 51.

[63] Act 22 of 1994.

of traditional lands (including its minerals and precious stones) and to the exclusive beneficial use and occupation of the land.[64]

The Constitutional Court relied on the same common law precedents as those used by the High Court of Australia and the Supreme Court of Canada to affirm that indigenous title survived the British Crown's assertion of radical title over the lands of the Richtersveld community through annexation in 1847. The difference in the South African situation however, was the Richtersveld community's dispossession of their lands under the Precious Stones Act of 1927. This enactment allowed the community's land to be proclaimed as unalienated Crown land.

Although the community's title to land was recognized in indigenous or customary law, this title was not registered by the state thereby allowing for the community to be dispossessed of its lands. The Richtersveld people sought to make their claim for land restitution on the basis of the limited retrospective provision of the Restitution of Land Rights Act arguing that they were dispossessed of their lands after 19 June 1913, and that this was a result of a racially discriminatory practice of the state not recognizing indigenous title to land.

The unique contribution of the *Richtersveld case* and in this sense the Restitution of Land Rights Act was that it established that, even if indigenous title was extinguished by an Act of state, it could be restored if the title were extinguished after 19 June 1913 which was when the Natives Land Act 27 of 1913[65] came into operation. (The latter Act deprived black South Africans of the right to own land and rights in land in large parts of South Africa). The Constitutional Court in the *Richtersveld* case also established the precedent that a claim of sovereignty by the Crown in 1847 did not extinguish indigenous title.

Perhaps one of the most significant assertions of the Constitutional Court was that indigenous or customary law title is sufficient to establish beneficial ownership and rights over land and that indigenous

[64] *Richtersveld*, paragraph 103; *See generally*, Ülgen Özelem, 'Developing the Doctrine of Aboriginal Title in South Africa: Source and Content', *Journal of African Law* 46(2002) pp. 131–54.

[65] Act 27 of 1913.

title must be understood on its own terms and not in accordance with common law. The Court citing the views of Viscount Haldane in *Amodu Tijani* concluded that:

> [W]e are of the view that the real character of the title that the Richtersveld Community possessed in the subject land was a right of communal ownership under indigenous law. The content of that right included the right to exclusive occupation and use of the subject land by members of the Community. The Community had the right to use its water, to use its land for grazing and hunting and to exploit its natural resources, above and beneath the surface. It follows therefore that prior to annexation the Richtersveld Community had a right of ownership in the subject land under indigenous law.[66]

In a radical pronouncement that went further than the decisions of the courts of Australia and Canada, the South African Court stated that actions of the state that did not recognize customary or indigenous land title would be tantamount to racially discriminatory practices if these actions tended to affect particular communities disproportionately. The Constitutional Court noted that:

> Accordingly, the Precious Stones Act and its Proclamations failed to recognise indigenous law ownership and treated the subject land as state land. On the other hand, registered ownership was recognised, respected and protected. For the most part, whites held their land under the system of registered ownership, though there were some black people and black communities who did acquire title of this sort. However, given that indigenous law ownership is the way in which black communities have held land in South Africa since time immemorial, the inevitable impact of the Precious Stones Act's failure to recognise indigenous law ownership was racially discriminatory against black people who were indigenous law owners. The laws and practices by which the Richtersveld Community was dispossessed of the subject land accordingly discriminated against the Community and its members on the ground of race.[67]

The Court continued:

> In this case, the racial discrimination lay in the failure to recognise and accord protection to indigenous law ownership while, on the

[66] *Richtersveld*, paragraph 64.
[67] Ibid., at paragraph 95.

> other hand, according protection to registered title. The inevitable impact of this differential treatment was racial discrimination against the Richtersveld Community, which caused it to be dispossessed of its land rights. Although it is correct that the Precious Stones Act did not form part of the panoply of legislation giving effect to 'spatial apartheid', its inevitable impact was to deprive the Richtersveld Community of its indigenous law rights in land while recognising, to a significant extent, the rights of registered owners. In our view, this is racially discriminatory ....[68]

While the decision of the Constitutional Court of South Africa is informed by common law, Roman-Dutch law and the South African Constitution, its judgment can be placed within the tradition of Anglo-American jurisprudence dealing with indigenous title beginning with *Mabo No. 2* and later continuing through to *Delgamuukw*. Each of these decisions symbolizes steps towards the recognition of customary land title and therefore, customary law itself.

Biocultural Rights and Customary Land Title

While the recognition of customary land title in Anglo-American jurisprudence is for the most part a result of challenges by indigenous or aboriginal peoples, these jurisprudential victories have added a significant momentum to biocultural rights. In a number of common law countries, the call for recognition of customary land titles is led by communities whose claims are not necessarily rooted in their aboriginal status but rather in the fact that they have been stewards of these lands for generations.

The recognition of customary land title in the form of native, aboriginal, or indigenous title is a significant advance in Anglo-American jurisprudence. As the Supreme Court of Canada in *Delgamuukw* pointed out, in many cases aboriginal rights are dependent on aboriginal title. Aboriginal title itself, while a beneficial form of interest in traditional lands is limited by a stewardship duty imposed on the tribes not to use the lands in a manner that is irreconcilable with those aspects of aboriginal culture that form the basis of the community's connection with the land.

[68] *Richtersveld*, at paragraph 99.

Both the Australian High Court and the Supreme Court of Canada emphasized that the state is not free to expropriate title or diminish it at will in accordance with its general power of eminent domain. Instead it has a fiduciary obligation to protect customary title realized in a requirement to consult and where necessary seek the consent of or compensate aboriginal communities where their title is to be diminished or extinguished. In addition of course, the state will be expected to pay compensation for the loss of rights. The Constitutional Court of South Africa went as far as to say that non-recognition of customary title when it disproportionately affects particular communities can be interpreted as racially discriminatory.

The line between recognition of biocultural rights and customary title to land is implicit although there is an overlap between the two. While the recognition of customary title to land usually involves remedying historical injustices, biocultural rights rely on stewardship of ecosystems for their justification. The point of overlap exists where both customary title and biocultural rights assert strong communal cultural and spiritual bonds to certain lands: bonds that render these lands as non-fungible, inalienable, and lie at the heart of peoplehood.

The Richtersveld community though belonging to the indigenous Nama community, grounded their claim not only on their indigeneity but also on historical occupation of their lands. In other common law countries such as India, it is clear that community rights to their traditional lands are no longer rooted in establishing indigeneity but in stewardship. The recent Indian *Scheduled Tribes and Other Traditional Forest Dwellers (Recognition of Forest Rights) Act of 2006* is an important case in point. The Act recognizes the customary use rights of all forest dwelling communities and in its preamble seeks to remedy the injustices caused to these communities during colonial times and post-independence. The biocultural dimension of this Act lies in the wording in its preamble where it affirms the responsibility and the authority of these communities to conserve biodiversity and maintain an ecological balance. Furthermore, the Act conclusively underscores stewardship duties of communities by including a section on 'Duties of Forest Rights Holders', which is unprecedented in any previous Indian law relating to forests.[69]

[69] Section 5 of the Forest Rights Act states that the holders of any forest right under this Act are empowered to:

The most explicit in recognition of biocultural rights in the form of stewardship duties is the 2010 Bolivian '*Law on the Rights of Mother Earth*', an unprecedented law to grant a personified Nature equal rights to humans.[70] The law establishes eleven new rights for Nature. These include: the right to life and to exist; the right to continue vital cycles and processes free from human alteration; the right to pure water and clean air; the right to balance; the right not to be polluted; the right to not have cellular structures modified or genetically altered; and the right not to be affected by mega-infrastructure and development projects that affect the balance of ecosystems and local inhabitant communities. In the same vein, Ecuador has changed its constitution to give Nature 'the right to exist, persist, maintain and regenerate its vital cycles, structure, functions and its processes in evolution'.[71]

Despite the differences between customary land title and biocultural rights, it is impossible to speak of either without seeing how the cases concerning both these concepts are fundamentally linked. In fact, the ethic that underlies both these concepts is one that sees land not purely as a tradable commodity but as the very soul of a people. Communities have slowly begun to innovate with legal instruments like trusts and biocultural community protocols to secure their biocultural rights. We shall explore these innovations in the concluding chapter.

(a) protect the wild life, forest, and biodiversity;
(b) ensure that adjoining catchments area, water sources, and other ecological sensitive areas are adequately protected;
(c) ensure that the habitat of forest dwelling Scheduled Tribes and other traditional forest dwellers is preserved from any form of destructive practices affecting their cultural and natural heritage;
(d) ensure that the decisions taken in the Gram Sabha to regulate access to community forest resources and stop any activity which adversely affects the wild animals, forest, and the biodiversity are complied with.

[70] *Ley de Derechos de la Madre Tierra*, Law 071 of the Plurinational State passed by Bolivia's Plurinational Legislative Assembly in December 2010.

[71] John Vidal, 'Bolivia Enshrines Natural World's Rights with Equal Status for Mother Earth', *The Guardian*, Sunday, 10 April 2011.

CHAPTER NINE

Biocultural Community Protocols

Towards a Pluralism of Property

Resources are fundamentally a matter of relationships, not things. They do not exist outside of the complex relationships between society, technology, culture, economics and environment in some pre-ordinated form.

— *Richie Howitt*, 'Frontiers, Borders, Edges: Liminal Challenges to the Hegemony of Exclusion'[1]

The focus thus far has been twofold: First, to deconstruct the notion of property and break it down to its building blocks, that is, that property is a legally enforceable claim or a relationship between people rather than a thing and that property rights must be justified in the context of human or community welfare. Second, through highlighting trends in international and domestic law it has been shown that international jurisprudence is beginning to recognize that stewardship of the land can be a stick in the bundle of property rights.[2] In fact, the trends over the last three decades

[1] Richie Howitt, 'Frontiers, Borders, Edges: Liminal Challenges to the Hegemony of Exclusion', *Australian Geographical Studies* 39(2) (2001), pp. 233–45.

[2] Justice Benjamin Cardozo has been credited with developing this metaphor: 'The bundle of power and privileges to which we give the name of ownership is not constant through the ages. The faggots must be put together and rebound from time to time' in Benjamin N. Cardozo, *The Paradoxes of Legal Science* (New York: Columbia University Press, 1928), p. 129. In several opinions, Justices of the Supreme Court of the United States have invoked this image to describe the fullest possible set of private property rights, *see Kaiser Aetna* v. *US*, 444 U.S. 164 (1979) at 176 (referring to 'sticks in the bundle of rights that are commonly characterized as property'); *US* v. *Craft*, 535 U.S. 274 (2002) at 278 ('A common idiom

suggest that the narrowing down of the concept of property in the seventeenth century from a set of enforceable relationships to a privately owned thing has been on the wane. Instead there has been a steady re-expansion of the grounds on which claims to property (whether land or natural resources) can be made.

Based on growing evidence that the environmental crisis is a result of delinking property rights (private property) from their social and environmental functions, law makers and judges have been forced to recognize property claims that go beyond pure legal title.[3] These claims are based on alternative ethical criteria that challenge ownership as the only criterion to justify a property claim. As discussed previously, all claims to property are based on a particular conception of personhood and the individual's well-being. A claim to private property is based on a conflation of personhood with the *homo economicus* thereby identifying human and societal well-being with the law's ability to secure the interests of the *homo economicus.*

The emergence of stewardship as an ethical justification for community property claims has sought to limit the unconditional nature of private property claims that abjure all environmental responsibilities. As shown earlier, Articles 8(j) and 10(c) of the CBD laid the foundations for stewardship as a legal ground for community property claims. Article 8(j) obliges state parties to respect, preserve, and maintain knowledge, innovations, and practices of indigenous and local communities embodying traditional lifestyles relevant for the conservation and sustainable use of biodiversity. Article 10(c) goes further by requiring state parties to protect and encourage customary use of biological resources in accordance with traditional cultural practices compatible with the conservation and sustainable use of biodiversity.

While multilateral environmental agreements, since the CBD entered into force in 1993, have ensured that community property claims based on stewardship are here to stay, it will be some time

---

describes property as a "bundle of sticks" ...') cited in Robert Ellickson, 'Two Cheers for the Bundle-of-Sticks Metaphor, Three Cheers for Merrill and Smith', *Econ Journal Watch* 8(3) (September 2011), pp. 215–22.

[3] *See* Chapter One.

before the decisions of regional tribunals and domestic courts entertain this principle as a standalone criterion to justify a property claim. However, it appears from the case law analysed above[4] that judges tend to support or deny a property claim based on a number of criteria ranging from legal title to long-term possession to cultural attachment to stewardship. In the highly contested community claims to property rights, it appears that the courts reason their decisions on an approach that seeks to bind together different kinds of claims all of which together make up a community's legally recognized right to property. In such an approach a property claim does not stand or fall based on just one factor but a multitude of factors *including* stewardship.

For this reason it would be difficult to make the case that we have reached a stage where *only* evidence of historical stewardship would ensure a better title to property (specifically land or natural resources) than a claim that is based on a title deed. However, evidence from case law shows that a claim of historical stewardship together with long occupation by a community or cultural attachment stands a strong chance of trumping a property claim that is based purely on legal title. The litmus test of whether evidence of historical stewardship actually contributes to strengthening a property claim would have to be based on whether an absence of that same evidence would weaken a claim notwithstanding proof of long occupation and use.

What comes through clearly in nearly all the cases of the regional and domestic courts discussed previously is that property claims led by indigenous or tribal communities invariably present evidence of historical stewardship resulting from strong cultural and spiritual bonds with the property in question. The subtext in the arguments presented by communities and the reasoning of the courts in these cases mirror Radin's argument that a personal property claim should trump a fungible property claim (that is, evidence by the state that the title to the land belongs to the government to lease freely to mining or timber companies).

In fact, what establishes the significance of evidence of stewardship is the courts' concentration on the nature of the community's

[4] *See* Chapters Seven and Eight.

relationship with its lands, and emphasis on its non-fungible nature. The final decision by the courts in the cases discussed previously upholds community claims of 'personal' property over competing claims by the state to the land as a fungible asset. The communities did not simply claim 'any land' but the territory of their ancestors dense with cultural and spiritual significance. The land, in fact, defined them as a people. The states on the other hand claimed the land as they would claim any other land within their jurisdiction to which there was no clear title.

Stewardship at its core implies an ethic of care and such an ethic is only realizable in situations where the relationship to property is, to use Radin's term, 'personal' with ties that go beyond the property as pure exchange value. Cultural and spiritual bonds to a land distinguish it from a mere piece of real estate and necessarily display a care ethic and hence stewardship. Radin, however, warns that every kind of attachment to property need not be given recognition. She notes:

> If there is a traditional understanding that a well-developed person must invest herself to some extent in external objects, there is no less a traditional understanding that one should not invest oneself *in the wrong way or to too great an extent* in external objects. Property is damnation as well as salvation, object-fetishism as well as moral groundwork.[5]

As we have seen in the cases discussed above however, the courts do not uphold a property claim merely because the claimant can produce evidence of a personal attachment to it, similar to an attachment to a pair of shoes or a car. On the contrary it is submitted that from the consistent judicial affirmation of certain kinds of property claims, a relationship of stewardship evidenced by strong cultural and spiritual bonds with a particular piece of land is likely to be upheld due to the larger societal benefits of conservation of Nature.

In any case a property claim based on stewardship can quite easily coexist with a competing property claim based on legal title. Both these claims do not necessarily have to be mutually exclusive. For the most part a property claim based on stewardship seeks a right to

[5] Radin, 'Property and Personhood' (1982), p. 961.

use, manage, benefit, and set limits on property rights derived from legal title. An example of such a situation would be a community's claim to use and care for their sacred sites on a land to which a private owner holds the title. While the private owner is still free to occupy and benefit from his land, the rights of the community as guardian of its sacred sites limit the extent of his rights of use.

Such a model is not necessarily radical in property jurisprudence, as Riley et al. have noted in their argument for 'cultural property rights'.[6] In fact, such models are gaining increasing currency especially in the context of trusts where a private owner sets aside for conservation portions of his property to be held in trust for perpetuity. The trustees may be a local tribe, a private owner, or in some cases the local government. The tribes commit to looking after the land for future generations who are the beneficiaries of the trust and the government may provide tax breaks since the land is set aside for conservation. The private owner financially benefits from the tax exemption along with having the land sustainably managed. The tribes are therefore able to carry on their traditional ways of life along with the necessary cultural and spiritual practices that are necessary for the flourishing of their peoplehood.

An arrangement of this sort explores the possibility of different kinds of property rights based on separate grounds (trusteeship/stewardship and ownership) coexisting, thereby challenging the popular myth that a private property right brooks no encumbrances. Mary Christina Wood has undertaken an extensive study on such stewardship trust models in the United States. The outcomes of this study were published in a two part series titled 'Tribes as Trustees' [7]

[6] Riley et al., 'In Defense of Property' (2009).

[7] Mary Christina Wood et al., 'Tribes as Trustees Again (Part 1): The Emerging Tribal Role in the Conservation Trust Movement', *Harvard Environmental Law Review*, Vol. 32 (2008), pp. 373–432; Mary Christina Wood et al., 'Tribes as Trustees Again (Part 2): Evaluating Four Models of Tribal Participation in the Conservation Trust Movement', *Stanford Environmental Law Journal*, Vol. 27 (2008), pp. 477–546. In Part 1, pp. 407–8, Wood provides an interesting example of the Yanix Ranch trusteeship model. The Yainix Ranch is a 788-acres parcel located in the Upper Klamath Basin of Southern Oregon. It sits near the confluence of the

which examines in detail innovative ways in which different property claims can coexist for the purposes of conservation. Studies of this nature have the beneficial impact of deconstructing reified notions of property as a 'right to exclude', and underscoring the truth that property is a relationship. The insights gained from such an understanding take us beyond the reductionist binary of absolute private property versus a complete open access to a more nuanced approach of the commons being a way of inclusively recognizing the different kinds of relationships people may construct with respect to property.

As Marx and Macpherson noted,[8] property as a concept is fluid and is in essence a set of enforceable claims. The kinds of claims that are legally recognized versus those that are not depend on a variety of factors. The rise of mercantilism from the seventeenth century onwards, that later evolved into free market capitalism in the nineteenth century, privileged claims to private property over common property claims. The work of John Locke shows clearly the difficult moral arguments that had to be made to justify enclosure of the commons and unlimited accumulation in the seventeenth century.[9]

Sprague and Sycan Rivers, both of which once held thriving populations of native redband trout as well as (now endangered) Lost River and shortnose suckers. The ranch land was originally part of the Klamath Indian Reservation. The land was sold to a series of non-Indian ranchers and owners of the land stocked far more cattle than was environmentally feasible. Years of overgrazing degraded the ranch and riparian erosion filled the river with sediment making the Sprague River the primary source of low water quality in Upper Klamath Lake. In 2002, the Hyde family purchased the Yainix Ranch, to demonstrate how cooperation could restore the ranch to productivity in a way that was good for ranchers, tribes, and fish. The Hydes worked with Sustainable Northwest, a Portland-based nonprofit organization, to create an innovative agricultural conservation easement. The Klamath Tribes hold the easement and are solely responsible for monitoring the ranch's ecological health in order to restore riparian vegetation and hence the water quality, habitat, and fisheries. The Hydes hold title to the ranch and live and pay taxes on the property, but manage the land in accordance with a restoration plan designed by the state, tribal, environmental, and neighbouring agricultural partners.

[8] *See* Chapters Five and Six.

[9] *See* Chapter Six.

Debates about the commons versus private property are in essence debates about different kinds of property claims. The right to private property is a right to exclude, whereas a right to the commons is a right of a community not to be excluded.

Growing public concern about the loss of biodiversity and its adverse effects on climate, food and health security, coupled with evidence of good conservation practices by communities has provided the impetus for historical stewardship to strengthen a community's claim to property. While the links between biodiversity conservation and the stewardship roles of certain communities is obvious in the various decisions of the Conference of the Parties to the CBD, it is interesting to note the strong participation of indigenous peoples' groups and supporting organizations in all the negotiations relating to multilateral environmental agreements. In fact, indigenous peoples and traditional communities have also begun to strategically present their claims over land, knowledge, and resources not merely as title claims but also as stewardship claims.

The environmental crisis has inadvertently had the effect of expanding the justificatory grounds for a legitimate property claim to include evidence of historical stewardship. Furthermore, evidence of stewardship under certain situations could actually trump a claim based purely on a legal title deed. This has resulted in a radical reconfiguration of the concept of property, and thus provided valuable ammunition for communities claiming the commons right or the 'right not to be excluded' against the hegemony of private property rights.

TRUSTS: SEPARATING TITLE FROM CONTROL AND BENEFITS

> *[I]n establishing a trust, a founder (or a court, in the case of 'imputed' trusts) can play a whole range of 'tricks' with three particular aspects of property ownership: nominal title, benefit and control. The founder (or the court) can juggle these around in a variety of ways.*[10]

[10] Graham Moffat Graham Moffat, Gerry Bean and Rebecca Probert, *Trust Law: Text and Materials*, 4th ed. (Cambridge: Cambridge University Press, 2005), p. 4.

One of the problems with the conflation of property with private property is the misconception that legal title, control, and benefit would all have to vest in the titleholder. Common law has produced legal instruments such as 'trusts' however, that allow for the separation between title, control, and benefits thereby allowing the coexistence of multiple claims over things. The history of trusts in common law extends back to the time of the crusades in the thirteenth century. They were developed to allow feudal landowners who went off to fight in foreign lands to pass the legal rights over their estates to someone they trusted (a trustee), who would then manage the lands on the understanding that the original landowner and his family would still have ultimate rights over the land as the beneficiaries. The trustee was expected to act in the best interests of the beneficiaries and in accordance with the agreement reached with the original landowner (the deed of trust).[11]

The concept of trust has obviously evolved since then and the modern trust can be created by anyone who is the absolute owner of a property (the settlor) by appointing a trustee to manage the property in accordance with a trust deed for a beneficiary (or beneficiaries, some of whom may be yet to be born). Once the trust is created, the legal title vests in the trustee, but the actions of the trustee are clearly limited by the trust deed and have to serve the beneficiaries who are said to have an 'equitable or beneficial interest' in the trust property. Thus, while the trustee has legal title over the property, the beneficiary has both the 'equitable property right' against the trust property and personal claims against the trustee to ensure that the trustee acts in accordance with the terms of the trust.[12]

The development of trusts owes its origins to common law's efforts to create the necessary flexibility in property jurisprudence to ensure equitable management of property. Courts have, therefore, imposed trusts in situations where the direct application of property law was likely to create an injustice. Such trusts, created irrespective of the

[11] Alastair Hudson, *Understanding Equity and Trusts*, 3rd ed. (London: Routledge-Cavendish, 2008), p. 13.

[12] Ibid., p. 14; There is nothing that prevents the settlor from also being a trustee and a trustee from also being a beneficiary of the trust as long as the trustee is not the sole beneficiary.

intention of the parties are referred to as 'constructive trusts'. In *Paragon Finance plc* v. *D.B. Thakerar & Co.*[13] Lord Justice Millett of the England and Wales Court of Appeal explained the institution as:

> A constructive trust arises by operation of law whenever the circumstances are such that it would be unconscionable for the owner of the property (usually but not necessarily the legal estate) to assert his own beneficial interest in the property and deny the beneficial interest of another.[14]

Courts have imposed constructive trusts whenever they felt that the common law owner of a property is acting unconscionably and such actions would adversely affect the rights of others. In the 1996 House of Lords decision of *Westdeutsche Landesbank Girozentrale* v. *Islington London Borough Council,*[15] Lord Browne-Wilkinson elaborated this rationale by stating that:

> Equity operates on the conscience of the owner of the legal interest. In the case of a trust, the conscience of the legal owner requires him to carry out the purposes for which the property is vested in him (express or implied trust) or which the law imposes on him by reason of his unconscionable conduct (constructive trust).

Lord Denning in the 1972 case of *Mrs. Emily Hussey* v. *P. Palmer*[16] provided perhaps the boldest exposition of a constructive trust when he stated that:

> Although the plaintiff alleged that there was a resulting trust, I should have thought that the trust in this case, if there was one, was more in the nature of a constructive trust: but this is more a pattern of words than anything else. The two run together. By whatever name it is described, it is a trust imposed by law whenever justice and good conscience require it. It is a liberal process, founded upon large principles of equity, to be applied in cases where the defendant cannot conscientiously keep the property for himself alone, but ought to allow another to have the property or share in it. The trust may

[13] [1999] 1 ALL ER 400, [1998] EWCA Civ 1249, also cited in ibid., at 98.

[14] [1999] 1 ALL ER 400 at 409.

[15] [1996] A.C. 669, [1996] 2 All E.R. 961.

[16] [1972] 3 All ER 744.

> arise at the outset when the property is acquired, or later on, as the circumstances may require. It is an equitable remedy by which the Court can enable an aggrieved party to obtain restitution.[17]

While the courts in both *Mabo* and *Delgamuukw* (discussed previously) did not explicitly assert that they were imposing a constructive trust on the Crown, the fact that they imputed a fiduciary duty on it to act in the best interests of the aboriginal communities underpinned the same principle of equity as in constructive trusts. The courts acknowledged that the Crown had radical title to all land in its jurisdiction. This radical title, though limited by common law, still implied that the Crown could acquire the land of the aboriginal communities for a public purpose. However, the fact that aboriginal or native title could only be transferred back to the Crown was sufficient ground for the courts to impute to the Crown a fiduciary duty to act in the interests of the aboriginal communities.[18] The power of the Crown to acquire aboriginal lands, according to the courts, necessarily imposed upon it the duty to act in the interests of the aboriginal communities.

While the Canadian and Australian courts have imputed a fiduciary duty to the Crown when dealing with aboriginal lands, they have also imposed another kind of trusteeship or stewardship on the aboriginal communities themselves in relation to their lands. Chief Justice Lamer in *Delgamuukw* explicitly noted that aboriginal title is limited by the fact that the range of uses to which the land can be put should not be irreconcilable with the nature of attachment to the land which forms the basis of the particular group's aboriginal title.[19] The Canadian Supreme Court further elaborated this duty of trusteeship when it reasoned that lands held pursuant to an aboriginal title could not be alienated since these lands are more than a fungible commodity. The Court explained that the relationship between the community and the lands has an important non-economic component based on the cultural and spiritual bonds of the community with its lands. It was

[17] [1972] 3 ALL ER, 747.
[18] *Mabo No. 2*, at paragraph 85, judgment of Toohey J.
[19] *Delgamuukw* (1997), at paragraph 124, judgment of Lamer, C.J.

on the basis of these bonds that the aboriginal title was recognized in the first place.[20]

The use of the trust model (without terming it thus) with legal title limited by stewardship requirements has been widely used in the context of 'community based natural resource management' (CBNRM) in eastern and southern Africa. Some of the best-known models have been Zimbabwe's Communal Areas Management Programme for Indigenous Resources (CAMPFIRE) and Namibia's communal conservancies. These CBNRM models in sub-Saharan Africa were devised to counter the colonial systems of centralized political authority over land and resources, systems that were later embraced by post-colonial states, decimating local institutions of land and resource governance. Resources were abused for private gain and patronage by centralized state authorities that had legal title over the land but lacked the capacity to manage the resources effectively. This led to the transformation of community managed wildlife, forests, and fisheries in the form of common property into de facto open access. The consequence was a rapid depletion of the resources since local users lacked the rights and therefore, the incentives to manage them.[21]

The late 1960s saw experiments by the governments of South Africa, Zimbabwe, and Namibia in developing wildlife management policies that sought to devolve stewardship of wildlife to white landowners. These landowners in turn managed the animals as a form of land use generating economic benefits from wildlife production thereby incentivizing stewardship and conservation. In Zimbabwe, 27,000 square kilometres of farmland shifted from cattle ranching to wildlife production, and Namibia saw an 80 per cent increase of wildlife on private lands between 1972 and 1992. In both Zimbabwe and Namibia, the successes of devolved stewardship led to adopting the same reforms on communal lands after their transition to majority rule in 1980 and 1990 respectively.[22]

[20] Ibid., paragraph 129, judgment of Lamer, C.J.

[21] Fred Nelson, 'The Politics of Natural Resource Governance in Africa', in Fred Nelson (ed.), *Community Rights, Conservation and Contested Land* (London: Earthscan, 2010), pp. 4, 8.

[22] Ibid., p. 9.

CAMPFIRE in Zimbabwe was a creative model of devolving stewardship over wildlife and benefits arising from their use to local communities. However, the extent of devolution was limited to the Rural District Councils rather than extended to communities on the ground. The CAMPFIRE model between 1989–2001 expanded to cover 37 districts with 43,000 square km of communal land being set aside for wildlife management, generating revenues of over 20 million USD shared evenly between the Rural District Councils and the communities. One of the main criticisms of the CAMPFIRE model was its limited devolution of stewardship rights to communities which hampered local incentives for wildlife conservation.[23] Namibia, on the other hand, through legislative reforms in 1996, empowered communities to form their own communal conservancies on communal lands with full stewardship rights.[24] Between 1996 and 2007 over 50 communal conservancies covering 118,000 square kilometres were formed in Namibia, with communities entering into joint ventures with tourism and hunting companies and keeping all revenues generated.[25]

The CAMPFIRE and conservancy models exemplify devolution of stewardship to the community level and have generated evidence of conservation best practice. They were in many respects the precursors of the discourse of biocultural rights with community stewardship rather than state-ownership, being the rallying cry.

BIOCULTURAL RIGHTS AND THE PLURALIZATION OF PROPERTY

While biocultural rights are a range of rights claimed by communities to secure their way of life as stewards of the land, they derive their primary justification as far as the broader society is concerned from the need to protect the environment. Hence, a property claim by a

[23] *See generally,* James C. Murombedzi, 'Devolution and Stewardship in Zimbabwe's CAMPFIRE Programme', *Journal of International Development* 11(2) (1999), pp. 287–93.

[24] *See generally,* Arthur Frederick Hoole, 'Place-Power-Prognosis: Community Based Conservation, Partnerships and Ecotourism Enterprise in Namibia', *International Journal of the Commons* 4(10) (2010), pp. 78–99.

[25] Nelson, 'The Politics of Natural Resource Governance in Africa' (2010).

community becomes an assertion of a biocultural right only if the claim is justified on the grounds of stewardship. One of the ramifications of an assertion of biocultural rights is the necessary pluralization of the grounds for a property claim to include stewardship. Stewardship as a ground for a property claim inherently limits the claimant to using the property only in ways that do not conflict with conservation.

The recognition of stewardship as a legitimate ground for claiming property in the context of the CBD does not always translate into greater preservation of biodiversity. This has to do with the delinking of the concept of property and the kind of rights it entails from the grounds on which the property claim is made in the first place. For example a community assertion of property rights over traditional knowledge is justified under the CBD as a way to recognize and incentivize the conservation practices of the community. The assumption of the CBD is that such recognition will lead to increased conservation of biodiversity. However, the common tendency when it comes to property rights is to conflate their exercise with the right to private property, that is, the right to freely use or dispose of the property with minimal restrictions. Thus, the exercise of a biocultural right may not always result in outcomes that affirm the biocultural relations of a community with Nature.

It follows that a community's cultural and spiritual bonds with its ecosystem must be emphasized in every situation where a community asserts property rights that have been established on the ground of stewardship. The greatest obstacle to viewing a property right as a right to stewardship is the common reduction of the different property relations to relations of private property. In many ways this is a problem that arises when the exercise of a right is divorced from discussions regarding its content and its origins. Rather the right tends to float freely in the sense that it is open to co-option by the dominant discourses, in this case, the discourse of private property. The San Hoodia case is an example of this conceptual conflation. Here the exercise of the San community's right over their traditional knowledge was delinked from the cultural and spiritual values of the community leading to conflicts within the community and friction between the San and the Nama.[26]

[26] Wynberg and Chennells, 'Green Diamonds of the South: An Overview of the San Hoodia Case' (2009).

This problem has also been widely debated under the broad theme of commodification of ethnicity and culture.[27] The problem with these debates, however, is a tendency to throw the proverbial baby out with the bathwater. Most tend to work on a reductionist binary of private property versus open access, where the only alternative to the excesses of private property is a kind of imaginary commons in which land, culture, and knowledge are all freely available to anyone who would like to use them. These commodification debates make the classic error of conflating property with private property and defining property as a thing rather than as an enforceable claim. A more considered response to the excesses of private property is to rescue property from its popular misconception and, in Polanyi's terms, to re-embed markets within society, where markets are an aspect of society rather than the other way round.

The call for biocultural rights is an effort to re-embed markets within society with an emphasis on the relevant community's stewardship of Nature. Society, however, is not homogenous and static but heterogeneous and dynamic, with different competing needs and interests. The values on which any society is based are a contested terrain. Without presuming any transcendental ethics outside of history and context, the growing influence of the discourse of environmentalism in the wake of the ecological crisis has given impetus to the recent legal manifestation of an ethic that was hitherto marginalized by capitalism. This is the ethic of stewardship, a principle that is vibrant amongst communities with strong cultural and spiritual bonds with Nature. These are communities that have sacralized Nature, where the identity of the community is tightly interwoven with the land and the deities and spirits.

The operative question at this stage, then, is one of strategy: How do we re-introduce and then privilege the ethic of stewardship within legal discourse? To state the question differently: How do we ensure that the collective is not individualized; how are we to ensure that property claims based on stewardship do not become empty receptacles which are filled by the values of private property?

[27] Comaroff, *Ethnicity Inc.* (2009).

THE NEW JURIDICAL SUBJECT: FROM THE *HOMO ECONOMICUS* TO THE *HOMO ECOLOGICUS*

Much of the discussion hitherto has critiqued the dominant legal approach to understanding property without reference to other legal concepts. The scholars and cases that have been analysed have sought to make the all-important link between property and personhood. At the same time, personhood or in this case peoplehood is an empty category which derives its meaning from what a society understands as well-being. One cannot speak of what it means to be a person or a people without necessarily describing certain ways of being.

These descriptions are rarely value-neutral. On the contrary they describe a certain kind of a person or people. In capitalist economies for example, the *homo economicus,* or in Adam Smith's terms 'our tendency to truck, barter and exchange one thing for another', is presented as the essence of personhood. This in turn forms the ground on which a legitimate property claim is made. In the case of capitalist economies, where profit and exchange is valued, personhood is conflated with the *homo economicus,* and property is conflated with private property.

It is therefore clear that conceptions of property are based on conceptions of personhood, and conceptions of personhood are based on conceptions of well-being. While it is our conception of what it means to be a person that informs our conception of property, the law tends to reify property, thereby doing the reverse, which is to define personhood or the juridical subject from the perspective of the dominant understanding of property. Thus, in capitalist economies, the dominance of private property results in a juridical subject with the right to private property with the right to exclude being the primary right. This leads to situations where both property and personhood are mutually reinforcing, and socially agreed conceptions of well-being are significantly influenced by dominant conceptions of property.

The *homo economicus* and its conception of Nature as pure exchange value have been blamed for the widespread loss of biodiversity and its adverse consequences. The tide is now turning; we have begun to mend the link between human well-being and the well-being of Nature. Communities where the ethic of stewardship is still strong are increasingly seen as repositories of a kind of well-being that mainstream society has sacrificed in favour of capitalism. The legal response to this shift in thinking has been greater recognition of the rights of communities to their traditional ways of life and different understandings of human and planetary well-being. While such rights are what are referred to here as biocultural rights, the single most important obstacle to their development is not recognition per se but rather the manner in which lawmakers and judges seek to recognize them.

Rights are merely enforceable claims, and well-being is what is sought through them. Hence, what lawmakers and judges understand to be well-being, significantly influences the manner in which rights are legislated, implemented, and adjudicated. Biocultural rights are a subset within the category of group rights, not because they create new rights but because they introduce new content into existing group rights and new grounds for claiming such rights. *In fact, the term 'biocultural right' is deployed in order to name a paradigm shift in our understanding of well-being rather than creating a new set of rights.* The essence of this type of right lies in the recognition of new types of claims based on stewardship as informing the content of pre-existing rights. The group right to property for example, becomes a biocultural right when this right recognizes the claim of a community based on evidence of historical stewardship.

If stewardship becomes the primary ethic on the basis of which biocultural rights are derived from group rights, then it is critical to explore how this ethic can be foregrounded in discussions that relate community rights to biodiversity. Such an exercise is crucial if we are to prevent biocultural rights from being co-opted by the discourse of private property. In this respect Balbus's arguments about the legal form mirroring the commodity form are relevant.[28] He noted that, in capitalist societies, the juridical subject as a self-enclosed bearer of rights imitates the commodity form, which is pure exchange value, delinked from use value. Just as the commodity form is a market abstraction estranged from the reality of the process of production, the juridical subject as the *homo economicus* is estranged from the

[28] Balbus, 'Commodity Form and Legal Form' (1977), pp. 571–88.

complexity of life, a life that is not motivated purely by economic imperatives but, rather is, informed by cultural and spiritual relationships.

Biocultural rights and their emphasis on stewardship reconfigure the juridical subject from the *homo economicus* to the *homo ecologicus*. The juridical subject evolves from an atomistic entity that interprets property rights as facilitating only free trade to a relational entity that views property rights as securing stewardship. The *homo ecologicus* then is the paradigm that emerges out of the environmental crisis seeking to stem the excesses of the *homo economicus*. The *homo ecologicus* underscores the fact that traditional ways of life result in the stewarding of biodiversity and these ways of life are rooted in strong cultural and spiritual relationships with Nature. The future of biodiversity conservation then rests in protecting these traditions through securing the concomitant biocultural rights.

Affirming Stewardship: Towards Biocultural Community Protocols

> *Landscapes are culture before they are nature; constructs of imagination projected onto wood, water and rock.*[29]

As noted at the beginning of this chapter, resources (or property) are a matter of relationships, not things, and can only be understood in the context of society as a whole, which includes the dominant cultural and spiritual values. Our understanding of property or Nature for that matter is mediated by our values; what is seen cannot be divorced from the spectator. How we understand Nature is discourse dependent; it does not exist waiting to be discovered by us, but rather our perception of the world is determined by how we

[29] S. Schama, *Landscape and Memory*, (London: Harper Collins, 1995), cited in Bas Verschuuren, 'An Overview of Cultural and Spiritual Values in Ecosystem Management and Conservation Strategies', in B. Haverkort and S. Rist (eds), *Endogenous Development and Bio-Cultural Diversity: The Interplay of Worldviews, Globalisation and Locality*, Series on Worldviews and Sciences, No. 6, (Leusden: Compas/CDE, 2007).

describe it. The dichotomy between Nature and culture is illusory to the extent that our culture informs how we perceive Nature.[30]

Biocultural rights seek in essence to ensure the conservation of biodiversity through the legal protection of a stewarding way of life, which includes the protection of relevant cultural and spiritual values. These rights show that Nature conservation cannot be a simple techno–bureaucratic exercise. Instead it is the protection of certain ways of understanding Nature as kindred (or sacred). But herein lies the challenge for biocultural rights, since they seek the protection of certain ways of being and knowing that result in the stewardship of Nature. While stewardship is integral to the cultural systems of certain communities, it is critical for lawmakers to appreciate these systems when they develop and implement laws and policies relating to conservation. As 'sacred natural sites' advocate Bas Verschuuren notes:

> The way people perceive nature depends on culturally defined value and belief systems that form an important, often intergenerational, source of information. Some of this valuable information, relating in particular to its spiritual dimensions, may not yet be considered in current ecosystem management. Part of the reason for this may be that such knowledge is inaccessible and difficult to be understood by outsiders such as western-trained conservationists and conventional ecosystem managers. Hence, accounting for the various worldviews and their corresponding cultural and spiritual values in the practice of ecosystem management forms a challenge for policy makers and local people alike.[31]

Since the early 1990s significant efforts have been made internationally to place the role of cultural and spiritual values in conservation in the foreground of our thinking.[32] Nevertheless, these efforts do not adequately consider how to ensure an effective

[30] A similar point is made on the distinction between 'facts' and 'values' by Hilary Putnam, *Reason, Truth and History*, cited in Radin, 'Market Inalienability', pp. 1882–3.

[31] Verschuuren 'An Overview of Cultural and Spiritual Values in Ecosystem Management and Conservation Strategies' (2007), p. 299.

[32] Examples of this include the IUCN World Commission for Protected Areas specialist task force on Cultural and Spiritual Values of Protected

interface between the stewardship values of communities that lead to conservation and the development and implementation of law and policy, both international and domestic, relating to biodiversity protection. The obligation on states to ensure biodiversity conservation through the recognition of the biocultural rights of indigenous people and local communities (through Articles 8(j) and 10(c) of the CBD and Article 16 of the African Model Law[33]) only takes us so far. This is because the content of these rights in domestic law is still provided by states and local administrators.

In the negotiations leading up to the Nagoya Protocol on Access and Benefit Sharing, one of the key debates relating to the rights of communities over their traditional knowledge concerned the way in which these rights should be recognized. Many states viewed them as something they would need to implement in domestic law, that is, ensure that communities, as with any other property owner, give prior informed consent for the commercial or research uses of their traditional knowledge. Indigenous peoples' representatives, however, argued that their right to the traditional knowledge had to be understood in the larger context of conservation and sustainable use of biodiversity. Traditional knowledge according to this argument is dynamic and is embodied in an active interface between the cultural and spiritual practices of a community, on the one hand, and the ecosystem they inhabit, on the other. Hence, for a law seeking to protect community rights to their traditional knowledge to be effective, it has to affirm an entire way of life.

An argument of this kind builds on first principles. It states that, if the object of recognizing the rights of communities to their traditional knowledge is to ensure conservation, then the flurry of activity around models of intellectual property rights to protect such knowledge, including its documentation, will not in themselves lead

---

Areas; and the Akwé: Kon Voluntary Guidelines for the conduct of cultural, environmental and social impact assessments on developments likely to impact sacred sites adopted by the 193 Parties to the CBD at their fifth Conference of Parties in May 2000.

[33] *The African Model Law for the Protection of the Rights of Local Communities, Farmers and Breeders and for the Regulation of Access to Biological Resources* (1997).

to the object of the right. Instead, the CBD's recognition of the right of communities to their traditional knowledge intends to protect a way of life that leads to conservation. This implies that the right to traditional knowledge is not akin to a private property right to trade freely in traditional knowledge, but a right to a way of life replete with knowledge, innovations, and practices that lead to the conservation and sustainable use of biodiversity.

Such a holistic interpretation of Article 8(j)[34] of the CBD led to further discussions on how states can effectively recognize the right to a stewarding way of life rather than a right that turned traditional knowledge into a tradable commodity. The African Group of countries in their submissions to the Working Group on ABS regarding the recognition of community rights to their traditional knowledge proposed 'biocultural community protocols'[35] as a useful method for protecting a way of life. This submission asked for recognition of such protocols in domestic ABS law so as to ensure that the rights of communities to traditional knowledge did not simply replicate the content of a private property right but rather promoted a way of life that would encourage conservation.

Biocultural community protocols—or what later came to be known as community protocols in the Nagoya Protocol on ABS—are community-led instruments that promote participatory advocacy for the recognition of and support for ways of life that are based on the sustainable use of biodiversity, according to customary, national, and international laws and policies.[36] In this sense, biocultural community protocols are community-specific declarations of the

[34] *See* Chapter One, footnote 47.

[35] UNEP/CBD/WG-ABS/7/INF/1.

[36] H. Jonas, K. Bavikatte and H. Shrumm, 2010. 'Biocultural Community Protocols and Conservation Pluralism', *Policy Matters*, 17, IUCN-CEESP, Malaysia, pp. 102–12; A significant amount of work on the development and elaboration of BCPs was done by Natural Justice (Lawyers for Communities and the Environment), an international NPO working on community rights and biodiversity and headquartered in South Africa. The submissions of the African Group regarding the protection of traditional knowledge benefitted from the inputs from members of the Natural Justice team.

right to diversity and claims to social pluralism. Their value and integrity lie in the process that communities undertake to develop them, in what the protocols represent to the community, and in their future uses and effects.[37]

It is worth quoting at length from the submission of the African Group to highlight the debates around the real meaning of Article 8(j) of the CBD, and hence the right of communities to their traditional knowledge. When referring to the need to safeguard the cultural and spiritual values of stewardship (or 'ecological values'), the African Group submitted that:

> Article 8 j is clear that the conservation and sustainable use of biological diversity in the context of ILCs (indigenous and local communities) is dependent on aspects of their TK (traditional knowledge associated with genetic resources) which is rooted in their 'ecological values'. This is the reason why Art 8 j does not refer to the protection and promotion of all the TK of all ILCs but specifically the TK of ILCs embodying traditional lifestyles relevant to the conservation and sustainable use of biodiversity. Such ecologically integral TK is based on a value framework that regulates the relationship between the cultures of ILCs and their lands. Thus TK relevant for the conservation and sustainable use of biodiversity rests on 'ecological values' which in turn rests on secure rights to land and culture. The truth of the matter is that ILCs have conserved and sustainably used biological diversity for thousands of years not because they have been able to trade in their TK but because they have been able to live on their traditional lands in accordance with their 'ecological values'. ABS in the context of ILCs focuses inordinately on an agenda of TK protection that perceives TK outside of the relationships which generate it, divorcing it from the ecological values that lead to its formation. The relations that the ILCs have with nature is one of a perpetual dialogue between land and culture each constituting and reconstituting the other. Ecological values are therefore rooted in an experience of relatedness between community and nature. Current intellectual property rights (IPR) systems perceive TK in a manner that is quite similar to conventional property systems where land

[37] H. Jonas, K. Bavikatte, and H. Shrumm , 'Community Protocols and Access and Benefit Sharing', *Asian Biotechnology and Development Review* 12(3) (2010), p. 62.

> for example is viewed as a commodity separate from the network of relations within which it operates. TK is also viewed as an object separate from the cultural and spiritual relationships with the land within which it is embedded. TK in reality is the manifestation of a particular kind of relationship with nature. TK is not just information but a set of relations that is embodied in traditional lifestyles of ILCs which ensure conservation and sustainable use of biodiversity .... To treat TK as a commodity and to assume that protecting this commodity will ensure conservation and sustainable use of biological diversity is akin to thinking that the sale of ivory will necessarily lead to the conservation of elephants and their habitats.[38]

The African countries elaborate their argument in the context of ABS by noting that, for the conservation and sustainable use objectives of the CBD to be realized, the process and outcome of ABS negotiations must uphold the spirit of Article 8(j). The emphasis therefore should not be solely on:

> (T)he sale of TK (traditional knowledge) but focus equally on the conservation and sustainable use of biological diversity and protection and promotion of traditional lifestyles including rights to land and culture. This implies ensuring that the ecological values of the ILCs in question are central to all stages of the ABS negotiation i.e. at the stage of 'PIC', 'MAT' and 'benefit sharing'.[39]

It should also be emphasized that: 'the process and the outcome of an ABS agreement between ILCs and the relevant stakeholders must affirm aspects of their traditional lifestyles that conserve and sustainably use biological diversity'.[40]

The African Group went on to explain community protocols in the context of ABS by stating that:

> A community protocol is an outlining of ecological values on which prior informed consent (PIC), mutually agreed terms (MAT) and benefit sharing would be based. A useful analogy for a community protocol would be the 'bill of rights' in the Constitution of a country that lists the core values of a people. It enunciates a community's

[38] UNEP/CBD/WG-ABS/7/5 28 January 2009 at p. 53

[39] Ibid., pp. 53, 54.

[40] Ibid., p. 54.

> core values and while it remains a flexible instrument, it provides community members and outside interests a level of certainty about the principles upon which any ABS agreement will be negotiated. Community protocols are perhaps the best chance for ILCs to ensure that their ways of life and values are respected and promoted. Merely relying on the benefits of ABS agreements without affirming their 'ecological values' would reduce ILCs to sellers of TK who warm themselves on the embers of a lifestyle that is fast dying out.[41]

One could proffer another possible explanation as to why the African Group of countries' proposal of community protocols was widely accepted by the other states. Research on management of common-pool resources had clearly shown that conservation and sustainable use of ecosystems depended on devolution of rights and sharing of benefits with communities that had historically managed these ecosystems. However, because these ecosystems were managed as commons with multiple claimants, the state or third parties were unable to identify these rights holders and beneficiaries. In the absence of a clear community led process that was able to identify the rights holders and beneficiaries, states or third parties took it upon themselves to pick and choose who the rights holders and beneficiaries were or in some cases did not recognize them at all. This led to business as usual that is, community commons were turned into open access due to centralization of control or private appropriation resulting in a tragedy of commons situation. Community protocols cracked this problem by developing a clear process of how multiple local claimants over common-pool resources can come together to reflect, consolidate, and articulate rules of how they govern and manage these resources (based on their values, etc.). This meant that communities were able to take the initiative in asserting rights through a process of establishing 'internal coherence and external interface'. This also facilitated communities in consolidating their various rights, fragmented through different laws, in a single process/ document. Effectively, community protocols eliminated all possible excuses of why rights and benefits cannot be devolved thus leading to a proper alignment of conservation theory and practice.

[41] Ibid., pp. 54, 55.

After intense negotiations, in October 2010 in Nagoya, Japan, the 193 states that are parties to the CBD adopted the Nagoya Protocol on Access and Benefit Sharing. This Protocol was a significant milestone for communities because it was the first time in international treaty law that states were obliged to give legal recognition to customary laws and community protocols of communities when it came to securing the rights of those communities to their traditional knowledge.[42] The implications of such recognition for biocultural rights as a whole are enormous since it lays strong foundations for the protection of a way of life (including cultural and spiritual values, customary laws, and traditional decision making structures) that leads to stewardship of Nature.

Biocultural community protocols are making their impact felt in the development of laws and policies that go beyond ABS, for example REDD+,[43] protected areas, etc., where the legislative

[42] Article 12 Traditional Knowledge Associated with Genetic Resources

1. In implementing their obligations under this Protocol, Parties shall in accordance with domestic law take into consideration indigenous and local communities' customary laws, community protocols and procedures, as applicable, with respect to traditional knowledge associated with genetic resources.
2. Parties, with the effective participation of the indigenous and local communities concerned, shall establish mechanisms to inform potential users of traditional knowledge associated with genetic resources about their obligations, including measures as made available through the Access and Benefit-sharing Clearing-House for access to and fair and equitable sharing of benefits arising from the utilization of such knowledge.
3. Parties shall endeavour to support, as appropriate, the development by indigenous and local communities, including women within these communities, of:
   (a) Community protocols in relation to access to traditional knowledge associated with genetic resources and the fair and equitable sharing of benefits arising out of the utilization of such knowledge; ...

[43] Reducing Emissions from Deforestation and Forest Degradation (REDD) is an effort to create a financial value for the carbon stored in forests, offering incentives for developing countries to reduce emissions

purpose of conservation of biodiversity intersects with the stewarding ways of life of communities.[44] It is submitted that the reason behind the success of these community protocols lies in their ability to challenge the widespread reification of the rights discourse, whereby states increasingly engage in rights talk but lack clarity or political will when it comes to defining the content of those rights and how their enforcement will lead to the greater goal of human well-being.

The dominant approach of the liberal rights discourse is piecemeal, meaning that each right — be it a right to property or culture or expression — is seen as self-contained and completely divorced from the fact that culture, property, or expression are all strands tightly woven into the rope of life. No single right has meaning in itself. It gains meaning only when interacting with other rights.

Biocultural community protocols developed by communities begin with the end in mind, which is conservation and sustainable use of biodiversity. They then describe the way of life of the community, its customary laws, cultural and spiritual values, governance and decision-making structures, etc., all of which contribute to the stewardship practices of the community. The community then identifies its current challenges and lays claim to a range of rights in domestic and international law. In essence, the broad rights claim allows the community to determine for itself its way of life, which in turn ensures the continuation of their stewardship practices. *The value of community protocols lies in their ability to act as the glue that holds together the total mosaic of a community life that is fragmented under different laws and policies, with the understanding that the conservation of Nature is a result of a holistic way of life.*

Jonas and Shrumm, legal practitioners working on community rights in the context of conservation confirm that even the manner

---

from forested lands and invest in low-carbon paths to sustainable development. 'REDD+' goes beyond deforestation and forest degradation, and includes the role of conservation, sustainable management of forests and enhancement of forest carbon stocks. From: http://www.un-redd.org/AboutREDD/tabid/582/Default.aspx (accessed 13 September 2011).

[44] Draft UNREDD Program Guidelines for Seeking the Free and Prior Informed Consent of Indigenous Peoples and other Forest Dependent Communities, Africa, 2011, available on file with author.

in which a protocol is developed can be used by the community to engage in a self-reflexive process regarding their way of life, values, customary laws, and priorities and how they would want to engage with a variety of supporting legal frameworks and rights. They refer to the entire process as a biocultural approach to the law that empowers communities to challenge the fragmentary nature of state law, and instead to engage with it from a more nuanced and integrated perspective.[45]

Biocultural Rights: Where to From Here?

A visual depiction of a discourse of biocultural rights would resemble a wheel with the circumference being the objective of conservation and sustainable use, the central hub being the ethic of stewardship and the spokes being the different biocultural rights that communities require to protect their ways of life which in turn are represented by the area of the wheel. This depiction seeks to emphasize the ethic of stewardship or care that pulls together the seemingly disparate rights in order to achieve the objective of conservation. The notion of stewardship is critical for a discourse of biocultural rights, for it provides the ethical content for these rights and thereby creates a paradigm shift whereby rights to land, culture, traditional knowledge, self-governance, etc. are informed by a set of values that are not market based.

Extensive research validates the strong links between cultural diversity and biological diversity, together with the stewardship role of indigenous peoples and local communities. In 1999 the United Nations Environment Program published a seminal collection of articles on the cultural and spiritual values of biodiversity,[46] a collection that was edited by the late anthropologist Darrell Addison Posey. Posey inspired an entire generation of anthropologists and community activists to begin mapping the role of cultures of indigenous peoples and local communities in ensuring biodiversity. He was one of the first to highlight the need for a bundle of rights

[45] Jonas et al., 'Biocultural Community Protocols and Conservation Pluralism', p. 109.

[46] Darrell Addison Posey (ed.), *Cultural and Spiritual Values of Biodiversity* (Nairobi: UNEP, 1999).

approach to conservation that would reflect the integrated nature of community life. He called these rights 'traditional resources rights' (TRR) and described them as:

> [T]he many 'bundles of rights' that can be used for protection, compensation, and conservation .... TRR is an integrated rights concept that recognizes the inextricable link between cultural and biological diversity and sees no contradiction between the human rights of indigenous and local communities, including the right to development and environmental conservation. Indeed, they are mutually supportive since the destiny of traditional peoples largely determines, and is determined by, the state of the world's biological diversity. TRR includes overlapping and mutually supporting bundles of rights.[47]

The concept of biocultural rights further nuances Posey's ideas on TRR by introducing stewardship as the fundamental ethos that binds together the different rights that communities need to protect their way of life. Biocultural rights are best described as a web. While the liberal rights discourse focuses on the juridical subject as an atomistic bearer of many separate rights, biocultural rights understand the juridical subject as a node in a web of biocultural relationships.

Biocultural rights focus less on free-standing rights and more on the linkages between rights required by communities to care for their lands and resources. Like language, where a word makes sense only in relation to other words (for example, light makes sense only in relation to dark which is non-light), within a biocultural rights framework, rights are meaningless on their own. They make sense only in relation to other rights and in the larger context of the well-being of communities and Nature.

The term biocultural right is ultimately a label for the legal tide moving towards securing the stewardship of Nature by indigenous peoples and local communities. This momentum is fuelled by the fact that it is these communities that can help humanity re-member its kinship with Nature and repair the dis-membering that has been caused from viewing Nature only as exchange value.

[47] Ibid.

We would do well to end with the words of Joji Carino who in 1997, representing the International Alliance of Indigenous-Tribal Peoples of the Tropical Forests, stated in her address to the UN General Assembly Special Session:

> Often, the campaigns of indigenous communities are misjudged as the ignorance of 'primitives' unschooled in modern economic realities. But make no mistake. We are not peoples of the past— we are your contemporaries and in some ways may be your guides towards more sustainable futures in the twenty-first century.[48]

[48] Joji Carino, 'Indigenous Peoples Address the UN General Assembly Special Session, 23-27 June, 1997', p. 67; Posey (ed.), *Cultural and Spiritual Values of Biodiversity* (Nairobi: UNEP, 1999).

Bibliography

Books

Amoore, Louise (ed.). 2005. *Global Resistance Reader*. Routledge: London.

Anaya, James. 2004. *Indigenous Peoples in International Law*. 2nd ed. New York: Oxford University Press.

Balbus, Isaac. 2009. *Governing Subjects*. New York: Routledge.

Balibar, Etienne. 2007. *The Philosophy of Marx*. London: Verso.

Bennett, Thomas W. 2004. *Customary Law in South Africa*. Landsdowne: Juta.

Bowers, Chet. 1997. *The Culture of Denial: Why the Environmental Movement Needs a Strategy for Reforming Universities and Public Schools*. New York: State University of New York Press.

Cardozo, Benjamin N. 1928. *The Paradoxes of Legal Science*. New York: Columbia University Press.

Child, Brian, Helen Suich, and Spenceley Anna (eds). 2009. *Evolution and Innovation in Wildlife Conservation: Parks and Game Ranches to Transfrontier Conservation Areas*. London: Earthscan.

Comaroff, John and Jean Comaroff. 2009. *Ethnicity Inc*. Chicago: University of Chicago Press.

Escobar, Arturo. 1997. *Encountering Development: The Making and Unmaking of the Third World*. Princeton: Princeton University Press.

Esteva, Gustavo and Madhu Suri. *Grassroots Postmodernism: Remaking the Soil of Cultures*. London: Zed Books.

France, Anatole. 2006. *The Red Lily*, e-book, www.gutenberg.org.

Geoff Tansey and Tasmin Rajotte (eds). 2008. *The Future Control of Food*. London: Earthscan.

Glowka, Lyle, Françoise Burhenne-Guilmin, and Hugh Synge. 1994. *A Guide to the Convention on Biological Diversity*. Gland: IUCN.

Gorz, Andre. 2008. *Ecologica*. Calcutta: Seagull Books.

Gramsci, Antonio (ed. By David Forgacs). 2000. *The Gramsci Reader: Selected Writings 1916–1935*. New York: New York University Press.

Harman, Chris. 2010. *Zombie Capitalism: The Global Crisis and the Relevance of Marx*. Chicago: Haymarket Books.

Harvey, David. 2005. *A Brief History of Neoliberalism*. New York: Oxford University Press.

Haverkort, B. and S. Rist (eds). 2007. *Endogenous Development and Bio-Cultural Diversity: The Interplay of Worldviews, Globalisation and Locality*. Series on Worldviews and Sciences, No. 6. Leusden: Compas/CDE.

Herskovits, Melville. 1952. *Economic Anthropology*. New York: Knopf.

Hobbes, Thomas. 1651. *Leviathan or the Matter, Form and Power of the Commonwealth*. London: Printed for Andrew Crooke at the Green Dragon in St. Paul's Churchyard.

Hudson, Alastair. 2008. *Understanding Equity and Trusts*. 3rd ed. Routledge-Cavendish: London.

Hyde, Lewis. 1983. *The Gift: How the Creative Spirit Transforms the World*. Edinburgh: Canongate.

Illich, Ivan. 1973. *Tools of Conviviality*. London: Boyars.

Kelman, Mark. 1987. *A Guide to Critical Legal Studies*. Boston: Harvard University Press.

Locke, John (ed. by Peter Laslett). 1965. *Locke's Two Treatises of Government: A Critical Edition with an Introduction and Apparatus Criticus*. New York: New American Library.

Lord Hailey. 1968. *An African Survey: A Study of Problems Arising in Africa South of the Sahara*. Revised to 1956. Oxford: Oxford University Press.

Lukacs, Georg. 1971. *History and Class Consciousness: Studies in Marxist Dialectics*. Cambridge: MIT Press.

Macpherson, C.B. 1962. *The Political Theory of Possessive Individualism: Hobbes to Locke*. Oxford University Press: Oxford.

——— (ed.). 1978. *Property: Mainstream and Critical Positions*. Basil Blackwell: Oxford.

Malinowski, Bronislaw. 1972. *Argonauts of the Western Pacific*. London: Routledge and Sons.

Malinowski, Bronislaw. 1965. *The Coral Gardens and Their Magic.* Vol. 1. Bloomington: University of Indiana Press.
Marx, Karl and Friedrich Engels. 1848. *The Communist Manifesto.* www.gutenberg.org (accessed 13 September 2011).
———. 1932. *The German Ideology.* http://faculty.rcc.edu/sellick/The German Ideology.pdf (accessed13 September 2011).
——— (ed. by Robert C. Tucker). 1972. *The Marx and Engels Reader.* New York: Norton.
Marx, Karl (ed. by Maurice Dobb). 1979. *A Contribution to the Critique of Political Economy.* New York: International Publishers.
———. 1967. *Capital.* Vol. 1. New York: International Publishers.
——— (tran. by B. Fowkes). 1976. *Capital: A Critique of Political Economy.* Vol. 1. London: Penguin.
———. 1975. *Early Writings.* London: Penguin Books.
———. 1973. *Grundrisse: Foundation of the Critique of Political Economy.* Harmondsworth: Penguin Books.
Mathiessen, Peter. 1984. *Indian Country.* Penguin: New York.
Mauss, Marcel. 1967. *The Gift: Forms and Functions of Exchange in Archaic Societies.* New York: Norton Library.
McGillivray, Mark and Matthew Clarke (eds). 2006. *Understanding Human Well-being.* Tokyo: United Nations University Press.
McManis, Charles (ed.). 2010. *Biodiversity & the Law: Intellectual Property, Biotechnology & Traditional Knowledge.* London: Earthscan.
Mead, Margaret and Nicolas Calas (eds). 1954. *Primitive Heritage: An Anthropological Anthology.* London: Victor Gollancz.
Moffat, Graham, Gerry Bean, and Rebecca Probert. 2005. *Trust Law: Text and Materials.* 4th ed. Cambridge University Press: Cambridge.
Mooney, P.R. 1979. *Seeds of the Earth: A Private or Public Resource?* London: International Coalition for Development Action.
Nelson, Fred (ed.). 2010. *Community Rights, Conservation and Contested Land.* London: Earthscan.
Niezen, Ronald. 2003. *The Origins of Indigenism: Human Rights and the Politics of Identity.* Berkeley: University of California Press.
Nijar, G.S. 1996. *In Defence of Local Community Knowledge and Biodiversity: A Conceptual Framework and the Essential Elements of a Rights Regime.* Penang: Third World Network.

Nishida, Kitaro. 1990. *An Enquiry into the Good*. New Haven: Yale University Press.

Nussbaum, Martha C. and Amartya Sen (eds). 1996. *The Quality of Life*. Oxford: Clarendon Press.

Osborne, Peter. 2005. *How to Read Marx*. New York: W. W. Norton & Co.

Ostrom, Elinor. 1990. *Governing the Commons: The Evolution of Institutions for Collective Action*. New York: Cambridge University Press.

Page, Kirby. 1936. *Living Courageously*. New York: Farrar & Rinehart, Inc.

Pashukanis, Evgeny. 1978. *Law and Marxism: A General Theory*. London: Ink Links.

Polanyi, Karl. 2001. *The Great Transformation: The Political and Economic Origins of Our Time*. Boston: Beacon Press.

Posey, Darrell Addison, and Graham Dutfield. 1996. *Beyond Intellectual Property: Towards Traditional Resource Rights for Indigenous Peoples and Local Communities*. Ottawa: International Development Research Centre.

Posey, Darrell Addison (ed.). 1999. *Cultural and Spiritual Values of Biodiversity*. Nairobi: UNEP.

Rahnema, Majid and Victoria Bawtree (eds). 1997. *The Post-Development Reader*. New York: Zed Books.

Rifkin, J. 1998. *The Biotech Century: Harnessing the Gene and Remaking the World*. New York: Jeremy P. Tarcher/Putnam.

Rousseau, Jean-Jacques (trans. by Roger D. Masters, ed. by Roger and Judith Masters). 1964. *The First and Second Discourses of Rousseau*. St. Martin's Press: New York.

Sachs, Wolfgang (ed.). 2010. *The Development Dictionary*. New York: Zed Books.

Sahlins, Marshall. 1972. *Stone Age Economics*. London: Tavistock Publications.

———. 2008. *The Western Illusion of Human Nature*. Chicago: Prickly Paradigm Press.

Schama, S. 1995. *Landscape and Memory*. London: Harper Collins.

Schroeder, Doris and Balakrishna Pisupati. 2010. *Ethics, Justice and the Convention on Biological Diversity*. Nairobi: UNEP.

Schumacher, E.F. 1973. *Small is Beautiful: Economics as if People Mattered*. London: Blond and Briggs.

Scott, James. 1990. *Domination and the Arts of Resistance: Hidden Transcripts*. New Haven: Yale University Press.

Segal, Howard P. 2005. *Technological Utopianism in American Culture*. New York: Syracuse University Press.

Shapiro, Stephen. 2008. *How to Read Marx's Capital*. London: Pluto Press.

Shiva, Vandana (ed.). 1994. *Biodiversity Conservation: Whose Resources? Whose Knowledge?* New Delhi: Indian National Trust for Art and Cultural Heritage.

———. 1993. *Monocultures of the Mind*. Penang: Third World Network.

Simon, Roger. 1991. *Gramsci's Political Thought-An Introduction*. London: Lawrence and Wishart.

Szalay, Miklos (ed.). 2002. *The Moon as Shoe: Drawings of the San*. Zurich: Scheidegger and Spiess.

Smith, Adam. 1986. *The Wealth of Nations*. Books I-III. New York: Penguin Classics.

———. 2000. *The Theory of Moral Sentiments*. New York: Prometheus Books.

Suneetha, M.S. and Balakrishna Pisupati. 2009. *Learning from the Practitioners: Benefit Sharing Perspectives from Enterprising Communities*. Nairobi: UNEP/UNU-IAS.

Swiderska, Krystyna, Alejandro Argumedo, Yiching Song, Jingsong Li, Ruchi Pant, Heraclio Herrera, Doris Mutta, Peter Munyi, S Vedavathy. 2009. *Protecting Community Rights over Traditional Knowledge: Implications of Customary Laws and Practices: Key Findings and Recommendations 2005–2009*. London: IIED. http://pubs.iied.org/14591IIED.html?c=biocon (accessed 13 September 2011).

Taussig, Michael. 2010. *The Devil and Commodity Fetishism in South America*. Chapel Hill: University of North Carolina Press.

Thompson, E.P. 1963. *The Making of the English Working Class*. London: Gollancz.

Titley, Brian E. 1986. *A Narrow Vision: Duncan Campbell Scott and the Administration of Indian Affairs in Canada*. Vancouver: University of British Columbia Press.

Tzu, Lao (trans. by Jonathan Star). 2001. *Tao Te Ching*. New York: Tarcher Cornerstone Editions.

Van der Walt, A.J. (ed.). 1991. *Land Reform and the Future of Landownership in South Africa*. Landsdowne: Juta.

Weber, Max. 1950. *The Protestant Ethic and the Spirit of Capitalism*. New York: Charles Scribner's Sons.

Wynberg, Rachel, Doris Schroeder, and Roger Chennells (eds). 2009. *Indigenous Peoples, Consent and Benefit Sharing*. New York: Springer.

Articles and Reports

Biocultural community protocol of the Gunis on the resources page of naturaljustice.org (accessed 13 September 2011).

Biocultural community protocol of the Maldharis is on file with the author. Copies of it can be requested from the Banni Pashu Uccherak Maldhari Sangathan, www.sahjeevan.org (accessed 13 September 2011.

Biocultural community protocol of the traditional healers of Bushbuckridge on the resources page of naturaljustice.org (accessed 13 September 2011).

Biocultural community protocol of the Vaidyas on the resources page of naturaljustice.org (accessed 13 September 2011).

Bio-cultural diversity conserved by indigenous peoples and local communities-examples and analysis, Companion document to the IUCN/CEESP Briefing Note No.10. Tehran: CENESTA.

Community well-being and biocultural diversity through endogenous development, COMPAS network: outcomes, impact and new initiatives, by request www.compasnet.org (accessed 13 September 2011).

Documenting Democracy, *Mabo* (No.2) http://foundingdocs.gov.au/item-did-33.html (accessed 13 September 2011).

Draft UNREDD Program Guidelines for Seeking the Free and Prior Informed Consent of Indigenous Peoples and other Forest Dependent Communities, Africa, 2011, available on file with author.

Economics of Ecosystems and Biodiversity-TEEB for Policy Makers, Summary-Responding to the Value of Nature. Wesseling: UNEP, 2009.

Ostrom, Elinor. 2010. Taking Sustainability Research Mainstream', FES, *Common Voices*, Issue 1: 6–9.

Payment for Ecosystem Services-Getting Started: A Primer. 2008. Nairobi: UNEP, Forest Trends, and the Katoomba Group.

Report of the First Part of the Ninth Meeting of the Ad-Hoc Open Ended Working Group on Access and Benefit Sharing, UNEP/CBD/WG-ABS/9/3.

Report of the Meeting of the Group of Technical and Legal Experts on Traditional Knowledge Associated with Genetic Resources in the Context of the International Regime on Access and Benefit-Sharing, UNEP/CBD/WG-ABS/9/2, 2009.

Summary of the Ad-hoc Open Ended Working Group on Access and Benefit Sharing of the Convention on Biological Diversity, 2010. Earth Negotiations Bulletin, http://www.iisd.ca/biodiv/abs9/ (accessed 23 March 2012).

Summary of the Ninth Conference of Parties to the CBD. 2008. *Earth Negotiations Bulletin*, 9(452).

Summary of the Interregional Negotiating Group on Access and Benefit Sharing, 18–21 September, 2010, Earth Negotiations Bulletin, http://www.iisd.ca/biodiv/absing/brief/absing_briefe.html (accessed 23 March 2012).

Towards a Green Economy: Pathways towards Sustainable Development and Poverty Eradication, http://www.unep.org/greeneconomy/Home/tabid/29770/Default.aspx (accessed 13 September 2011).

Anaya, James S. and Claudio Grossman. 2002. 'The Case of Awas Tingni v. Nicaragua: A New Step in the International Law of Indigenous Peoples', *Arizona Journal of International and Comparative Law*, 19(1): 1–15.

Balbus, Isaac. 1977. 'Commodity Form and Legal Form: An Essay on the Relative Autonomy of the Law', *Law and Society*, 11: 571–88.

Bavikatte, Kabir and Daniel F. Robinson. 2011. 'Towards a Peoples History of the Law: Biocultural Jurisprudence and the Nagoya Protocol on Access and Benefit Sharing', *The Law, Environment and Development Journal*, 7(1): 37–51, available at http://www.lead-journal.org/content/11035.pdf (accessed 13 September 2011).

Bavikatte, Kabir, Harry Jonas, and Johanna von Braun, 'Shifting Sands of ABS Best Practice', naturaljustice.org (resources page), (accessed 13 September 2011).

Bennett, Thomas W. and Cathleen Powell. 1999. 'Aboriginal Title in South Africa Revisited', *South African Journal of Human Rights*, 15: 449–85.

Bennett, Thomas W. and Cathleen Powell. 2000. 'The State as Trustee of Land', *South African Journal of Human Rights*, 16: 601–22.

Bouckley, Ben. 2010. 'Phytopharm CEO Insists Hoodia Still "Interesting" Despite Patent Disposal', http://www.nutraingredients.com/Industry/Phytopharm-CEO-insists-Hoodia-still-interesting-despite-patent-disposal (accessed23 March 2011).

Bowers, Chet. 'Towards an Eco-Justice Pedagogy', http://www.cabowers.net/CAbookarticle.php (accessed 13 September 2011).

Bragdon, S.H. 1996. 'The Evolution and the Future of Law of Sustainable Development: Lessons from the Convention on Biological Diversity', *Georgetown International Environmental Law Review*, VIII(3): 389–513.

Bragdon, S., Kathryn Garforth, and John E. Haapala Jr. 'Safeguarding Biodiversity: The Convention on Biological Diversity (CBD)', in Geoff Tansey and Tasmin Rajotte (eds.), *The Future Control of Food*, (London: Earthscan, 2008).

Brunner, Lisl. 2008. 'The Rise of Peoples' Rights in the Americas: The *Saramaka People* Decision of the Inter-American Court of Human Rights', *Chinese Journal of International Law*, 7(3): 699–711.

Carpenter, Kristen. 2008. 'Real Property and Peoplehood', *Stanford Environmental Law Journal*, 27: 313–95.

Chhatre, Ashwini and Arun Agrawal. 2008. 'Forest Commons and Local Enforcement', *Proceedings of the National Academy of Sciences*, 105(36): 13286–91.

Ellickson, Robert. 2011. 'Two Cheers for the Bundle-of-Sticks Metaphor, Three Cheers for Merrill and Smith', *Econ Journal Watch*, 8(3): 215–22.

FPP, KLIM, SCPDA, IMPECT, OKANI, CED, and Unnayan Onneshan. 2010. Customary Sustainable Use of Biodiversity by Indigenous Peoples and Local Communities: Examples, Challenges, Community Initiatives and Recommendations Relating to CBD Article 10(c), A Synthesis Paper by the FPP and Partner Organizations, http://www.forestpeoples.org/topics/convention-biological-diversity-cbd/publication/2010/synthesis-paper-10c-case-studies (accessed 13 September 2011).

Gabel, Peter. 1980. 'Reification in Legal Reasoning', *Research in Law and Sociology*, 3: 25–6.

Glowka, Lyle. 1997. 'Emerging Legislative Approaches to Implement Article 15 of the Convention on Biological Diversity', *RECIEL*, 6(3): 249–62.

Hardin, Garrett. 1968. 'The Tragedy of the Commons', *Science*, 1243–48.

Hardin, Russell. 2003. 'The Free-Rider Problem', *The Stanford Encyclopedia of Philosophy*, http://plato.stanford.edu/entries/free-rider/ (accessed 13 September 2011).

Hoole, Arthur Frederick. 2010. 'Place-Power-Prognosis: Community Based Conservation, Partnerships and Ecotourism Enterprise in Namibia', *International Journal of the Commons*, 4(10): 78–99.

Howitt, Richie. 2001. 'Frontiers, Borders, Edges: Liminal Challenges to the Hegemony of Exclusion', *Australian Geographical Studies*, 39(2): 233–45.

Hurley, Mary C. 2000. *Aboriginal Title: The Supreme Court of Canada Decision in Delgamuukw v. British Columbia*, Law and Government Division, Parliamentary Information and Research Service.

IIED, ANDES (Peru) and the Potato Park Communities. 2011. 'Community Biocultural Protocols: Building Mechanisms for Access and Benefit Sharing Amongst the Communities of the Potato Park Based on Quechua Customary Norms'. London: IIED.

Ishizawa, Jorge. 2009. 'Affirmation of Cultural Diversity-Learning with Communities in the Central Andes', *Development Dialogue*, 2: 105–39.

James, William. 1904. 'Does Consciousness Exist?', *Journal of Philosophy, Psychology, and Scientific Methods*, 1: 477–91.

Jonas, H., K. Bavikatte, and H. Shrumm. 2010. 'Community Protocols and Access and Benefit Sharing', *Asian Biotechnology and Development Review*, 12(3): 49–76.

———. 'Biocultural Community Protocols and Conservation Pluralism', *Policy Matters*, IUCN-CEESP, Malaysia, 17: 102–12.

Kohler-Rollefson, Ilse. 2010. 'Biocultural Community Protocols: A Tool for Pastoralists to Secure Customary Rights to the Commons', FES, *Common Voices*, 2: 16.

Köhler-Rollefson, Ilse and Evelyn Mathias. 2010. 'Livestock Keepers' Rights: A Rights-Based Approach to Invoking Justice for

Pastoralists and Biodiversity Conserving Livestock Keepers', *Policy Matters*, 17: 113–15.

Korten, Fran. 2010. 'Elinor Ostrom wins Nobel for Common(s) Sense', *Yes! Magazine*, http://www.yesmagazine.org/issues/america-the-remix/elinor-ostrom-wins-nobel-for-common-s-sense (accessed 13 September 2011).

Landes, Elisabeth M. and Posner, Richard. 1978. 'The Economics of the Baby Shortage', *Journal of Legal Studies*, 7: 323–48.

Lynch, Owen J. 2011. *Mandating Recognition: International Law and Native/Aboriginal Title*. Rights and Resources Initiative: Washington DC.

Marx, Karl. 1844. 'A Contribution to Hegel's Philosophy of Right', http://www.marxists.org/archive/marx/works/1843/critique-hpr/intro.htm (accessed 13 September 2011).

McNeil, Kent. 1998. *Defining Aboriginal Title in the 90's: Has the Supreme Court Finally Got it Right?*, 12th Annual Robarts Lecture, 25 March 1998, York University: Toronto, Ontario.

Murombedzi, James C. 1999. 'Devolution and Stewardship in Zimbabwe's CAMPFIRE Programme', *Journal of International Development*, 11(2): 287–93.

Ng, Irene and Lu-Ming Tseng. 2008. 'Learning to be Sociable: The Evolution of Homo Economicus', *The American Journal of Economics and Sociology*, 67(2): 265–86.

Ostrom, Elinor and Harini Nagendra. 2006. 'Insights on Linking Forests, Trees, and People from the Air, on the Ground, and in the Laboratory', *Proceedings of the National Academy of Sciences*, 103(51): 19224–31.

Özelem, Ülgen. 2002. 'Developing the Doctrine of Aboriginal Title in South Africa: Source and Content', *Journal of African Law*, 46: 131–54.

Pearson, Noel. 1997. 'The Concept of Native Title at Common Law', *Australian Humanities Law Review*, http://www.australianhumanitiesreview.org/archive/Issue-March-1997/pearson.html (accessed 13 September 2011).

Price, Richard. 'Contested Territory: The Victory of the Saramaka People vs. Suriname.' Paper prepared for *Simpósio Internacional: Territórios Sensíveis: diferença, agência e transgressão*, Museu Nacional, Rio de Janeiro, 15 June 2009, available at www.richandsally.net.

Putnam, Hilary. 1981. *Reason, Truth, and History*. Cambridge University Press: Cambridge.

Radin, Margaret Jane. 1982. 'Property and Personhood', *Stanford Law Review*, 34(5): 957–1015.

———. 1987. 'Market-Inalienability', *Harvard Law Review*, 100(8): 1849–1937.

Riley, Angela, Kirsten Carpenter, and Sonia Katyal. 2009. 'In Defense of Property', *Yale Law Journal*, 118: 1022–1125.

Sandel, Michael J. 1998. 'What Money Can't Buy: The Moral Limits of Markets', *The Tanner Lectures on Human Values*, Oxford, www.tannerlectures.utah.edu/lectures/documents/sandel00.pdf (accessed 13 September 2011).

Schroeder, Doris and Balakrishna Pisupati. 2010. 'Justice and the Convention on Biological Diversity', *Ethics and International Affairs*, 23(3): 267–80.

Shrumm, Holly and Jessica Campese. 2010. 'Exploring the Right to Diversity in Conservation Law, Policy and Practice', *Policy Matters*, 17: 10–14.

Secher, Ulla. 2008. 'Implications of the Crown's Radical Title for Statutory Regimes Regulating the Alienation of Land: "Crown Land" v "Property of the Crown" Post-*Mabo*', *Monash University Law Review*, 34(1): 9–52.

Singer, Joseph. 2006. 'The Ownership Society and Takings of Property: Castles, Investments and Just Obligations', *Harvard Environmental Law Review*, 30: 309.

———. 2007. 'How Property Norms Construct the Externalities of Ownership', Harvard Law School Public Law Research Paper No. 08–06, http://ssrn.com/abstract=1093341 (accessed 28 February 2012).

Stevens, Stan. 2010. 'Implementing the UN Declaration on the Rights of Indigenous Peoples and the International Human Rights Law through the Recognition of ICCAs', *Policy Matters*, 17: 181–94.

Tierny, John. 2009. 'The Non-Tragedy of the Commons', *The New York Times*, 15 October 2009, http://tierneylab.blogs.nytimes.com/2009/10/15/the-non-tragedy-of-the-commons/ (accessed 14 March 2012).

Tobin, Brendan and Emily Taylor. 2009. 'Across the Great Divide: A Case Study of Complementarity and Conflict between Customary

Law and TK Protection Legislation in Peru', Initiative for the Prevention of Biopiracy, Research Documents, IV(11).

Tobin, Brendan and Emily Taylor. 2010. '"Law Giveth and the Law Taketh Away": The Case for Recognition of Customary Law in International ABS and Traditional Knowledge Governance', *Policy Matters*, 17: 16–24.

UNFCC. 2011. *An Introduction to the United Nations Framework Convention on Climate Change (UNFCCC) and its Kyoto Protocol.* Fact Sheet.

Vasak, Karel. 1977. 'Human Rights: A Thirty-Year Struggle: the Sustained Efforts to give Force of law to the Universal Declaration of Human Rights', *UNESCO Courier*. 30(11): 29.

Vaughan, Greg. 2010. 'Swidden Agriculture: Sustainable Slash and Burn?', *Good Eater Collaborative*, http://www.goodeater.org/2010/07/02/swidden-agriculture-sustainable-slash-and-burn/ (accessed 13 September 2011).

Vermeylen, Saskia. 2007. 'Contextualizing "Fair" and "Equitable": The San's Reflections on the Hoodia Benefit-Sharing Agreement', *Local Environment*, 12(4): 423–36.

———. 2008. 'From Life Force to Slimming Aid: Exploring Views on the Commodification of Traditional Medicinal Knowledge', *Applied Geography*, 28: 224–35.

Vidal, John. 2011. 'Bolivia Enshrines Natural World's Rights with Equal Status for Mother Earth', *The Guardian*, Sunday 10 April.

Vuotto, Jonathan P. 2004. 'Awas Tingni v. Nicaragua: International Precedent for Indigenous Land Rights?', *Boston University International Law Journal*, 22: 219–43.

WIPO Publication No. 920(E). *Intellectual Property and Traditional Knowledge*, Booklet no.2. New York: WIPO Publication.

Secretariat of the Convention on Biological Diversity. 2000. *Sustaining Life on Earth: How the Convention on Biological Diversity Promotes Nature and Well-Being*, Montreal: Secretariat of the Convention on Biological Diversity.

Wood, Mary Christina and Zachary Welcker. 2008. 'Tribes as Trustees Again (Part 1): The Emerging Tribal Role in the Conservation Trust Movement', *Harvard Environmental Law Review*, 32: 373–432.

Wood, Mary Christina and Mathew O'Brien. 2008. 'Tribes as Trustees Again (Part 2): Evaluating Four Models of Tribal Participation in the Conservation Trust Movement', *Stanford Environmental Law Journal*, 27: 477–546.

Wood, Peter, Olivier Rukundo, and Johanna von Braun. 2010. 'REDD Community Protocols: A Community Approach to Ensuring the Local Integrity of REDD', *Outreach*, Special Post-COP 15 Issue:7.

Zeigler, Jean, Grégoire de Kalbermatten, Liliane Ortega, Christophe Golay, Claire Mahon, Sally-Anne Way, and Michaela Büschi. 2008. 'Human Rights and Desertification: Exploring the Complementarity of International Human Rights Law and the United Nations Convention to Combat Desertification', Issue paper 1, *Desertification, Land Degradation and Drought*, Bonn: UNCCD.

International and Regional Laws, Processes and Resolutions

African Model Law for the Protection of the Rights of Local Communities, Farmers and Breeders and for the Regulation of Access to Biological Resources

Akwé: Kon Voluntary Guidelines for the Conduct of Cultural, Environmental and Social Impact Assessments on Developments Likely to Impact Sacred Sites

American Convention on Human Rights

Convention on Biological Diversity (CBD)

International Labour Organization (ILO) Conventions No. 107 and 169 on the Rights of Indigenous and Tribal Peoples in Developing Countries

Program of Work on Protected Areas (PoWPA)

Reducing Emissions from Deforestation and Forest Degradation (UN-REDD)

Takrihwaie:ri Ethical Code of Conduct for Respecting the Cultural and Intellectual Heritage of Indigenous and Local Communities

The African Charter on Human and Peoples' Rights

The International Covenant on Civil and Political Rights (ICCPR)

The International Covenant on Economic, Social and Cultural Rights (ICESCR)

The International Treaty on Plant Genetic Resources for Food and Agriculture (ITPGRFA)

The Nagoya Protocol on Access to Genetic Resources and the Fair and Equitable Sharing of Benefits Arising from their Utilization to the Convention on Biological Diversity

The Statute of the International Court of Justice

The Universal Declaration on Human Rights (UDHR)

United Nations Convention on Combating Desertification (UNCCD)

United Nations Declaration on the Rights of Indigenous Peoples (UNDRIP)

United Nations Framework Convention on Climate Change (UNFCCC)

World Intellectual Property Organization Intergovernmental Committee on Intellectual Property and Genetic Resources, Traditional Knowledge and Folklore (WIPO-IGC)

The Bonn Guidelines on Access to Genetic Resources and the Fair and Equitable Sharing of Benefits Arising out of their Utilization

Index

About the Author

Sanjay Kabir Bavikatte has practised as an international environmental lawyer for several years, assisting communities to secure rights to their territories and heritage. He is the founder and former co-director of Natural Justice, an international organization of environmental lawyers providing legal assistance to indigenous peoples in Africa, Asia, and Latin America.

Bavikatte was the legal advisor to the African Group of Countries through the negotiations towards the Nagoya Protocol on Access and Benefit Sharing (ABS). He has also provided legal advice to a number of governments including those of South Africa, Namibia, India, Bhutan, and the Federated States of Micronesia towards the development and implementation of community centred environmental law and policy. He has published extensively on environmental law and was awarded the Shuttleworth Fellowship in 2011 for his work on Biocultural Community Protocols.

Bavikatte is currently the Japan Society for the Promotion of Science Fellow at the United Nations University-Institute for the Advanced Study of Sustainability. He coordinates the Heroes Project, a grassroots initiative that works with indigenous peoples to complement legal empowerment strategies with culturally sensitive psychosocial interventions to heal collective trauma.